the

STORY

of

YIDDISH

Also by Neal Karlen

Take My Life, Please (with Henny Youngman)

Babes in Toyland: The Making and Selling of a Rock and Roll Band

Slouching Toward Fargo: A Two-Year Saga of Sinners and St. Paul Saints at the Bottom of the Bush Leagues with Bill Murray, Darryl Strawberry, Dakota Sadie and Me

Jen X (with Jenny McCarthy)

Shanda: The Making of a Self-Loathing Jew

the

STORY

of

יודישע

How a *Mish-Mosh* of
Languages Saved the Jews

Neal Karlen

WILLIAM MORROW
An Imprint of HarperCollinsPublishers

HarperCollins books may be purchased for educational, business, or sales promotional use. For information please write: Special Markets Department, HarperCollins Publishers, 10 East 53rd Street, New York, NY 10022.

FIRST EDITION

Designed by Nicola Ferguson

Library of Congress Cataloging-in-Publication Data has been applied for.

ISBN: 978-0-06-083711-2

08 09 10 11 12 WBC/QWF 10 9 8 7 6 5 4 3 2 1

ON EARTH . . .

For my sister, Bonnie, the planet's bravest soul and biggest
yiddishe hartz
You'll be laughing and running by the time this comes out!
and
For Suzanne Gluck, agent, friend, protector
Thanks for thinking this one up!

AS IT IS IN HEAVEN . . .

And in memory of my mother, Charlotte Karlen
(1926–2005)
I hope you like this one!

1. Steve McQueen's first professional line, delivered
   in a 1952 all-Yiddish production of *Molly Picon*,
   played on "Knish Alley," Yiddish theater's Broadway.

   McQueen [enters, grim look on his face]:
   "Alles iz forloren."
   "All is lost."

2. "What are you, a *meshuggener*? We're all *mishpocha*!"
   Jenny McCarthy to Pamela Anderson (*Stacked*,
   the Fox Television sitcom, 2005)

3. "That *shmendrick* keeps looking over here. And that
   guy has a gun. And you have to do what you have
   to do."
   Harvey Keitel in a mid-2007 Gatorade commercial

4. "I would tell you, ladies and gentlemen, how much
   better you understand Yiddish than you suppose."
   Franz Kafka

5. "Did someone call me *shnorrer*?"
   Groucho Marx in *Animal Crackers* (1930)

CONTENTS

the
STORY
of
YIDDISH

CHAPTER 1

You Don't Have to Be Jewish
to "Get" Yiddish

To begin to understand the soul of Yiddish, one needn't understand the homely language as much as its bipolar worldview. Mere answers of how this mutt language saved the often fatally stubborn and proud Jews over the last thousand years doesn't begin to tell the full tale of the *mamme-loshn* (mother tongue) any more than the correct answers on *Jeopardy!* reveal anything beyond the memorization of trivia.

Over the centuries, experts have thought Yiddish had as many linguistic meanings as the word *oy*. At various times it was considered a jargon, dialect, vulgar street slang, language, secret code, medium of high art, punishment, Jewish Esperanto, or even an embarrassment to its people. Yet it's always been anything but trivial.

Not that Yiddish doesn't bear enough Neat Facts to titillate Alex Trebek. How could it possibly be, for example, that Steve McQueen, Jimmy Cagney, American war hero General Colin Powell, and Nazi war criminal Adolf Eichmann all knew Yiddish—while few of Israel's prime ministers have had even a passing knowledge of the language.

Yet this is not a *history* of Yiddish, but the *story* of Yiddish. True, there are names, dates, and places important to the language's development lurking not too deeply in its one-thousand-year history as perhaps the world's most loathed and loved patois.

These historical truths are critical. Still, this is really the story of how Yiddish's heart and spirit evolved from its status as the worst-ever, quasi-linguistic equivalent of the 1962 New York Mets into, simultaneously, the most sonorous, wisest, ironic, funereal, and joyous language in the world.

Yiddish has forever been granted least-favorite-nation status by the Jews' enemies. Never mind that *der yidn* (Jews), wandering forever in Diaspora, never even *were* a nation, as they were kicked around like an always-deflating soccer ball in a match of global proportions that was never good for the Jews.

Yet there were good times, many of them, and all reflected in Yiddish. I hope that joy will be captured in these pages; Yiddish is as much about the humor and magic of life as it is about seemingly never-ending pogroms and cataclysm. Many of those laughs have come through clenched teeth and lost hopes. Yet Yiddish, in all of its feeling, longing, and laughter, is available to anyone. You don't have to be Jewish to enjoy Levy's rye bread, as in the famous ad read in New York subways; nor do you have to be Jewish to read this book.

In fact it might be better if you're not. Besides gaining a further insight into the Yiddish-based mind of many Jews, there is always the enjoyment that comes with going up to a group of Chasidic or ultra-Orthodox men at a gas pump or convenience store, and begin talking to them in Yiddish.

For Jews, Yiddish is the easiest way to see who we and the world are, and were, to *der yidn* and *der goyim* (Gentiles). It is understanding Yiddishkeit—the spirit and essence of living life like a Jew—at a time when too many *yidn* have forgotten or never knew the story of the language that saved them more than any rabbi ever did.

The book can be read out of order, by pages, paragraphs, or sentences. This is a book to be carried and tattered; in a world of A.D.D. and short attention spans, including my own, I have tried to write in digestible giblets as well as chunks. Five hours of reading time? Fine. Five-minute intervals, just long enough to learn a filthy Yiddish phrase? Also fine. As the Band sang, "Just take what you need and leave the rest"—but in this book please feel free to take whatever you feel is Yiddish's very best.

The oft-repeated tale, complete with names, is a staple of Yiddish: It was how Jewish history was memorized and one's own dead relatives kept alive. I include a couple of twice-told tales in honor of that tradition. I believe German poet Heinrich Heine's declaration of insincerity after he converted from Judaism to Catholicism is worth hearing twice. (Heine, who switched teams for social mobility, said no such conversion to Christianity could be honest, because no Jew could believe any other Jew was Divine.)

The question this book tries to answer is short, as many Yiddish queries are. Not long ago, this *mish-mosh* of other peoples' languages and worlds was thought to be a dialect of Jewish pig Latin. How could such a mongrel tongue save the Jews at the same time it was so derided?

The answer is this: The Story of Yiddish.

DURING THEIR DIASPORA, in place of a spot on the map, Jews made Yiddish into an invisible homeland with unmarked boundaries, encompassing virtually any place on the planet where *yidn* lived, or were violently bounced, whether they were in a cluster of three million, or three. With no place to turn as they wandered a world that largely despised them, Jews had to settle on the *mamme-loshn* (mother tongue), wrote journalist Miriam Weinstein, as their borderless "nation of words."

"Yiddish culture was more than ever an international culture," wrote Irving Howe, author of the magisterial *World of Our Fathers*, "a fraternity of survivors across the globe."

To foes of the Jews, Yiddish was the chicken-squawk gibberish of a historically chickenhearted people literally demonized as horned Christ killers with yellow stripes down their backs. That might be expected. Curiously, however, Yiddish is also the story of a language almost equally loathed by its own.

Nevertheless, Yiddish saved the Jews from assimilation or disappearance. Yiddish—this forever-dying language with no mother, father, or, as with Hebrew, Divine roots. Instead, it sprung naturally from the Jewish experience and need to survive the murderous sabers of Crusaders on the way to Jerusalem. The language, for good *and* rotten over the last thousand years, held the Chosen together with their own Esperanto as they were chased and kicked around the world.

The story of Yiddish is not nearly just the history of the language, though the past of course will be more than limned. That history frames one of the world's most colorful and beautiful languages encompassing the invisible and forever-changing borders of world Jewry.

NEVER MIND THAT by 1939, Yiddish was the *lingua franca* of eleven million *lantzmen* (fellow Jews from the same continent or village). Those eleven million represented the 75 percent of world Jewry who spoke Yiddish as their only or first language.

Jews were the unlikeliest survivors of all the Bible's peoples to wander into the world's vicious time-tunnel and somehow escape through history. Along the way, for the last one thousand years, the worst part of the Diaspora, Yiddish joined them in that tunnel.

Rulers were forever outlawing Yiddish where the putatively "Saved" nomads were begrudgingly, temporarily, allowed to settle. Almost always, repressing Yiddish ultimately proved itself just one more failed attempt by kings, queens, czars, and despots to make the reviled Jews assimilate and disappear into the maw of the host countries' masses.

Sometimes, the *ganze macher goyim* (big-shot non-Jews) found their own selfish reasons to keep "their" Jews a bit longer than they normally might. Yet for the Jews' own good, the monarchs and rulers of the fiefdoms where the *yidn* were allowed to stay usually felt their tribe had to be rid of the seemingly incomprehensible babble of Yiddish that separated the Jews from the world as much as their damnable refusal to accept Jesus as their Messiah.

Until the 1880s, Yiddish didn't even have a name among Jews besides the linguistic epithet *Jhargon* (jargon). Ironically, for the world's most historically tortured people, Yiddish has always been the most ironic language.

Even more ironic, this most wiseassed and mournful language not only saved the Jews from their enemies—but themselves as well.

THE *MAMME-LOSHN* WAS conceived as slang meant for illiterate Jewish peasants, women, children, and intellectual nincompoops—all of which were in plentiful supply in Europe's *shtetls* and ghettos. Still, Yiddish was voted least likely to succeed at anything, even by its own people, as it slowly began morphing into a linguistic sponge that borrowed from every country from which the Jews were evicted as they wandered the world during their mostly hideous Diaspora.

Lucky to scrounge a living wherever they went, the Jews had better luck scrounging words and phrases from even dead languages they ran into on their triptych through the universe of anti-Semitism.

"Yiddish is the Robin Hood of languages. It steals from the linguistically rich to give to the fledgling poor," wrote Leo Rosten, author of *The Joys of Yiddish*, the 1968 secular, best-selling, and controversial classic. Part of the *mamme-loshn*'s unique, inspired, and bent charm is its *mish-mosh* of vocabulary swiped from and traded with peoples who would rather kill the Jews than lend them a home for fifteen minutes.

Over centuries of making use of other people's words, Yiddish became much like the Johnny Cash song "One Piece at a Time," the tale of a poor auto-factory worker who felt he wouldn't be able to survive unless he had his own Cadillac. That blue-collar worker does indeed survive, by slowly building over the years a rich man's ride put together with mismatched parts he'd "borrowed" from the auto plant every day in his lunchbox.

The results, like Johnny Cash's *mish-mosh* Cadillac, were breathtaking. In 1978, Isaac Bashevis Singer became the only Yiddish writer ever to win the Nobel Prize in Literature. After accepting his medal from Sweden's king, Singer made his address in the language in which he composed.

"The high honor," he said,

is also a recognition of the Yiddish language—a language of exile, without a land, without a frontier, not supported by any government; a language which possesses not words for weapons, ammunition, military exercises, war tactics; a language despised by the gentiles and emancipated Jews.

Yet . . . one can find in the Yiddish tongue expressions of pious joy, lust for life, longing for the Messiah, patience and deep appreciation of human individuality. There is a quiet humor in Yiddish and a gratitude for every day of life, every crumb of success, each encounter of love.

The Jews *needed* Yiddish, and its descriptions in mismatched words that made sense of incomprehensible, almost universally, unfriendly worlds. Even when Jews kicked Yiddish into the gutter, the *Jhargon* bore obvious magic. How else to explain a disreputable *mish-mosh* of borrowed words woven into an often-upside-down language that the lowliest, most illiterate *shlemiel* (one who falls on his back and bruises his nose) could understand—but which left the brightest *goyishe* philologists stamping their feet in frustration and incomprehension?

The Jews needed lowly Yiddish far more than even their hallowed religious rituals, customs, and rote repetitions of ancient prayers that supposedly kept them bonded no matter the miles that separated *lantzmen*. Those rituals could actually *alienate* Jew from Jew; leaving tiny *shtetls* located perhaps only fifteen miles apart, warring over the proper expression of ritual and tradition.

The ultra-Orthodox Jews on one side of town might use *tefillin* (prayer phylacteries) different from the ultra-Orthodox Jews on the other side. Meantime, the Jews in the middle might attempt (sometimes successfully) to have the other two groups excommunicated. (In the sixteenth century, the Gaon of Vilna, literally "the smartest Jew in Vilna," did just that, excommunicating the Chasidim for allegedly turning somersaults during prayer.)

Oh, the religious debates. In old world Eastern Europe, word filtered back from the new world United States that *der greener* (greenhorns) were getting right off the boat at Ellis Island—and against all rabbinic-based Jewish law, shaving off the beards they'd spent all their lives growing. Apostasy!

In response, their newly Americanized *mishpocha* would write back one sentence in Yiddish:

Beser a yid on a bord eyder a bord on a yid.
"Better a Jew without a beard than a beard without a Jew."

Yiddish, besides being a shrill and/or poetic form for Jews to bicker in, expressed a particular Jewish view of the world during a Diaspora that would have killed off a weaker people—or perhaps a stronger one whose religion didn't preach running away today to live to run away again tomorrow.

With a population wandering in a seemingly never-ending journey to nowhere, Yiddish evolved into *the* critical way for Jews to codify and explain to one another their ever-changing laws and worlds. Yiddish was Esperanto exclusively for Jews, a code with few rules that turned into a language virtually impossible to break.

Despite what the Jews *wanted*—their own Messiah—they *needed* Yiddish. Until their God came, Yiddish served as the Jews' shared and mythical homeland. Though Yiddish had no flag, it served as the uncollected encyclopedia that explained why their enemies tortured them. It also provided the plain words to clarify among themselves why God was waiting so long to save them from this world grown so *verkakte* (screwed up). In the Hebrew bible, God is described as a comic book Messiah, all thunderbolts and miracles, reverently smiting and smoting, ordering the death penalty for masturbators, and turning Lot's wife, who merely wanted to sightsee, into a pillar of salt.

The Yiddish God, however, was treated more as a *shlemiel* of

an underachiever who'd forgotten where the button for miracles was. One could talk to Him in Yiddish and even give him
the *zetz* (verbal needle) for His shortcomings. (All Jews reserved
the right to give any other Jew the *zetz*, and for no reason.
Further, many Jews mirror Sicilians in their ability to carry
grudges—especially toward former business partners—to the
grave.)

And so, this new-school sort of God of the Eastern European
shtetl was a *zetz*-able kind of Divine presence, whom even Tevye
the milkman in *Fiddler on the Roof* could ask proudly, on un-
bended knees, with a sprinkle of self-righteousness, "Couldn't
You choose someone else for a while?"

As they say:

Az got volt gelebt oyf der erd volt men im ale fenster oysgeshlogen
"If God lived on earth, all His windows would be broken."

Yet though the Jews might rib Him unmercifully, the God
who would save them was never far from the Yiddish mind. He
might be tardy—Jews are often tardy—but He *would* show up.

SO YIDDISH THRIVED and the peasant *yidn* who spoke it never
stopped fleeing. The Jews' everyday language always came
along on the next stop of their unwanted world tour, as much as
their limbs or consciences. Often, these Jews-on-the-run didn't
even have enough time to grab their *bubbe*'s (grandmother's)
most prized possession, usually her *Shabbos* (Sabbath) candle-
sticks, or their *zayde*'s (grandfather's) prayer shawl.

Usually all of the Jews' worldly possessions had to be left behind as they alchemized into instant refugees by formerly relatively friendly hosts who'd suddenly had enough of this strange

people with their bizarre babble and weird beards. Usually the Jews were given five minutes to pack up and flee one more time somewhere else.

"Somewhere else" would be anywhere the Jews could rest, even for a spell. Yiddish, needing no luggage, was the one thing the Jews always could and did bring along. Before fleeing another land, they usually had managed to take as lovely parting gifts some vocabulary and slang that they could incorporate into the Yiddish.

Yiddish was Jewry's Silly Putty. Like the toy dough, Yiddish lifted off the image of the words it was borrowing from other cultures, leaving an impression on the clay that could be bent and stretched for the Jews' own linguistic needs.

As Yiddish journalist Charles Rappaport said over a generation ago: "I speak ten languages, all of them Yiddish."

Rappaport was underestimating.

According to conservative estimates, Yiddish contains medieval and modern German, the Jews' own antiquated holy Hebrew and Aramaic, Russian, Polish, Czech, Romanian, Ukrainian, Lithuanian, Galician, Hungarian, Judean, Ladino (the "Yiddish" of Jews along the Iberian Peninsula, South America, and Mexico), and American English.

Yiddish has pieces of the Italian with which Venetians used to jeer Shylock; English, which Britain used to expel the Jews in the thirteenth century for allegedly practicing voodoo; French, the language used to evict Jews from the oh-so-cultured Normandy coast half a dozen times since medieval days; along with traces of the languages of virtually every country in northern and western Europe and well beyond—wherever the Jews settled and were eventually kicked out.

(Some have added to this *mish-mosh* "Hollywood western,"

where "stick 'em up" is translated into "hold up de *hends*—please!")

Yiddish even *shnorred* (mooched) from Latin, the Vatican's own language, where even the precept that the Jews killed Jesus has barely been rescinded. In perhaps a subtle form of revenge beyond Latin's unholy death, and as payback for all of the Crusades and Inquisitions, the *yidn* took Latin's most reverent reference to God—Divine—and revised it into *dah'-ven*, Jewish prayer.

Eventually, it was shown possible to make a Yiddish sentence of five words comprising five different root languages:

"Guten erev Shabbos, Madame Chairman"—the phrase in *mamme-loshn* for wishing a pleasant Sabbath eve to a high-standing woman, utilizing, consecutively, German, Hebrew, Yiddish, French, and English.

HISTORY'S CENTRIFUGE OF de-evolution, lost wars, and forced or wanted assimilation seems a likely reason for the passing of any people, let alone their languages. Yet of all the mighty tribes and peoples of the Old Testament who've had starring roles over the last three thousand years, seemingly only the Jews are still alive.

Where are all the Babylonians, Hellenists, and Romans, who spent centuries battering the bejabbers out of the *yidn*, yet somehow lost the long-term war of survival against the Jews, who lacked both the strength or will to fight? What happened to the Jews' fellow tribes of the Old Testament, the Hittites, Moabites, and Canaanites?

The Jews traversed back and forth across the world for three thousand years over almost universally unfriendly lands. They should have disappeared or been killed off dozens of centuries ago, when most of their mightiest foes passed into dust and ancient history.

But the Jews survived. As did Yiddish, which stuck to the Jews' sandals and shoes like a discarded piece of not-quite-kosher bubblegum.

Beyond its own survival, Yiddish is stocked with curiosities. They are highly ironic curiosities, appropriate in that the gold standard of irony has always served as the attitude, underpinnings, and emotional ballast of Yiddish. For no matter that Yiddish has been Judaism's savior while the Jews wait for their Messiah, a significant number of *yidn* have never been able to stand hearing the language, never mind considering the story of how Yiddish saved the Jews who relied on it.

"Who knew?" as goes the Yiddish construction, borrowed by American English. The story of that evolution is one of glory and horror, of laughter and tears, and simultaneously, in one of the language's multitude of double meanings, of the endless optimism and pessimism inherent in Yiddish-based Judaism.

Yiddish is not just another Jewish language, although there have been dozens that never quite caught on. Yet Yiddish is the survivor, the language with which the Jews waited out their world's assorted attempts at genocide upon them— or the day-to-day gossip of the vicious *shtetl yenta* (village gossip) on a tear about the rabbi and the *shtetl nafke* (village whore).

The word "Yiddish," translated into Yiddish, means "Jewish," and the language is still called "Jewish" by many first-generation American old-timers, now mostly in their eighties and nineties. It is an appropriate moniker. Spoken of as "Jewish," the *mamme-loshn* is indeed a reflection of Judaism's history, heart, and soul—a warmth that allowed Yiddish to first peek out, like a daisy breaking through a crack in the sidewalk.

While Yiddish was born as that bright weed, ancient Hebrew, meantime, was reverently referred to as the *Lushen Kodesh*, (the holy language). Antiquated Hebrew, utilizing the exact same words God dictated the Old Testament to Moses on Mount Sinai, was the unalterable language to be used strictly for prayer in the synagogue, by only the wisest of Jewish men. Holy Hebrew, over its thousands of years, was purposely mummified and pickled in its own ancient juices.

So, there was always a heartbeating vitality to Yiddish that immutable Hebrew always lacked. This language with seemingly no rules of grammar or usage bore a vocabulary that could change as recently as yesterday's sojourn into the town square of an all-Gentile city.

Yiddish, bending to the Jews' ever-changing reality, never stopped reflecting the world and themselves *to* themselves. Whether those reflections were from ten centuries ago, or next *Shabbos* (Sabbath), Yiddish kept the Jews alive and together, their religion and dreams of someday going home intact.

Yet how could Yiddish save the Jews? How could this jargon save *anything*?

The *mamme-loshn* was for the *shtetls'* untutored. Besides women and children, who couldn't help their ignorance, Yiddish was, for a people self-dubbed "the people of the book," aimed at its veritable village idiots.

Yiddish was for the *shtetl* stable hands shoveling *drek* (shit), and for ignorant fieldworkers strapped into their plows sweating eighteen-hour days to *macht a leben* (make a living). In the ghetto, the jargon was meant for unschooled *bulvons* (vulgarians), with soup in their beards and an eye for the *shiksas*; *shtarkers;* and *shleppers* (men-beasts best used for heavy lifting).

Yiddish? Saving the Jews?

It happened.

For, as is said in Yiddish:

Mentsh tracht, Gott lacht.

"Man plans, God laughs."

CHAPTER 2

שװעגעבאװנעשבאנבאבאגעװש

Yiddishkeit

Now could millions of Jews find a voice in Yiddish, this hybrid language of glory, horror, laughter, and tears?

Still, there are a handful of points that should be addressed about the language, nature, and spirit of Yiddish, called Yiddishkeit, a word that literally means the essence of "Jewishness."

Yiddishkeit's soul has always breathed on in the attempts of people, no matter what their religion, prejudices, or limitations, to live life as a *mentsh*, a human being, not a *vilde chaye*, a wild beast. To even near becoming a *mentsh* is the greatest achievement one can reach in the Yiddish language's understanding of the Sisyphean task of staying alive, while living honorably as just such a human being, not a nonconscious animal.

AND A LIFE is a precious life, from whomever and wherever it descends, according to the tenets of Yiddishkeit. And that human life *matters*.

Take the story of the Jewish soldier during World War I, lost at night, wandering between the lines, trying to remember what "side" he was on.

"Who goes there? Stop or we'll shoot!" a soldier, also on who knows what side, yells into the dark at the Jew.

"What do you mean?" the Jew shouts back. "Don't you see there's a *human being* here?"

TO TRY AND be—and treat all people as—a *mentsh*, a human being and not a wild animal, is not a Pollyannaish concept. To live within Yiddishkeit also means bearing the bittersweet knowledge—and the ability to forgive, as is said in the language with which Yiddishkeit speaks—that:

> *A mentsh iz nebek, nit mer vi oykh a mentsh un amol dos nit.*
> "People are just people—and sometimes not even that."

THE STORY OF Yiddish—a people's language that for better *and* worse was literally to the manure-born—has many interpreters and prophets, almost none of whom get along. Yiddish-style wisdom is not nearly based just on holy scholarship, though one of my two most important wise men and teachers into the heart of Yiddish is Chasidic rabbi Manis Friedman.

Friedman is a pious man with a graying beard to his chest and a Sam Spade–style fedora always on his head. He is also one of the language's most incisive technical, scholarly experts, among the last group of people on earth to speak the *mamme-loshn* in daily discourse.

In modern times, rabbis like Manis Friedman don't even have to be ordained to be secular rabbis. For several decades, the term has been adopted into the English vernacular to describe any adviser and powerful mentor who can grease the skids of ascension up any and all treacherous political terrain between academic, nonprofit, communistic, and corporate realms.

To make things even more complicated—complexity being a favorite trick of Yiddish—the great ordained rabbis (the term means "teachers") were always commanded to work other jobs. "Beginning with Rabbi Ezra, Jewish scholars established that no man should use the Torah as a 'spade' with which to dig for wealth."

Rabbi Hillel chopped wood for a living, despite inventing around the beginning of the Common Era the Golden Rule as described in the Babylonian Talmud: "What is hateful to you, do not do to your fellow: this is the whole Torah; the rest is explanation; go and learn." With these wise words, Hillel the wood-whacker recognized the fundamental principle of the Jewish moral law, the biblical precept of brotherly love.

Rabbi Shammai, contemporaneous to Hillel, was a land surveyor. Abba Hoshaiah washed others' dirty laundry to be able to achieve that all-important Yiddishkeit principle of *macht a leben*—"make your own living."

AFTER CHASIDIC RABBI Manis Friedman, the second rabbi who over the years has led me toward a deeper understanding of the soul and substance of Yiddish and Yiddishkeit is a dead comedian, Lenny Bruce. Bruce has for so long been hung on the cross of postmortem martyrology that people no longer know if he was funny—or, in the usual backlash of the hipster cognoscenti, is considered merely as just a boring preacher and overrated junkie.

It's nauseating. Bruce didn't dive through society's plate-glass window of Eisenhower-era normalcy asking to die for anybody's sins with his foul-mouth *shpritz* of Yiddish-hepcat patois. Whatever he did, Bruce understood and described for mixed audiences of *yidn* and *goyim* the hilarious heart of both Yiddish and Yiddish-keit. But his forte was enunciating the *mamme-loshn's* inherent darkness.

"People should be taught what is, not what should be," Bruce contentiously contended. "All my humor is based on destruction and despair. If the whole world were tranquil, without disease and violence, I'd be standing in the bread line—right back of J. Edgar Hoover."

He left as a legacy more than a haunting photograph of his 1966 death, lying naked in his bathroom with a heroin spike still in his arm. It was a picture snapped by dozens of news photographers who'd been allowed in by the police who'd harassed Bruce to his most un-Yiddishkeit-like final moments.

Those photographs are ghoulishly reminiscent of the Georgia cracker families photographed waving clumsily in front of the still-hanging lynched corpse of Jewish pencil maker Leo Frank, who'd been set up by Atlanta's hata's that-be for raping and killing of teenage girls.

Still, Lenny Bruce left an appropriately Talmudic-style, if utterly profane, commentary on Yiddish, Yiddishkeit, and the Jews and Gentiles who didn't give a *kak* (shit).

IT IS FINE to use Lenny Bruce as a rabbi of Yiddish, says my primary Yiddishkeit source, Manis Friedman, the apostle of Yiddish's holy light. "Even if someone is profane," said Rabbi Friedman, my favorite ordained scholar of the *mamme-loshn*, in his home in St. Paul, Minnesota, "their commentary should be analyzed if they have words and thoughts of wisdom to share."

We now live in a world where even Ph.D.s holding endowed chairs in Yiddish studies almost always deliver their papers to fellow scholars of the mother tongue in English. Almost none of them can actually *speak* the language.

WHEN I FIRST rang Rabbi Manis Friedman's doorbell in St. Paul, I faintly heard a man with a strong Yiddish accent address in Yiddish his son Nissan, one of his fourteen children. Rabbi Friedman, a world-famous *mentsh* (human being), the ultimate Yiddish compliment, also ranks as a leading Yiddish scholar among the Chasidim.

"*Nissan, du herst aymeter bein tier?*" I heard the distant voice ask.

("Nissan, do you hear someone at the door?")

I peeked through a glass panel and saw a boy of about ten, a skullcap on his head, *tzit-tzit* (religious tassels) flying from his waist, take a running start on a wooden floor and slide ten yards to the door.

"How ya' doin'?" I asked the youngster in English when he opened the door. His impish, freckled grin turned quizzical when he saw that before entering I hadn't first kissed my fingers and touched the *mezuzah* (the tiny box holding holy scripture on the doorframe), then returned my middle and index fingers to my mouth. The same ritual is supposed to be done upon leaving. (Lenny Bruce had a routine where he said, "A *mezuzah* is Jewish chap stick. That's why Jews are always kissing it when they go out.")

That, and the fact I wasn't wearing a *yarmulke* (skullcap), indicated I was most definitely a *goy*—a *goy*, in proper Yiddish, not a slur against Gentiles, but merely a word signifying a stranger or one from another nation. (Mormons also use the word "Gentile," to indicate a "heathen" who disbelieves the story of Joseph Smith being that of Jesus coming to America.)

"*Baruch HaShem*," Nissan said shyly in response to my English greeting of "How ya' doin'?" He turned his eyes and hesitated, then offered the standard Chasidic reply of "Fine, *Baruch HaShem*," literally "fine, praise the Name," the "Name" being God.

"The Name" was a Chasidic moniker indicating His identity, which was not to be uttered outside of prayer. Chasidically speaking, I am using a misnomer by saying "Him," not the gender-neutral *HaShem*.

Chasidic scholars, as per the mystical texts their people live by, study the ancient Kabbalah sixteen hours a day for decades and believe God is made up of equal male and female components. (The Chasidic Kabbalah, as opposed to Madonna and Britney Spears' ridiculous rendition, cannot be understood by wearing red string bracelets or using "Kabbalah water." Nor does the Chasidic Kabbalah reveal how one can increase the net worth of one's land holdings via DVDs mailed from Hollywood for $199.99.)

"*TATEH!*" ("FATHER!") THE little boy yelled in the direction of the study after I'd entered their house *sans yarmulke* (skullcap) or respect for the front-door *mezuzah*. Then he reversed his course, gliding back to a spot in the kitchen near the family's dining room table that could hold twenty-five.

There, jumping around with an apparent dose of *shpilkes* (ants in the pants), young Nissan began boisterously entertaining his little sister, Muschka, by doing handstands, his *yarmulke* held in place with bobby pins.

Rabbi Friedman, Yiddish *ganze maven* (high, high expert), shook my hand. "How ya doin'?" he said, breaking the silence. (Normally he'd say, "*Vos macht a yid?*"—"How you doing, Jew?"—a Yiddish phrase dating back one thousand years, when the chances of a Jew being allowed to actually even *speak* to a non-Jew were approximately a thousand to one.)

"Mentsh tracht, HaShem lacht, Baruch HaShem," Rabbi Friedman tells me after listening wordlessly as I weepily regale him for an hour with the sordid details of my broken marriage engagement. "Man plans, God laughs, Praised Be God."

Ten minutes after I at last dry my eyes, he tells his impish ten-year-old son Nissan, in Yiddish, "Mamme is at a meeting tonight, so we'll be bachelors and have hot dogs for dinner, okay? I'll be cooking, so listen for your brother Moitel at the door."

Ten minutes later, Moitel arrives, and Nissan exclaims once again, *"Tate."*

Moitel, who runs the national Chasidic *yeshiva* (religious high school and college) designed for troubled Lubavitchers, asked me in English what my Yiddish name was. *("Vus iz dein Yiddisher nomen?"* he would have normally asked.)

I looked at his little brother bouncing off the walls. I actually shared something important with the boy. His name.

"Nissan," I said. *"Mein nomen iz Nissan."*

"How are you Nissan?" asked Moitel, still in his early twenties, whose beard now only barely passed his chin. It would grow, *Baruch HaShem* (which in Yiddish may also mean, "God willing").

"Goot," I said (good).

After dinner, I asked Rabbi Friedman the elder what one should say in Yiddish if you were doing lousy.

"In that case," he said, "if someone asks you, 'Vos macht a yid?' you should answer, 'Baruch HaShem, nisht so goot.' "

"Praise God, not so good."

I WAS IMMEDIATELY reminded by the rabbi's greeting of *"vos macht a yid"*—"how you doing, Jew"—of the late Leybl Londer, who drove rabbis without drivers' licenses around town for free and *macht a leben* (made a living) as a beer vendor at the Minnesota Twins' major league baseball games. Leybl was a childhood friend from the Minneapolis Jewish ghetto of my father, Markle. (Like Leybl, my father was born with an actual Yiddish name given by my grandparents, who only spoke Yiddish.)

Markle, my dad, would wait for Leybl (pronounced "Lay-buhl") to hustle down the aisle, whereupon he'd raise his hand for the single cup of *shnapps* he'd drink during the game (*shnapps* is Yiddish for any kind of potent potable, including shitty ballpark piss beer like Grain Belt).

"*Vos macht a yid?*" Leybl would scream across the ears of dozens of dumbstruck Scandinavian fans.

"*Nane, Leybl, du vaist ich bin nisht a shikker,*" my father would reply. "You know I'm not a drunk."

IT IS CRITICAL that both Rabbi Manis Friedman and Lenny Bruce, my two rabbis of Yiddishkeit, actually spoke Yiddish, unlike most of today's academic scholars, who only read the language.

Bruce learned to speak Yiddish sixty years ago at Hanson's drugstore in midtown Manhattan. (Rabbi Friedman learned as a tiny child held behind wire after World War II in a Czechoslovakian refugee camp.)

At Hanson's, Lenny Bruce picked up the bulk of the Yiddish he'd use in his stage act. Hanson's was his comedy yeshiva, and his peers were the young, undiscovered Jewish comics who hung out near the offices of their Broadway Danny Rose–like agents, waiting for a call for a last-second fill-in engagement at a third-rate Borscht Belt hotel or a skanky, mob-owned strip club like the one in Passaic, New Jersey, called The Lido Venice.

At that joint, the Yiddish-spouting young Jewish comics said to each other, the management drove you *zu arbeit* (to work)—with a whip! The hatcheck girl was a *shlammer* (leg breaker) named Rocco! When you finished, they stabbed you *a guten avent* (good night).

Along with Lenny Bruce (ne' Leonard Schneider), the comics' booth at Hanson's was filled with wannabes who were virtually all born Jewish and poor in New York, a heavy percentage from Brooklyn. Some grew up speaking Yiddish fluently with their proletarian parents; others had a vocabulary of several hundred words of *mamme-loshn* they would eventually profanely sprinkle into their acts. Among the then-unknown comics elbowing one another for *shpritzing* space at Hanson's were Buddy Hackett (ne' Leonard Hacker), Rodney Dangerfield (ne' Jack Roy), and Jackie Gayle (ne' Jack Patovsky). At Hanson's, the undiscovered held court amongst one another, unaware of the sun rising or setting, for the price of a twenty-five cent cup of coffee and the ability to keep up with the Gatling gun patter of the desperately funny.

Using Yiddish as a base, the young Jewish comics helped develop only the second art form indigenous to the United States: the *shpritz*, a.k.a. "Jewish jazz." (African-American jazz is often thought of as the only such legitimate claimant. Curiously, "jazz" is slang for ejaculate; *shpritz* is Yiddish for "spray." Talk amongst yourselves.)

No less a cross-cultural authority than Mezz Mezzrow himself found profound similarities between the secret languages of jazz jive and Jewish Yiddish. (Mezz, born Jewish as Milton Mezzrow, is most famously remembered for the uniquely potent marijuana he provided the most famous jazzmen and hipsters of his generation. Louis Armstrong, stoned virtually every second of his life since adolescence, thanked Mezzrow in recorded song

for his never-ending supply of righteous product that a hall of
fame of African-American jazz improvisers dubbed "Mezz." To
the Jewish jazz *shpritzers* at Hanson's, "Mezz" was the *"richtige
vare"*—Yiddish for "the right stuff.")

Jive, like Yiddish, Mezz wrote, is "a secret code . . . that re-
sembles no regular words in any regular language. [Black] guys
talk that way when they don't want to be spied on, and to prevent eavesdropping when they're jealously guarding their private lives, which are lived under great pressure, and don't want
the details known to outsiders."

Jazz, Mezzrow continued in his 1946 autobiography, was first
cousins with Yiddish, especially Yiddish *klezmer* music. Wrote
Mezz, "I found out more how music of different oppressed peoples blends together. Jewish or Hebrew music is mostly minor, is
in a simple form, full of wailing and lament.

"When I add Negro inflects to it they fit so perfect, it thrills
me. I just sing 'Oh, oh, oh,' over and over because I don't know
the Hebrew chants, but I give it a weepy blues inflection and the
[black] guys are all happy about it. They can't understand how
some [white] guy digs the spirit of their music so."

That spirit is what rang out in Jewish jazz at Hanson's Broadway coffee shop, where the comic *pishers* (young upstarts) didn't
tell the guy next to them that his pants were ugly but *chaloshes*
(disgusting). One didn't just bring over to the Hanson's comics'
table a round of coffee, you *shlepped* the cups. Testicles and
courage were *batzim*. Inveterate moochers of cigarettes, change,
and Mezz Mezzrow's *richtige ware*, right stuff marijuana, were
shnorrers.

And a *tuchus leckher,* an ass kisser, was anybody who over-
flattered Jerry Lewis, the first of the Hanson's gang to achieve
fame. When Lewis, né Joseph Levitch, came in to say hi to his
old buddies, picking up everybody's check while his limo was

idling outside, you were supposed to remind him of the time he *shtupped* a woman in a Hanson's phone booth, not ask for employment help.

The Hanson's *shpritzers* had no idea they were helping midwife perhaps Yiddish's greatest contribution to American popular culture. Lenny Bruce's breathless biographer Albert Goldman wrote that unlike the comics of old, the *shpritzers* would talk "like you'd squeeze the trigger on a machine gun. Words like bullets. Jam[med] together in fugues of impatience. Never bothering to makes sentences, paragraphs, pauses."

Like Yiddish itself, forever *shnorring* from other languages, the comics at Hanson's unabashedly stole material from one another. Take impressionist Will Jordan, whose Ed Sullivan imitation caused the real Ed Sullivan to start adopting Jordan's over-the-top impersonation of his own tics. At Hanson's, Jordan, afraid his colleagues would steal an imitation, would go outside and try out new voices on the sidewalk.

It didn't matter that Lenny Bruce lifted most of his Yiddish at Hanson's from his buddy Joe Ancis, the funniest *shpritzer* of all. Ancis was too frightened ever to go on stage. Bruce's pilferage was okay. Yiddish was born to borrow. And it also gave back.

UNDERSTANDING YIDDISHKEIT PROVIDES a glimpse into the heart and very essence of the amanuensis that feeds the homely, humble *mamme-loshn*.

So it is an act of Yiddishkeit for non-Jews such as Jimmy Cagney or Steve McQueen to know even a smattering of Yiddish.

Young Cagney learned Yiddish while working for Jews as a *Shabbos goy*.

A *Shabbos goy* was a Gentile lad paid a few kopeks in the old country, and a few nickels in the new, to turn on the oven and lights in an observant Jewish home where the family was forbidden to make any sort of fire on the Sabbath.

Cagney used his fluent knowledge of the *mamme-loshn* to good use in Hollywood, and not just in films such as *Taxi!*, the 1932 movie where he plays a Yiddish-spouting hack. Serving as his own agent, Cagney was famous, perhaps apocryphally, for using his *mamme-loshn* to outnegotiate Hollywood moguls, almost all Eastern European *bulvons* (vulgarians) like Samuel Goldwyn, né Samuel Goldfish, né Shmuel Gelbfisz.

So, using *goy* and *goyim* are fine. *Shiksa*, meantime, says Rabbi Manis Friedman, my Chasidic Yiddish expert, should never be uttered. It doesn't matter, says Rabbi Friedman, that even *shiksas* now call themselves *shiksas*. The word, he relates, has a definition so cruel toward Gentile women that he won't even tell me what it is.

Shvartze, which has evolved into the Yiddish "N" word, is of course unspeakable. The feminine *shvartze* or masculine *shvartzer*, killing words indeed, are actually the innocent Yiddish words for the color "black."

Unfortunately, the actual Yiddish word for a black person is *neger*. This was a problem. Eager not to offend anyone, immigrants quickly switched to *shvartze*. Though the word is proper Yiddish, it is as far from Yiddishkeit as Notre Dame football.

One of the saddest, most profound losses to Yiddishkeit has been the death of Ladino, the Yiddish-like language used by Jews in countries along the Iberian Peninsula. Yiddish speakers, if they'd heard of Ladino at all, considered the tongue the little sister of the *mamme-loshn*.

Jews in Spain, Portugal, Greece, Turkey, and eventually France, North Africa, the Middle East, and South America had a different idea. Despite their myriad similarities, Yiddish was thought by Ladino speakers to be a vulgar *mish-mosh* of verbal nothingness.

It was snobbery. Ladino speakers were Sephardim taken from the word "Sepharad" (Obadiah 9:20), which means Spain, and "Zarephath," France. The Shephards' lives, beliefs, and manner of practicing Judaism, as well as preserving their Iberian Jewish heritage, was not communicated via Yiddish.

Yet Ladino and Yiddish were similar in intent and philosophy.

Ladino, like Yiddish, sponged words from Spanish, Portuguese, ancient Hebrew, the Talmud, Greek, Castilian, Arabic, Serbo-Croatian, and English.

Ladino, like Yiddish, was usually written in scripted Hebrew letters. As in Yiddish, Ladino had no rules of grammar or sentence structure. Yiddish was forged out of necessity by the Crusades; Ladino was birthed following the Jews' expulsion from Spain in 1942.

Like Yiddish, Ladino was always considered a third-rate gutter language by the Jewish elite, who preferred Castilian. Now flat-lined as a living language, Gloria Ascher of Tufts University is the only professor teaching courses in Ladino in the United States.

Born in Turkey, Ascher emigrated with her family to the United States. "[My mother] didn't think much of the language," Professor Ascher said. "To her it was a kitchen language."

THE SEPHARDIM VIEWED themselves as Judaism's royalty, and looked down upon even the notoriously snobbish and hyper-assimilated German and Austrian Jews. These Western European Jews, in turn, were horrified by their un-Enlightened, unschooled, and poverty-stricken brethren in Eastern Europe, especially Poland and Russia.

All of these European groups, from Berlin to Warsaw to Odessa, were Ashkenazi (the word "Ashkenaz "appears in Genesis 10:3, referring to Germany).

In Russia and Poland, Jews were barely ever able to survive. In Germany and Austria, Jews had to convert to Christianity to be admitted to the best salons of high society. But, along the Iberian Peninsula, the Sephardim had no reason to change a thing to find prominence. One of the most successful and lauded Shephards was Maimonides, the beyond brilliant, twelfth-century Jewish law codifier and philosopher whose most famous work was the *Mishneh Torah*. He was also a gifted physician. Born in Spain, Maimonides, a.k.a. the Rambam, spent most of his life in Cairo, where he was house physician to the Egyptian court. His life was proof that there was no limit to how high a Sephardic Jew could fly. Indeed, Maimonides' schedule reads like the daily planner of a modern manic entrepreneur:

I live in Fostate and the sultanate in Cairo; the two cities are a Shabbat's distance from one another, or so four thousand cubits. My obligations insofar as the monarch is concerned are the most time consuming. I must visit him daily and when he, one of his children, or one of the harem dwellers is ill, I spend most of the day at the palace. I do not return to Fostate by which time I am dying of hunger. All of the waiting rooms are full of Jews and Gentiles alike, important and humble people, theologians, bailiffs, friends and enemies, all sorts of people await my return. The flow of patients continues until nightfall and on occasion continues to eight o'clock or even later. I receive them lying on my back, overwhelmed by weariness. Given this schedule, I never have a free moment during the week to meet the Jews who like to discuss the affairs of the community of private matters with. I therefore devote my *Shabbas* to this.

Eventually, Maimonides' Ladino was utterly swamped by Yiddish; there were twenty times more Ashkenazim than Sephardim.

AT SOME POINT over the centuries, Yiddish became the most sonorous, funny, beautiful, sad, occasionally guttural, and alternately laugh-splattered and gut-wrenching language on earth. There are so many theories about the birth of Yiddish, its growth, rise, fall, rise, fall and rise and fall again, that nothing like a conventional wisdom concerning the *mamme-loshn* exists.

Still, would it hurt like a hole in the head—one of the hundreds of Yiddish phrases translated and transfused into English since the 1880s—to know that the following sayings come from the *mamme-loshn*?

"Get lost." "You should live so long." "My son, the physicist." "Who *needs* it?" "So why do you?" "All *right* already." "It shouldn't happen to a dog." "Okay by me." "He knows from nothing," and "From that he makes a *living*?"

Pulitzer Prize–winner Art Spiegelman's comic book *Maus* is the deepest and most haunting example of Yiddish's influence on English. Spiegelman's father, Vladek, survived Auschwitz, and his son created a brilliant pictorial metaphor of history's most grotesque horrors. When his Polish father spoke in *Maus*, Spiegelman quoted him directly in the Yiddish/English the survivor used in his adopted country.

"He did a good job, no?"; "But I haven't with whom else to talk!"; "It's a shame my son would wear such a coat!"; "But now is dark out! I wanted you would climb to the roof, it's a leak in the pipe"; "Ach. When I think now of them, it still makes me cry . . ."; "To your father you yell this way?" "I'm telling you, Mala makes me *meshugah!*"; "*Nu?* With my life now, you know it can't be everything okay!" "*Hooh!* I made too fast, our walking!"

LIKE SPIEGELMAN'S FATHER, Yiddish is always making too fast.

> *A yid felt tomed a tog tsu der vokh.*
> "A Jew is always short a day in the week."

> *Der yid hot tsayt krank zu zayn.*
> "A Jew has time only to be sick."

BUT YIDDISH, IS IT not dead?

According to Isaac Bashevis Singer, it might not even *matter* if Yiddish was in fact clinically dead. Shortly after Singer won his Nobel Prize, a journalist pressed the old man with the see-through skin as to why he had never stopped writing stories in such a decrepit and moribund language as Yiddish.

Singer, who'd spent his entire life writing mostly about other-worldly *dybbuks, golems,* and sex, lots of *sex,* looked at the reporter as if he were a dunce. Finally, he explained what he considered the obvious. Singer said he always wrote in the *mamme-loshn,* because: "Ghosts love *Yiddish,* and as far as I know, they all speak it." "When the resurrection comes," he continued,

> I am sure that millions of Yiddish-speaking corpses will rise from their graves one day, and the first question everybody

will be asking is "Are there any new books in Yiddish to read?"

In 1978, satirist Gary Rosenblatt got it right when he published, in the Jewish magazine *Moment*, a faux edition of the *Jerusalem Post* called the *Jerusalem Roast*.

The article was datelined May 14, 2048.

YIDDISH STILL DYING

New York: An urgent appeal has gone out to Jews all over the world to save the daily [now weekly] Yiddish newspaper, the *Forward [Forverts]*, now in its 200th year of continuous publication.

A *Forward* staffer deplored the fact that the Yiddish language is dying, and cited as proof that 42 books, 67 magazine articles and 2,800 doctoral dissertations have been published this year alone on the tragic theme that Yiddish is a forgotten language.

IN 1984, I was a pup reporter at a New York–based weekly newsmagazine. One day, without anything to do and not wanting to look idle, I wrote a preobituary for Yiddish, hooked to the surely imminent-seeming demise of the *Forverts*, a.k.a. the Jewish *Daily Forward*.

The *Forverts* certainly looked to be on life support. "DNR"—medical lingo for "Do Not Resuscitate"—was scrawled on its chart. The paper, and Yiddish itself, seemed to be waiting only for a doctor of linguistics to pull the plug and put the Yiddish newspaper and language out of its own misery.

It had once been the leading Yiddish paper in the world with a circulation of over 250,000. Now, the *Forverts* skimped along with octogenarian writers who were no longer able to find Yiddish typewriters; ninety-year-old typesetters who couldn't find replacements for their worn-down metal letters; and one-hundred-year-old editors who'd forgotten the names of their great-grandchildren, yet still hadn't buried grudges against Yiddish enemies from seventy years before.

Yet the *Forverts* didn't die. The publication was like Karen Ann Quinlan, the comatose young woman whose life-or-death fate captured America's civil libertarians, churches, the courts, and the press's attention in the 1970s. After almost a year of debate, her parents, in 1976, finally won the right to pull the plug on their daughter.

She didn't die until 1985.

Similarly, my obituary for the *Forverts* and Yiddish never ran. I realized I would be dust long before Yiddish.

The *mamme-loshn* will live on, as the Yiddish saying goes, "if only out of spite."

SPITE IS NOT at all a tenet of living in Yiddish. While German has the word *Schadenfreude*, the pleasure one gets from another's misfortune, Yiddish, has *kvelling*, the vicarious rush of good feeling when a friend or relative does well. Even gossip, as long as it bore at least the appearance of seemliness, was considered an often-proper means of communication through the preprinting-press *shtetls* and Jewish ghettos of Europe.

Gossip probably wasn't any more or less important in any other culture. In Yiddish, however, it seemed almost officially sanctioned.

Az ikh tuvos ikh vil, meg dokh yener zogn vos er vil.
"If I do as I choose, then another may say what he pleases."

Soon after I was unable to bury Yiddish, I began taking lessons in the *mamme-loshn* and Yiddish-style gossip. I'd learned
just the language at home and college. This time I attended the
Inlingua Institute on Fifth Avenue in midtown Manhattan. The
magazine was paying for the lessons out of its generous education allowance, and I enrolled in the language institute whose
clientele was composed mostly of foreign-bound businesspeople
who needed to quickly learn how to say, "Madame Premier,
may you pass the monkey brains and hot sauce?"

It took Inlingua six months to find me an individual tutor in
Yiddish. Who they came up with was a delightful octogenarian,
Dr. Joseph Levitz, a renowned American Yiddish poet.

He'd come to America from Russia as a young man, and he
still spoke with a thick European-Yiddish accent. He'd earned
his Ph.D. in New York, and was currently an emeritus professor
of Yiddish studies at Brooklyn College.

We spent most of our sessions cramming the usual language
drills; whenever I made a mistake, he'd say, "Not so simple, Mr.
Gimpel!"

Dr. Levitz liked to spend the last twenty minutes of each of
our thrice-weekly tutorials teaching me filthy Yiddish metaphors.

He taught me that the phrase for "she's good in bed" is:

Zi veys take vi tsu tantsn matratsn-polke!
"She really knows how to dance the mattress polka!"

He also enjoyed gossiping about the good old days when Yiddish was king among American Jews. When we got to that end
point of our lesson—he called it my introduction to Yiddishkeit—
he would lower his voice conspiratorially. He was convinced we
were being spied upon by agents of the *goyim*: For proof, he
would point silently at an internal Inlingua phone that hung on

the wall next to the table where we sat facing each other in our assigned room.

Soon, though, he'd forget about potential spies in our midst on Fifth Avenue, and talk animatedly of life half a century before, when he was a young poet and regular at the Café Royal, histrionically joining in the never-ending debates—held at a decibel level approximating that of Kennedy Airport.

Yiddish actors, writers, and journalists congregated in the cafés along "Knish Alley"—Second Avenue, between 1911 and 1915 the Yiddish equivalent of uptown's Tin Pan Alley. The man who opened the Royal quickly lost it to Oscar Szatmarie, the café's headwaiter, in a game of Hungarian *klabyash*.

Besides such frequent luminaries from the Yiddish stage as Boris Thomashevsky and Jacob Adler, the café was also visited by the likes of Leon Trotsky, Charlie Chaplin, and Theodore Dreiser. The Royal became so famous that in 1942 Elia Kazan put on a production called *Café Crown*, a fictionalized account of the real thing.

As with the young, foul-mouthed, Yiddish-spouting comedians at Hanson's drugstore a few decades later, the price of admission to the arguments was a single cheap purchase. Instead of a twenty-five-cent cup of Hanson's coffee, the Royal demanded a few pennies for a *glah-zel tay*, a glass of tea, drunk in the traditional Yiddishkeit manner through a sugar cube placed between the front teeth.

There was one other requirement for the right to stay: The café proprietor had to be impressed with one's level of discourse or you were out on the street, like the loser of a playground game of one-on-one basketball. Such was not the case, however, at one noted Second Avenue emporium: Segal's Café.

Segal's clientele were not Yiddish revolutionaries or *littéra-*

teurs; they had no interest in arguing Hegelian dialectics or Nietzsche's nihilism. They were Jewish gangsters, and discussions tended toward yesterday's or tomorrow's score. In Professor Albert Fried's seminal *The Rise and Fall of the Jewish Gangster in America*, he quoted the 1912 findings of Abe Shoenfeld's inquiry into the no-goodniks who congregated at the café of ill repute.

Shoenfeld was the chief investigator of the New York *Kehillah*, the experiment in pragmatic social organization whose founders hoped to unite all the city's multifarious Jewish factions into one model community. Shoenfeld's list of Segal's regular patrons included:

Sadie Chink, ex-prostitute, owner disorderly house; Dopey Benny, gorilla, life taker; Little Mikie Newman, gangster; Sam Boston, gambler, owner, former fagin, fence, commission bettor; his wife, a pickpocket; Crazy Jake, gun (pickpocket); Little Natie (not the one from Broome Street), gun, right family name is Lubin being related to Lubin the Philadelphia Moving Film Company; Jennie Morris, alias Jennie the Factory, former Prostitute and at present disorderly house owner, her mack is Henry Morris, owner 249 Broome Street; Tillie Finkelstein, gun-moll from Bessie London's School, married to Candy Kid Phil, do not know his family name.

My tutor Dr. Levitz, however, preferred the gossip tossed back and forth at the more intellectual Jewish salons. Sex and envy from fifty years ago seemed his primary nostalgic interests. He laughed remembering the priapic wanderings of a young Yiddish actor named Julius Garfinkle, who was consistently late to rehearsals because he was always *shtupping* someone's wife while the husband was working at the sweatshop or the family candy

store. Said Dr. Levitz, explaining Garfinkle/Garfield's love of the
illicit affair:

"Eyner hot lib dem rov, der anderer hot lib di rebetsin."
"One person likes the rabbi, another likes the rabbi's wife."

Later, Garfinkle moved to Hollywood and changed his name
to John Garfield. He became a star in *Body and Soul*, where he
played a haunted boxer—a *box-eh* as distraught *mammeles* called
the profession when they discovered what their boys were training to be after school. Boxing was one of those endeavors Jewish
parents thought the height of *goyishe nachas*—activities that
brought pride only to non-Jews. (This would all change with the
arrival of such Jewish champions and contenders as Battling
Levinsky, Benny Leonard, and Leach Cross, a.k.a. Dr. Lewis
Wallach, a dentist who in 1910 knocked out the tooth and consciousness of Knockout Brown, then replaced the tooth the next
day in his dental office.)

Perhaps Julius Garfinkle/John Garfield's most important
role was playing the actual Jew in the 1947 film *Gentleman's
Agreement*, perhaps the first major production to tackle anti-
Semitism. The film was made by the non-Jewish moviemaker
Dore Schary, and starred Gregory Peck as an investigative reporter posing as a Jew (!) to expose restricted hotels and other
sorts of less-casual anti-Semitism. Peck, talking slowly, inex-
pressively, and without waving his hands, seemed as Jewish as
lobster.

Garfield had heart trouble—and, as Dr. Levitz correctly announced, had died literally *zetzing* in the sack. "Very appropriate," said my octogenarian tutor.

Clifford Odets and Isaac Bashevis Singer also had trouble

keeping their *shmeckels* (penises) in their pants, my tutor informed me. "Mr. Clifford Odets was a ladies' man who liked to step out," Dr. Levitz said.

Singer, meantime, was always so depressed that women of a maternal bent fell all over the unknown author then trying to ride the coattails of his famous brother, Yiddish writer I. L. Singer, who serialized his novels in the *Forverts*. Dying young, I. L. Singer authored the universally acclaimed *Yoshe Kalb* and *The Brothers Ashkenazi*.

"I never understood how Bashevis performed," Dr. Levitz said. "He was so suicidal whenever I saw them that I don't know how he could get his *petzel zu stehen* [penis to stand]."

"*Az der kleyner vil nisht shtey mus men zik mit a finer bageyn*," he said, wonderingly.

"If the little one won't stand, you have to do it all by hand."

AND THEN THERE was the green monster of *mamme-loshn* letters. Cynthia Ozick nailed it when she titled her *roman à clef*, "Yiddish: Or, Envy in America," without question the best short story about the mother tongue written in English.

"Somehow word had leaked, and everyone knew a Yiddish writer was going to get the Nobel Prize in Literature that year [1978]," Dr. Levitz told me. The short list was thought to consist of two undisputed masters.

First was the world-famous Isaac Bashevis Singer, whose oeuvre had been fully translated. An even bet with Singer was the novelist Chaim Grade, whose realistic tales of old-world Jewry had earned him a lifetime of critical plaudits. Yet he'd had trouble finding translators, and his work was little known, even in the United States.

"So then Grade found out he'd been passed over for Singer," Dr. Levitz said. "And BOOM!!" the old poet said, banging his hand on the table. "Grade dropped dead of jealousy that day!"

Not quite: Singer's prize came in 1978; Grade died in 1982.

Yet Yiddish tales rarely let facts get in the way of a good story. Especially when the tale is about Jew-versus-Jew.

Another facet of Yiddishkeit tradition is the repeating of old tales. "The best way to remember and plug into the past is to re- member our ancestors and tell their stories, and stories about them," says Chasidic rabbi and Yiddish wise man Manis Friedman.

So, in the story of Yiddish, old stories are often told in the truncated words of those very souls. Special attention is placed on many whose names have been forgotten: the writer Dovid Bergelson; the intellectual Simon Dubnow and fools like David Friedlander and the Wise Men [sic] of Chelm; the Gentile Jacob Riis; and the (should be forgotten) anti-Semites Henry James and Charles Lindbergh.

ANOTHER CONVENTIONAL PIECE of Yiddish-based wisdom is that there is no true real blood to keep the *mamme-loshn* alive. Not true.

There is a virtually publicly unknown movement called "Queer Yiddishkeit," wherein young gay Jews are injecting des- perately needed new plasma into the mother tongue, helping reinvigorate the language with a new generation of fluent speak- ers actively trying to *live* their lives in Yiddish.

Gay Yiddishists naturally despise the use of the word *faygel- lah* to describe their orientation.

It is very important not to call a gay Jewish person a *faygellah*, Yiddish for a little bird with a beautiful song.

Rather, say *fray-lech*, Yiddish for "happy" or "gay."

Yet "Queer Yiddishkeit" is fine to say when used by members, friends, or sympathizers to the cause. Queer Yiddishkeit is a barely publicized movement and lifestyle, and, outside of Yiddish insider circles, a virtually-until-this-second-unspoken-of secret that is only now breaking into the mainstream Jewish press.

And thank goodness. Every convert to the cause is another bellowful of air into spoken Yiddish's wheezing lungs. And any particular group drawn in any significant numbers to the *mamme-loshn* should be cheered.

Masha in Chekhov's *The Seagull* said she dressed in black because "I'm in mourning for my life." Yiddish, too, has always worn bereavement clothes fit for a people so often, it seemed, living in wait for its own funeral.

Many times, reports of Yiddish's imminent demise seemed far from exaggerated. And though the language has seemingly thousands of words at its command to indicate a human dipshit, it has names for only two flowers (rose, violet) and none for wild birds.

Yiddish needs extra hues in its tiny Crayola box in order to draw a new world for itself: Its survival as a breathing language needs more than academics in their ivory towers and octogenarians in their Sunday-morning Yiddish clubs at the local Jewish community centers. If transfusing other kinds of lives into the pale, old hacking *mamme-loshn* means adding a shade of pink, so be it. Yiddish certainly needs the color in its *cholent* (a slow-cooked Sabbath stew consisting of everything and tasting like nothing).

Yiddish has always had forty-seven different splinter groups debating its meanings and detesting each other, so what's the problem with adding one more? This diversity of disunity is one of the primary ways Yiddish has saved the Jews. It has given

them the words, which somehow transmuted into the strength
to hold on as they debated endlessly among themselves in the
most colorful language on earth.

The topics of discussion were, and are, every conceivable human act, hope, or atrocity on that earth, especially the never
firm Jewish terra firma. Arguments have raged for centuries
about the idiocies and wisdom of assorted rabbis; the wandering
evil eye of the *shtetl* philanderer and the mitigating factor of his
unbearably shrewish wife; why every Jew had to belong to two
synagogues—one in which to pray, and a second which they
wanted it known they'd never be caught dead in.

And, most important, Yiddish provided the armor of words
and passion in which Jews could endlessly toss back and forth to
each other the question of if, and why, it was worth the often
unbearable wait for their world on this earth to get unfucked,
and their Chosenness proven.

After all, as the *mamme-loshn* put it:

Di tsung iz nit in goles.
"The tongue is never in exile."

DESPITE ITS REPUTATION, Yiddish has never been a poor or
stupid man's consolation language. What can be poor or stupid
about a tongue that not only describes the universe in words,
but in short phrases, unbelievable metaphors, and both simple
and dense stories that encompass entire worlds via tears strained
through laughter; idealism siphoned through cynicism; wisdom
as filtered by idiots; and *shmendricks* observed by wise men?

"A man should live if only to satisfy his curiosity."

"The tavern can't corrupt a good man, the synagogue can't reform a bad one."

"A job is fine but it interferes with your time."

"All cantors are fools, but not every fool can sing."

"If my *bube* had balls she'd be my *zayde*."

"The rabbi drains the bottle and tells the others to be gay."

"God never told anyone to be stupid."

"Dead-shmed; is he earning a living?"

"Shrouds are made without pockets."

"'For dust thou art, and unto dust thou shalt return'—in between, a drink comes in handy."

CHAPTER 3

אידיש פֿון נשמה די אידיש פֿון נשמה די

The Soul of Yiddish

ere facts don't even begin to tell the story of Yiddish: Yet they do make for smart cocktail chat that in some ways keeps a Band-Aid on this supposedly always dying language until the doctorates in linguistics show up.

Yiddish, in the one thousand years of its mischievous, bastardized life, has served as more than merely a mirror and self-descriptor for Jews. It also provides a great shaggy dog story of a language, and a history of the people who own it. The tale is a millennium-old, up-and-down plot line waiting for a final act that has never been written, and never will be as long as there are two Jews left, as Michael Wax has it, to *kvetch* about everything.

The story of Yiddish is a nonlinear tale that at first seems as complicated and impossible to solve as an all-blue-sky jigsaw puzzle. Yet it is easily assembled once its secrets and style become apparent. The puzzle can be cracked with both the rational and counterintuitive reasoning known as a *Yiddishe kopf*, a "Jewish head."

That's not necessarily an insult to Christians. One can be Gentile and have a *Yiddishe kopf,* and likewise you can be a Jew and have *a goyishe kopf,* a non-Jewish head. But a *Yiddishe kopf* isn't just about being an algebra whiz in junior high school, and sharing with the *goyishe kopfs* all the answers to all the tests in exchange for making one's shop projects. A *Yiddishe kopf,* of whatever denomination, knows instinctively, for example, the meaning and soul of the word *feh!*

Feh!, always spelled with an exclamation point, is the disrespectful equivalent of the Bronx cheer, the sound offered by fifty-five thousand Yankee Stadium fans after Alex Rodriguez grounds into a game-ending double play. And *feh!,* when repeated three or a dozen times in a row, results in what Lenny Bruce referred to as the call of the "Jewish seagull."

Feh! emanates in a dismissive, hysterical, exasperated spirit, the kind of noise one hears when the same Alex Rodriguez grounds into a game-ending *triple* play. *Feh! feh! feh! feh! feh! feh! feh!* is what Lenny Bruce's old-world *Yiddishe* auntie shrieked when her beloved nephew told her he was marrying a stripper named Honey Harlowe.

Feh!, a prominent Yiddish dictionary details, has seventeen different definitions, only one of them positive:

"*Feh!* I salute you!"

Oy, meantime, is a language complete in itself, describing and defining all of life's grandiosity and perils in one word. Or two words, if you include, which you must, *Oy gevalt!* Generally, each additional *oy* amplifies the enunciated distress by a power of *finf un zwanzig* (twenty-five).

Oy is what one's mother says when she discovers her fourteen-year-old son is missing from Yom Kippur services. *Oy gevalt!* are the words she yells when she finds said son smoking a cigarette on the synagogue steps with his cronies during the Kol Nidre prayers, the beginning of Yom Kippur, the most solemn day of the year.

The meaning of *oy* can be deceptive, as can *oy, oy; oy yoy yoy;* and *oy gevalt*. Appropriate usage often depends on a shrug of the shoulders, two palms turned upward, and correct body language: a Groucho Marx lifting an eyebrow or an innocent Harpo Marx leer.

Oy gevalt! is what Al Jolson's cantor father must have at the very least thought before he died of heartbreak in the 1927 movie *The Jazz Singer*, when Al Jolson, the cantor's fictional son and protégé, failed to show up for Kol Nidre in order to chase his dream of becoming a secular singing sensation by kneeling like a *shnorrer* (mooch) and emoting like Sophie Tucker while tastefully made up with the burnt cork of a minstrel maestro slathered on his face.

GREAT FAILURE IS in the grand Yiddish tradition.

Just as Eskimos reputedly have hundreds of ways to say "snow," so Yiddish has a seemingly unending vocabulary used by Jews to their brethren to indicate a failure: a fool, an idiot, or a *meshuggener* who shouldn't be out *sans* a day pass.

Charlie Chaplin didn't mean for his little tramp character to be mistaken for a Yiddish *luftmentsch* (literally an "air man," the kind of airhead with no visible means of support who seemingly lives on nothing but oxygen). Yet, to the horrified dismay of the resolutely British-not-Yiddish comic genius, he was forever assumed to be Jewish.

It didn't help that his little tramp was an utter, if unconscious, homage to the vaudeville "Hebe" acts that began flourishing before the turn of the twentieth century. Decades before Chaplin, these hack comics appeared onstage dressed as unemployed Jewish pants pressers, with moth-eaten derbies and vests, toothbrush mustaches, and flowers in their lapels thrown in for effect. For whatever reason, Chaplin made no nod to the existence of concentration camps in *The Great Dictator*.

Not so with The Three Stooges in *You Nazty Spy*, the first Hollywood-approved attack on Hitler that came out months before Chaplin's classic. In their spoof of the Nazis, the proudly Jewish Moe, Larry, and Curly slipped a profane Yiddish question concerning the already-begun Holocaust into the script:

> *"Alle menschen muss zu machen, jeden tug a gentzen kachen?"*
> "Who do you have to fuck in this town to get somebody to help?"

Yiddish failure.

Max Bialystock and Leo Bloom in *The Producers*.

Onetime wonder boy record producer Phil Spector, reduced to a ridiculously bewigged Jewish munchkin with lifts in his heels, was on trial in 2007 for allegedly murdering, in meaningless cold blood, a C-level actress in his Hollywood mansion-cum-fortress.

Yiddish failure is director Sidney Lumet casting Melanie Griffith to play a Chasidic woman in *A Stranger Among Us*.

There is the failure of living off your father-in-law while pursuing advanced studies, forgetting this tradition died as a *mitzvah* (good deed) for elder *reichers* (rich ones) in the old country. In America, one must *macht a leben* or risk being accused of *shnorring*, being a *luftmentsh* living on someone else's air.

The failure of a Jewish magnate never reading a book or giving *tzedakah* ("charity.")

★ ★ ★

AND THEN THERE is the general failure of Jews in sports. In baseball, forget Hank Greenberg and Sandy Koufax for a moment. No one knows how many talented Jewish ballplayers were waylaid by old world *Yiddishe* tradition from the path of New World athletic *goyishe nachas*. (Koufax had always planned to be an architect and was always the most reluctant of sports heroes, and Greenberg's parents only allowed him to sign with the Detroit Tigers because the team promised to let their Henry graduate from New York University before making him play.)

Saul Bellow understood the twin currents pulling young, gifted Jewish athletes. He wrote in *Humboldt's Gift* that the Jewish

> Humboldt could hit like a sonofabitch on the sandlot. With his shoulders, just imagine how much beef went into his swing. If I had my way, he would have ended up in the majors. But he started hanging around the Forty-Second Street library . . . first thing I knew he was printing highbrow poems in the magazines.

Yet non-Jewish baseball men remained always on the lookout for *yidn*. New York Giants manager John McGraw, forever searching for Jewish ballplayers to attract the multitudes of Manhattan Jews to his Polo Grounds, was the most obvious.

McGraw failed most spectacularly with the putative slugger Moses "the Rabbi of Swat" Solomon, who disappeared into oblivion after four at-bats in 1923. McGraw had more luck with Andy Cohen, falsely advertised in his 1928 debut as the "Jewish [version of baseball superhero] Rogers Hornsby."

One New York tabloid was especially not impressed by Cohen's brilliant prospects, printing doggerel that read:

And from the bleachers
The cry of "Oy oy" rose.
And up came Andy Cohen
Half a foot behind his nose.

Meantime, immediately after Hank Greenberg signed with Detroit, he was greeted with a headline in *The Sporting News*, the undisputed "Bible of Baseball," of—"OI OI OI [sic], OH BOY! HAIL THAT LONG-SOUGHT JEWISH STAR." Accompanying the article was a cartoon of a large-beaked man who looked like Fagin saying "Oy yoy-yoy."

In the 1960s, columnist Don Riley of the *St. Paul Pioneer Press* wrote that Sandy Koufax threw "*matzoh* balls." In 1998, *Elysian Fields*, a literary and scholarly baseball journal, printed a piece by respected baseball writer Peter J. Bjarkman that said "the handsome and refined [Koufax] at first seemed to wipe away a common notion about Jewish athletes as essentially inferior, second-rate, and feeble; then his sudden retirement at the pinnacle of glory seemed to confirm a popular conception and also certify a time-worn myth."

Then there is the ultimate failure of Jewish professional basketball players. Though Jews once dominated the "City Game" on the court, now one is more likely to *own* an NBA team than play on one.

Yiddish, as Isaac Singer said in his Nobel speech, was the language of struggling for any scrap of success. Yet failure was everywhere, as was worrying about problems so profound they were insoluble. For:

Der goy iz tss-oom go'-les nit ge-voint.
"*Goyim* aren't used to Jewish troubles."

* * *

A FEW OF the Jews' biggest historic troubles have been self-inflicted. Primary amongst them have been the perils of working professionally with their *mishpocha*. There are illustrations going at least as far back as the Maccabees, a few centuries B.C.E., of the perils of going into a Jewish family business.

All looked swell at first. The Maccabees, a family of brothers-in-arms, beat back a massive Greek army, saving the Temple, and providing an excuse for Hanukkah. The Maccabees disintegrated not in further battle, but because of meaningless intramural bickering between the former spiritual brothers. Their nonstop *kvetching* proved once again that if one must work with one's own Jewish family, make sure and place all responsibility and, when necessary, blame on one of your relatives.

Take the four Jewish sons, all lawyers, and the story of how to avoid entanglement. One day, a would-be customer telephones the law firm of Schwartz, Schwartz, Schwartz, and Schwartz.

"Is Mr. Schwartz there?" the would-be client asks the man who answers the law firm's phone.

"I'm sorry, Mr. Schwartz is at the Bar Association convention."

"Well, can I speak to Mr. Schwartz?" the customer asks.

"I'm sorry, Mr. Schwartz just retired."

"Well, is Mr. Schwartz there?"

"I'm afraid not, he's on vacation and won't be back until next week."

"Well, is Mr. Schwartz there?" the potential customer asks.

"Speaking."

As is said in *Yiddish*:

Voynen zol men tsvishn yidn, handlen zol men tsvishn goyim.
"Live among Jews, do business with Gentiles."

Yet, as always, there is an alternate Yiddish viewpoint:

Mit a yidn iz nor gut kugl tsu esn, davenen fun eyn sider un lign of eyn beysakvores.
"Togetherness among Jews is only good for eating pudding, praying from prayerbook, and lying in one cemetery."

THOSE WHO UNDERSTAND the secret power of Yiddish words *must* also know the meaning and feeling of Yiddishkeit, which again technically translates to "Jewishness." Yet Yiddishkeit is not an outlook restricted to Jews, and every Jew doesn't carry it in his or her heart.

Yiddishkeit means breathing in the spirit of an all-encompassing language and worldview. It carries an intuitive code of proper conduct and karmic intentions toward oneself, other Jews, and larger society.

Yiddishkeit is by definition *not* holy laws—it's everything about being a Jew that *isn't* a commandment or legal precept. Yiddishkeit is the warmest feelings—and sometimes curious habits—of "Jewishness." Yiddishkeit denotes bearing a Yiddishe *hartz*, a loving Jewish heart.

Yiddishkeit is a rabbi who memorizes the names and individual problems of all twelve hundred members of his or her congregation. Or the old-time Jewish gangsters—none of whom have existed for more than a generation—never discussing business at the dinner table.

Yiddishkeit is those gangsters fighting harder for their European brethren during the Holocaust than the official Jewish organizations afraid of rocking the Gentile world's boat. They donated money to their synagogues and illegally ran guns to Israel that they heisted from shipments bound for the Arabs after Israel was immediately attacked upon being named an independent Jewish state.

Yiddishkeit is these Jewish gangsters being uniformly successful in keeping their sons from entering the business. (In one of the goofier incidents, federal agents, forever tailing Meyer Lansky, swooped down upon the old gangster in Miami, when they saw him writing out a check on a car roof to a suspicious-looking man. Sure they had finally caught Lansky making a payoff for criminal malfeasance, it turned out the retired gangster was paying for a new set of the encyclopedias so his Wolfie's Delicatessen comrades of retired *shlammers* could determine more accurately the correct answers to each other's trivia questions.)

That's Yiddishkeit.

What isn't Yiddishkeit is David Ben-Gurion, the legendary first prime minister of Israel, ordering the sinking of a ship in state waters, resulting in the killing of dozens of Jewish sailors carrying illegal armaments to the new state. Nor are the actions of Rabbi Stephen Wise, head of all the official Jewish organizations in the country, refusing to press his friend Franklin Roosevelt to take action during the Holocaust in order not to make World War II look like a "Jewish" conflict; nor is the state of Minnesota naming their international airport after Nazi sympathizer Charles Lindbergh.

Nor is Richard Nixon an example of Yiddishkeit, who told Henry Kissinger, "It's the Jews, Henry, the Jews" who were out to get him; nor is Henry Kissinger, the German-Jewish refugee from World War II, who replied, "Zer are Jews, Mr. President, and zer are Jews."

Academic and professional Yiddishists may know the linguistic and grammatical nuances within the words *shmuck* and *putz*. Yet if they, or any gay *klezmer* ensemble, have no notion of abiding in their heads and hearts the soul of Yiddishkeit, they are, well, *shmucks* and *putzes*.

According to the rules of Yiddishkeit, any Jew is usually well within their rights to tell another Jew:

Zol du vaksn vi a tsibele: mitn kop in dre'erd un di fis farkert!
"May you grow like an onion: with your head in the
    ground and your feet in the air!"

Or:

*Zol dein zeyger bay in krikn, dos harts loyfn,
di gal ibergeyn, di bayb antloyfn, un der noz
shtendik rinen!*
"May your clock run slow, your heart fast,
your bile over, your wife away, and your
nose always!"

After all, as one of the most famous old Yiddish saws goes:

Tzvay yidn, drei meinungen.
"Two Jews, three opinions."

Jews often disbelieve even their own attempts at apostasy. Take the case of Heinrich Heine, the great nineteenth-century Jewish poet, who, like many other German Jews, converted to

Christianity for social mobility into the restricted salons of the Gentile cognoscenti and aristocracy.

Despite Heine's proud, haughty, and debonair demeanor among his non-Jewish friends, the poet could never erase his roots. That failure toward one's own blood is symbolized best by Heine's inability even to look in his mother's eyes, to whom he feels, "shamed by your presence . . . for I have brought your heart to tears."

Heine's poem was oft translated for the Yiddish stage, a melodramatic warning to those who would dare discard their heritage, like Heine, for the approval of the *goyim*. Realizing his conundrum between genteel assimilation and abandonment of his own blood, Heine wrote:

Stubborn and proud I carry my head high;
Haughty by birth, inflexible by mood,
I would not bow to any king; I would
Not even veil my candid gaze, not I.
But, mother, never let me dare deny
How soon my pride, my boastful hardihood
Shamed by your presence and solicitude,
Leaves me without one small departing sigh.
Is it your spirit that o'ermasters me,
Your lofty, penetrating soul that clears
The earth and cleaves to heaven, flying free?
Memory burns and rankles, for I know
How often I have brought your heart to tears,
The soft and suffering heart that loved me so.

Shtolz bin ich, eingeshpart, halt hoich die kop;
Geboiren mazeldik, vil zich nit boigen;
Tzu keynem neyg ah kni—nit tzu ah kenig,

Und ich kuk alemen gleich in die oigen.
Ober, mein muter, ich ken nit ferneigen
As mein shtolzieren und berimerei,
Veren ferloren, in gantzen oisgemekt,
Vibald du kumst doh mit dein edelkeit,
Is dos dein geist vos ibermechtigt mir,
Dein forshendeh neshomeh, vos hoibt zich
Iber erd, uhn nehntert zich tzum himel?
Die erinerung erbitert mir, veil
Ich veys vie oft 'chob ful gemacht mit treren
Dein veycheh hartz, vos hot mir azoi gern.

Even with that, Heine went on to publicly debase himself and other Jews who were converting for social reasons. He doubted the sincerity of any such conversions, because "it is extremely difficult for a Jew to be converted, for how can he bring himself to believe in the divinity of another Jew?"

THIS PART OF Yiddish—teasing or lancing your *lantzmen's* hubris or sincerity—has been for the millennium of Yiddish's existence proof (as the *mamme-loshn* reports) that words can be as deadly as arrows.

Yet self-deprecation to the point of masochism was often the only weapon the defenseless Diaspora *yidn* ever had.

As Kenneth Tynan wrote in a *New Yorker* profile in the 1970s of Mel Brooks, "On the streets, where Irish, Italian, and Polish gangs roamed only a few blocks away, Brooks was funny in self-defense. 'If your enemy is laughing' [Brooks said], 'how can he bludgeon you to death?'"

"I do not know of a people making fun to such a degree of its own character," observed Sigmund Freud.

Still, a fierce camaraderie among Jews was forged through the vessel of Yiddish—largely because of segregationist decrees in their host countries that made sure the odds were prohibitive a Jew would ever be speaking to a Gentile.

So it is easy to see why, when saying "hello," Yiddish speakers, so isolated from the world, would greet friends with:

Vos macht a yid?
"What's up, Jew?"

Even that hints at the universality of Yiddish. There is the old joke, recounted in Cynthia Ozick's *"Yiddish*: Or, Envy in America," about an international conference of speakers of Esperanto, the man-made language meant to combine the basics of all languages to create one tongue that could be used by the entire world.

During a break in the conference, the attendees wandered out into the hall and began informally chatting in their special language. An Esperanto expert saw an old friend and went up to say hello in their global language:

"Vos macht a yid?"

THE STORY OF Yiddish makes *War and Peace* seem as straightforward and linear as *Green Eggs and Ham*. Yet there is a simplicity to Yiddish that explains the Jews to themselves, and to the outside world, why Jews must stick together and why they react to the *goyim* with a *mish-mosh* of unalloyed fear, wistful contempt, and grateful appreciation for those perceived on the Jews' side.

That simplicity, often grounded in self-protective self-deprecation, is another reason Jews have historically looked down upon the language, even as it became one of their most precious belongings, a jewel that helped save the Jews both from their enemies and the invariable splintering of most any tribe that has managed to stay together for three thousand years.

Probably Leo Rosten's wisest sentence came while he was speaking as a scholar and professor of linguistics, before he authored *The Joys of Yiddish* (1968), perhaps the most populist and popular, loved and loathed book concerning the *mamme-loshn* in history.

According to Rosten, everyone in the world "sees things as *we* are, not as *they* are."

So what is so special about Yiddish? And why is it so easily left behind by Jews? Part, as mentioned, is the glory and strength of modern Hebrew, arming Israel's troops with the words for the actual weapons they now possess. Though two Jews, have three opinions, apparently one people can only handle one language. Yiddish knew it:

> *Mit ain tuchus ken mer nisht tanzen auf tzvay chasenes chos'-en-eh.*
> "With one ass you can't dance at two weddings."

Seeing the positive side of Yiddish was Israel Zangwill, the British writer of such turn-of-the-twentieth-century classics as *The King of the Shnorrers*. "Yiddish," he said, "incorporates the essence of a life which is distinctive and unlike any other."

On the self-loathing side are the words of David Friedlander (1750–1834), a zealous acolyte of Moses Mendelssohn, best known for his *Epistle to the German Jews*. His 1788 screed clanked as Friedlander attempted to show his *lantzmen* the way of the Enlightenment—in Yiddish, the *Haskalah*.

Irving Howe wrote about Friedlander's Enlightenment that

"the Haskalah has sometimes been described as a forerunner of 'assimilation'—a loaded word in Jewish discourse that suggests the Jews surrender their identity and lose themselves in the non-Jewish world."

Friedlander—a German Jew, one of the leading assimilationists in the world—wrote in fear and self-loathing:

> The [Yiddish] that is common among us has no rules, It is vulgar, and it is an incomprehensible language outside of our own circles. It must be eradicated completely . . . only then will it be possible to lay the foundations for a useful and rational education for our youth.

ON THE OTHER side of the spectrum are the still Yiddish-speaking ultra-Orthodox Chasidim, those of the long beards who are adherents and scholars of the non-Madonna Kabbalah. They are those black-hatted, wild, and ecstatic dancers who cut their rugs on hard cement as part of their prayers in their bare-bones synagogues, unable to afford most amenities save a few extra *tallises* (prayer shawls) for the empty-handed.

Chasidic Bar Mitzvah parties, meantime, usually consist of a *shnapps*, *kichel* (plain cookie), and maybe an extra piece of herring speared with a toothpick.

These Jews look like they've just walked out of an eighteenth-century painting of an Eastern European ghetto still believing in Frankenstein-like Golems and fiendish *dybbuks*.

Yiddish will never die, say the Chasidim, because we are simultaneously living in the past, present, and future. So why bother worrying?

Meshuggas? Craziness from *meshuggeners*, crazy people?

Not to William Faulkner, who even though he was, as they

used to say in Yiddish, a *shikker goy* (drunk Gentile), understood, just like the Chasidim, that "the past isn't dead. It isn't even past."

Indeed. After all, as they say in Yiddish:

Es iz laykhter aroystunemen dem yidn fun dem goles eyer dem goles fun dem yidn.
"It's easier to take the Jew out of exile than the exile out of the Jew."

CHAPTER 4

שעסטנ־ַלֶיעטַרשעטנ־ַלֶיעטַרש

History of the Mother Tongue

We will walk through the valley of the Shadow of Death,
for God . . .
On second thought, let's flee through the valley of the
Shadow of Death.
—Woody Allen, *as the nineteenth-century Boris*
in the film Love and Death, *preparing to die*
in his faux-Russian adaptation of an overlong
Tolstoy or Dostoevesky novel

There is a joke most Jews know that putatively offers a nine-word history of their people:

They tried to kill us, we won, let's eat.

Unfortunately, the true story of the last two thousand years of the Jewish Diaspora is more like:

They tried to kill us, they almost did kill us, and when they saw that too many Jews were still alive, they violently kicked God's supposed Chosens out of their country.

Notwithstanding a few intervals of peace and prosperity, the centuries since Yiddish began inventing itself have generally been completely, utterly *verkakte* for the Jews. Relative to what was coming, the thousand years before 1000 C.E. were a *mechaye*, a blessing.

True, there were unprovoked outbreaks of massive, violent anti-Semitism going back dozens of centuries before in the first millennium C.E., when Yiddish began incubating.

Again one must return to the eternal question of why God couldn't Choose someone else for a while.

In fact, God did. By some Talmudic reckonings, this Chosen-ness business had all been a big mistake. According to one important *midrash* (commentary on Jewish scripture), God first approached the children of Esau with the Five Books of Moses and the chance to go Chosen.

Asking for a CliffsNotes version of what was inside, they bridled at the words "Thou Shalt Not Kill," pointing out that in the selfsame Torah, Isaac tells Esau, "By thy sword shalt thou live [Genesis 27: 40]." Thank you, the descendants of Esau said, but no thanks.

God, the *midrash* continues, then approached several other tribes, but none wanted any part of a five-part rule book that included proscriptions on seemingly every pleasurable human activity, civilized or not. Finally, as with the scrawny bespectacled kid chosen last at a pickup game of playground baseball, He came to the Jews.

FOR THIS SEEMING consolation prize of being Chosen, there would be hell, literally, to pay. Still, there were some notable victories.

In antiquity there was Haman, who attempted perhaps one of history's first go's at genocide. His try led to the Purim war, and Jewish victory in 525 B.C.E. It all sounds like a fairy tale. Yet the fairly accurate story is told in the Book of Esther.

The plot revolves around Haman, the bad guy, a wily anti-Semitic Snidely Whiplash. Haman served as the puppet master to the dopey Persian king Achash-vay-rosh, and was brilliantly outwitted by Esther, the king's (secretly Jewish) knockout bride.

She used her *Yiddishe kopf*, centuries before Yiddish existed. And what's especially interesting in this old story are the words themselves, an early vocabulary of the Jews' enemies who would return time and again to try to destroy them.

According to the Book of Esther, Chapter 3, verses 8–9, Haman advised the king that Jews were "a certain people scattered abroad and dispersed among the peoples in the provinces of your kingdom; their laws are different from those of every other people, and they do not keep the king's lot, so that is not for the king's profit to tolerate them. Let it be decreed that they be destroyed."

And so there's the holiday of Purim, the only occasion on which Jews truly let go and celebrate (usually, as Lenny Bruce pointed out, Jews "observe" holidays. It's the non-Jews who "celebrate").

But not on Purim, when Yiddishkeit decrees a Jew must get so drunk he can't tell Haman from Mordecai, Esther's cousin, who is a key co-star in the story.

And yet, even in this day of utter joy, Yiddish won't let the Jews forget:

A sakh homens un nor eyn purim.
"So many Hamans and only one Purim."

Later, the Babylonians came to the holy land, destroying the First Temple in 586 B.C.E. Then came the Greeks, ruling all the way to Alexander the Great. The Maccabees won back greater Judea in 165 B.C.E. and provided a war story worthy of a holiday—Hanukkah. Then came the Romans, who took over Jerusalem as the Maccabees disintegrated from within between 67 and 63 B.C.E.—not an especially long feud between battling Jews.

Then, about 650 years after the First Temple turned to cinders, the Romans took care of the Second Temple in 70 C.E. Greeks, Persians, more Romans, and then, forty years after the death of Jesus, Jews made their last stand and killed themselves on the Judean desert hill called Masada.

Still, European Jews were relatively safe for the first seven hundred years of Christianity. Generally speaking, if they stayed out of harm's way . . . they could stay out of harm's way. Yet as the old blues song had it, "Don't go lookin' for trouble, trouble will find you."

Indeed.

Trouble found them.

So, as they say in the *mamme-loshn:*

Tsum shlimazel darf men oykh hobn.
"Even for bad luck, you need luck."

The First Crusade ran into the Jews in 1096 C.E., when the holy Christians practiced their chops on the *yidn*—literally—on their way to recapturing Jerusalem from the heathen Arabs. Isolating themselves from the rest of civilization and its killing fields proved a good answer for the Jews, and a new language began forming around them that would provide even greater autonomy.

In such a situation, it made good sense that an ever-malleable jargon that non-Jews couldn't understand began evolving. And the First Crusade was as good a time as any for the Jews to get as far away as they could from the Gentiles.

As mentioned, *"Yiddish,"* in Yiddish, means "Jewish."

And "Jewish" is what Yiddish is: the heart and soul, for better *and* for worse, a reflection and mirror of the forever-wanderers' condition.

For decades, the theory that held sway among most scholars was that Yiddish began in France, then moved with the ever-migrating Jews to the banks of the Rhineland. From there, supposedly, Yiddish moved into the heart of Europe, the people and their jerry-built language forever heading eastward, until the Jews and their vernacular tongue settled largely in Russia, Poland, and Romania.

The problem with this long-held notion that the Jews and their Yiddish pushed ever eastward is one of numbers. Three million Jews eventually settled in Eastern Europe; only a fraction of that kind of population could have possibly migrated east from Germany.

More likely, goes a rising tide of opinion, Yiddish spread in the opposite direction, westward from Russia. The population explosion in Eastern European Jews can probably be accounted for by the voluntary mass conversion to Judaism in 740 C.E. by the Turkish Khazars, who had settled on the steppes of southern Russia.

In time, Yiddish began mirroring Jewish existence. The *mamme-loshn*, wrote William Novak and Moshe Waldoks, is "optimistic in the long run, but pessimistic about the present and the immediate future," with "twin currents of anxiety and skepticism that can become so strong that even the ancient sources of Jewish optimism are swept up in them."

Yiddish has always been considered malleable to any language, with new usages declared not by an academy of philologists, but by the people themselves who need to discuss some idea, happenstance, or words of encouragement and compliment. But the *mamme-loshn* is no *shnorrer*. Throughout its history, Yiddish has also given as much as it has received.

Take, just the "sh" words that have become as American as bagels after Sunday church.

Shmuck. Shmegegge. Shmendrick. Shlimazel. Shlemiel. Shlepper. Shnook. Shmo. Shikker. Shagetz. Shiksa. Shlump. Shtick. Shtunk. Shtup. Shlong. Shtuss. Shnook. Shlub. Shnorrer. Shabbes goy. Shnapps. Shmek Tabik. Shteyger. Shlock. Shlockhouse. Shmaltz. Shmooz. Shnoz. Shmattes. Shammes.

And is there any language more nuanced? Take the sentence:

Tz-vay' bill-et'-en fahr zein konzert zohl ich kaufen?

Translated, the question is:

"Two tickets for his concert I should buy?"

In English, the number of attitudes one can express by that Yiddish construction is astonishing. Leo Rosten's noble delineation:

1. "*Two* tickets for his concert I should buy?" (In other words, "it's trouble enough deciding if it's worth buying one ticket to the show.")
2. "Two *tickets* for his concert I should buy?" ("You mean he isn't giving out free passes? If not, no one will come!")
3. "Two tickets for *his* concert I should buy?" ("Did he buy tickets to my nephew's concert?")

4. "Two tickets for his *concert* I should buy?" ("You mean, they call whatever he does a 'concert'?")
5. "Two tickets for his concert *I* should buy?" ("After what he did to me?")
6. "Two tickets for his concert I *should* buy?" ("Are you giving me lessons in ethics?")
7. "Two tickets for his concert I should *buy*? ("I wouldn't go even if he gave me complimentary tickets.")

FOLLOWING THE FIRST Crusade, countries that had once abided or even given Jews fractionalized citizenship began another round of expulsions. Though many lands would grudgingly allow Jews and their services again and again, even the short list of notable banishments over the four hundred years after the First Crusade is, well, notable.

In 1182, France gave Jews the boot, to be followed in 1290 by England, which claimed the Jews were practicing voodoo. France apparently had let some Jews back in occasionally because they evicted them again in 1306, and once more in 1394.

Hungary also had double decrees tossing the Jews out, in 1349 and 1360. Germany sent the Jews scurrying like Steinbeck's Okies in 1348 and 1498.

Austria, Spain, and Portugal only needed one edict apiece (in 1421, 1492, and 1497, respectively), while Lithuania twice ordered their Jews to go, in 1445 and 1495.

After a while, the numbers and years of the evictions become statistics; contemporary accounts of some of the expulsions make human the horror of dispersion. Almost always the Jews were stripped of their land and assets before they fled; all they generally were allowed to take were some personal possessions—and untold numbers of words, sayings, and locutions they'd picked up from the native population's language.

Spain was one land that kept "their" Jews around for political, economic, and cultural advice. Indeed, in 1491, Queen Isabella had a court of Jews who fancied themselves almost Spanish. A year later, however, Isabella was seizing money from Spanish citizens to pay for the voyage of Christopher Columbus (who many still say was a Jew).

In Spain, the royal decree of March 30, 1492, was nothing if not to the point: "The hands of the inquisitors are still stretched forth to investigate the evil of their deeds and . . . We have therefore seen fit to totally banish the Jews from all places in our kingdom, even though they deserve a greater punishment than this for what they have done."

The Jews had three months to get out, the decree continued, "and whoever disobeys us and does not leave will be sentenced to death."

The most powerful Spanish Jew at the time was Don Isaac Abravanel (1437–1508), treasurer of the entire country, working on behalf and at the pleasure of King Ferdinand and Queen Isabella. Abravanel escaped the Inquisition to Italy, where his account of the Jews' ouster gives perhaps a taste, a whiff, of life through the Diaspora as a wandering Jew. He wrote:

"At the time I was in the king's court [and] I met with the king three times, begging him: 'Save us, O King. Why do you do thus to your servants? Impose a large payment on us, one of gold and silver, and every Jew will give.'"

Such appeasement didn't work, nor did argument: "I did not rest and did not remain silent and did not let up," Abravanel continued, "but the decree remained."

Nor did the supposed influence of "all my [Gentile] friends who were close to the king, asking them to intercede . . . so that the decree to destroy all the Jews might be rescinded. But [the king] remained completely deaf."

Abravanel continued:

When [the Jews] heard the decree they all mourned, and wherever the news of the king's word and order was heard, the Jews despaired, and all feared greatly, a fear unequaled since the exile of Judah from its land to a foreign land. . . . In the end there left, without strength, three hundred thousand people on foot, from the youngest to the oldest, all at one time, from all the provinces of the king, to wherever they were able to go.

"God [was] at [the Jews'] helm, and each pledged himself to God anew," Abravanel continued.

But where could they actually go?

Some went to Portugal and Navarre, which are close, but all they found were troubles and darkness, looting, starvation and pestilence. Some traveled through the perilous ocean, and here, too, God's hand was against them, and many were seized and sold as slaves, while many others drowned in the sea. Others again were burned alive, as the ships on which they were traveling were engulfed by flames.

In the end, all suffered: some by the sword and some by captivity and some by disease, until but a few remained of the many. In the words of our fathers (Num. 17:28), "Behold we perish, we die, we all perish," may the name of the Lord be blessed.

I, too, chose the way of the sea, and I arrived here in the famed Naples, a city whose kings are merciful.

Abravanel was, of course, Sephardic. Meantime, the largest mass of Ashkenazic Jews ended up in almost always virulently, and violently, anti-Semitic Russia and Poland.

True, the situation there wasn't exactly Miami Beach, but after centuries of repression things were looking up. In 1861, the new czar, Alexander, released the serfs, an act as charged as Lincoln freeing the slaves. Alexander instituted a modern census; this was when Jews were to take surnames, instead of just being known as "Moishe ben Mordecai" or "Rachel bas Yankl." The census would count Jews as Russian citizens, but it was too difficult to count them if you couldn't properly name them.

Things changed.

In 1881, the major waves of Jewish immigration from Eastern Europe to the United States began in the wake of the assassination of Czar Alexander II by six plotters, including one Jew, Jessie Helfmann. On May 6, 1881, the Vienna bureau chief of the *Daily Telegraph* in London telegraphed news of a hideous pogrom that ran under the headline OUTRAGES UPON JEWS IN RUSSIA.

[The Russians] have represented the Jew as the source of all the evils with which Russia is afflicted. They are held up to popular [opinion] as the assassins of the Czar and Jessie Helfmann, the Jewess who was implicated, as having been the soul of the whole plot. The Czar's assassination happened on a day that is kept up festively by the Jews of Russia, and after the event they were charged having made merry. . . . The atrocities committed at Elizabethgrad, said my informant, must have been fearful to witness, as an officer who traveled a short distance with him and who was present at the time said he had seen things that sickened him to think of. Neither women nor children were spared, and had not many of the Jews been armed a wholesale massacre would certainly have taken place. . . .

That assassination resulted in the 1882 "May Laws," which in effect officially sanctioned pogroms, overlooked spontaneous eruptions of killing Jews, and stepped up the humiliating repression of the *yidn*.

Another mass of Jews fled to the United States after the failed Russian Revolution, fueled largely by Yiddish-speaking, neonatal trade unionists. Proud and atheistic young Jews, the revolutionaries had dared begin forming Socialist labor unions such as Der Algemayner Yidisher Arbeter-Bund.

The failure to overthrow the czar in 1905 hastened the departure to America of a highly politicized group of young Jews who were now being conscripted in the Russian army for enlistments of twenty years.

Then came 1920, when the United States Congress, in the wake of alleged Jewish war profiteering during World War I, and the ensuing postwar "Red Scare" fanned by Attorney General A. Mitchell Palmer to stamp out "Bolsheviks" and "anarchists," enacted prohibitively restrictive immigration laws. These laws virtually stopped the flow to America of Eastern European Jews, two million of whom had fled from Russia, Poland, and Romania to the United States in the preceding forty years.

THE IMPOVERISHED *SHTETL* immigrants who'd made it to America actually carried more than the clothes they were wearing and knowledge of Yiddish. They also brought remembrances of every little village's stock characters.

Two of the most interesting—both which have been siphoned off by English: the *shnorrer* and the *luftmentsh*. Often they were titles shared by the same person.

In all of the Marx Brothers films, Groucho, Harpo, and Chico almost always played roles representing *shtetl luftmentshen*. Enterprising con men with no visible means of support, the *luftmentshen* lived by their cunning, double talk, and ability to cleverly and outrageously manipulate *shlemiels* bearing money and *goyishe kopfs*, to both finance their lives of happy indolence and take advantage of the hospitality offered by (usually Christian) dumbbells who couldn't see through their daffy impersonations of whomever their rich hosts would accept on their scene.

"Can't you see I love you?" Groucho asks Margaret Dumont, playing her usual role as the rich, quickly-aging-past-midlife high-society dowager. "Will you marry me? Did your husband leave you any money? Answer the second question first."

Ms. Dumont, speaking in the rich, marbles-in-the-mouth cadences of Willliam F. Buckley, says her late husband did indeed leave her riches. Groucho's eyebrows rise. Says Dumont, "He died in my arms."

"Aha!" Groucho says, "so it was murder!"

GROUCHO, BESIDES PLAYING the wisecracking *luftmentsh* too fast for any WASPs to understand he's making fun of them, also enacts in film after film the ultimate Yiddish-style, self-entitled mooch called a *shnorrer*, a word long part of the American vocabulary. In the old country, the *shnorrer* was an accepted part of the community: He didn't ask for alms, he demanded them.

His reason for *shnorring* (there is no record of female *shnorrers*) was that he was helping the people he put the touch on to fulfill the commandment to give *tzedaka* (translated literally to

"righteousness," but used to denote "charity"). The *shnorrer* felt
his *chutzpah* (balls-out gall) in demanding money was aiding in
the *shtetl* residents' ability to perform a mitzvah and do right
by God.

The *shnorrer* viewed his job as almost a holy calling. He
thought of it as a profession, similar to jobs requiring special ordi-
nation in Orthodox and Chasidic communities, such as rabbis,
scribes who handwrite the Torah, and *shochets*, the ritual slaugh-
terers who oversee the strict koshering of the town's meat.

There was the old-world story of a *shnorrer* who was unable to
make an appointment to see Rothschild, one of the tiny number
of European Jewish millionaires. The *shnorrer* finally stands outside Rothschild's mansion and begins shouting repeatedly, "The
Baron refuses to see me, and my family is starving to death!"

To finally shut the *shnorrer* up, Rothschild goes outside and
gives him thirty rubles.

"Here you are," he says. "And I want to tell you that if you
hadn't made such a scene, I would have given you sixty rubles."

"My dear Baron," the *shnorrer* said self-righteously, "you're
a banker and I don't give you banking advice. I'm a *shnorrer*, so
please—don't give me *shnorring* advice."

OR:

In the *shtetl*, Mrs. Krasnov, feeling sorry for a *shnorrer* who
appeared at her door, invited him in and gave him a substantial
meal: chicken, *kugel* (noodle pudding), wine, and two kinds of
bread, black bread and challah (the tasty twist bread usually
saved for the Sabbath).

The *shnorrer* devoured everything he was given, except the
black bread. "The challah was wonderful," he said, "do you
have any more?"

"My dear man," said Mrs. Krasnov, "we have plenty of black bread, but challah is very expensive."

"I know," said the *shnorrer*, "but it's worth every cent!"

AS IN THE old world, Groucho Marx's character proudly claimed the historic, dubious, yet accepted title of *shnorrer* bestowed upon the most forward shake-down artist in the *shtetl*. The most obvious example was in the brothers' Yiddish-tinged *Animal Crackers* (1930).

This time, they have managed to sneak into the most aristocratic mansion of their careers. Groucho, after gaining entry into Margaret Dumont's house under the guise of a famous WASP adventurer named Geoffrey Spaulding, is greeted by a chorus of precious *goyim* who look like they've just graduated from Princeton.

They regale him at the beginning of the movie with a song that starts, "Hooray for Captain Spaulding, the African explorer!"

"Did someone call me *shnorrer*?" Groucho sings, *sotto voce*, directly toward the screen.

Or, dining with Clara "the It Girl" Bow in an expensive restaurant, Groucho is presented with a mountainous bill.

"This is an outrage!" he says, acting in proper *shnorrer* fashion by handing the tab to the sex kitten of the times, "if I were you I wouldn't pay it!"

A more modern *shnorrer* walks into one's house uninvited, doesn't ask permission as he opens the refrigerator, and in an accusatory tone demands, "You don't have *Diet* Dr Pepper?" Or he takes your cigarette pack and expresses disappointment when he finds they aren't filterless Lucky Strikes, the kind of smoke last seen in World War II vending machines.

In 1977, Joan Micklin Silver—before directing the Yiddishkeit classics *Hester Street* and *Crossing Delancey*—presented the best modern film depiction of the *shnorrer* and *luftmentsh* in *Between the Lines*, the story of a Boston alternative newspaper called *The Back Bay Mainline*.

In it, a still baby-faced Jeff Goldblum, in his best role ever, plays Max Arloff, the ultimate modern, hip *luftmentsh* forever spouting Yiddish (he answers the paper's phone with, "Back Bay *Shmeckel*").

Arloff is finally confronted for his lack of productivity by the paper's business manager. "You never do any work around here, you never do anything!"

"You don't call that *work*?" the *luftmentsh* self-righteously retorts, hurt.

Forever stoned (on other people's *shnorred* dope), Max begins asking for a raise from the publisher with a *shnorrer*'s air of properly outraged self-entitlement: "And I demand—demand!!" he exclaims,

> that my entire family be flown in for every major Jewish holiday, *especially Pay-sach* [Passover], because there I am alone in my apartment, running around by myself looking for the *afikomen* [children's matzoh search] all by myself— and it's sad!

The *luftmentsh* and the *shnorrer* were but two of the occupations that made it safe and sound from the *shtetl* to Ellis Island.

CHAPTER 5

The Sounds of Yiddish

There are some who call Yiddish a dead language, but so was Hebrew called for two thousand years. . . . Yiddish has not yet said its last word. It contains treasure that has not been revealed to the eyes of the world. It was the tongue of martyrs and saints, of dreamers and Cabalists—rich in humor in memories that mankind may never forget. In a figurative way, Yiddish is the wise and humble language of us all, the idiom of frightened and hopeful Humanity.

—Isaac Bashevis Singer, 1978

Melvin Kaminsky, a.k.a. Mel Brooks, learned Yiddish from his mother, a Ukrainian immigrant (his father had died at thirty-four, when the future comedian was two and a half). She had come from Kiev only speaking the *mamme-loshn*, not even knowing Russian.

By the time she reached Ellis Island, and for over the next half-century, Mrs. Kaminsky never learned English. She assumed simply that Americans should behave like the Irish cops. They were

the first people she saw in America, the authority figures who pro-
cessed the immigrants with contempt and sometime brutal efficiency.

The result? What happened, Brooks said, was that "[my
mother] speaks no known language, and speaks it with an Irish
accent."

Brooks fears that the entire language he terms "American Yiddish" will soon be lost. American Yiddish, he says, has a certain
timbre, a sometimes grating insistence and roll of the tongue that
separates the Yiddish of the *shtetl* from the Yiddish of Brooklyn. He
mourns for those sounds that ring more of Fanny Brice than Tevye
the milkman.

"Within a couple of decades, there won't be any more accents like that," he said, back when he was riding high on the
heels of *Blazing Saddles*. "They've been ironed out by history,
because there are no more Jewish immigrants. It's the sound I
was brought up on, and it's dying."

Several Jews arguing in Yiddish at once can sound like a
symphony of incomprehensibility to those who don't know the
code. Even befuddled was John Shaft, the famous movie *shamus*
and all-knowing wise man of the street, "a black private dick"
for whom, Isaac Hayes sang, "danger is no stranger."

Shaft, the man "who won't cop out/when there's danger all
about," was, for once, at a loss for private-eye *sachel* (street wisdom) when confronted by a gaggle of Yiddish speakers who'd
come to him regarding robbery and murder most foul in the
Chasidic Jew–dominated diamond district of Manhattan's Forty-
seventh Street.

In the unfortunately named novel *Shaft Among the Jews*, by
Ernest Tidyman, the private detective is surprised in his office by
seven Chasidic Jews, the last people in the world who when not

praying in *shul* speak Yiddish, like their ancestors, on a day-to-day basis.

They want Shaft to investigate, but first the baker's half-dozen of Chasidim shoehorned into the badass snoop's office have to argue.

"The chairman of the group asked Shaft, 'Do you understand Yiddish?'"

"What?" Shaft replied.

"Yiddish."

"'No.'"

"The elder nodded and turned to the others again to begin. Shaft expected it would be a few exchanges that would decide whether they wanted to tell him what it was all about and then maybe a request that he handle their problem, whatever the hell it might be. What he got, or felt he was getting, was a debate on the beginning and end of mankind with serious review of the causes—and all of it in a language he could not understand."

"Each one of the seven men in the room apparently had a speech to make. And each one had a strong counterproposal and counter-counterproposals. Shaft sat back in his chair and listened for a while. He couldn't understand a word."

How does one describe the almost ineffable sounds and rhythms of a language as beautiful as a minor-key sonata, and as bitter as three *yentas* gossiping about everybody else's business; a language seemingly frightened by mankind, yet powerful enough to casually rib God, as if He's a poker buddy, for His never-ending failures?

Got veyst shoyn oykh nit vos er tut.
"God Himself doesn't even know what He does."

It is the sound of the perfect metaphor. Instead of simply saying one has a sexually transmitted disease, Yiddish declares:

Er hot in di hoizen a ya-reed.
"He has a carnival in his pants."

It is onomatopoetic:

Koosh mir in tuchus.
"Kiss my ass."

Or the language can be found in its entirety in one syllable:
Nu?

Yiddish is often worried:

Es iz gut fur yidn?
"Is it good for the Jews?"

Other times, Yiddish is just plain depressed:

Es iz zu zeinen a yid.
"It's hard to be a Jew."

Yiddish is a tongue ironic and knowing about death, birth, and life—yet verges on hysteria in dealing with day-to-day existence. Today, the echo of this vernacular was once used by millions isn't a death rattle, but the sound of an ocean heard in a tiny, jaggedly formed seashell that has floated onto some beach from anywhere and everywhere.

Perhaps John Steinbeck came closest to describing Yiddish while he was actually writing about the denizens living on the borderline of society on Cannery Row in Monterey, California. Cannery Row, like Yiddish, was "a poem, a stink, a grating noise, a quality of light, a tone, a habit, a nostalgia, a dream."

Sometimes, Yiddish rings beautiful, in the most unlikely places. *The Merchant of Venice* was a mainstay of the Yiddish theater in New York; Jacob Adler, one of the greatest Yiddish actors, directors, and producers ever, played Shylock to great acclaim for decades.

Shylock:
Ich bin ein Yid.
Hot a Yid nisht kine oigen?
(I am a Jew.
Hath not a Jew eyes?)

Hot a Yid nisht kine Hent, dimensye, gefel, liebshaft?
Gekormet mit die zelbe essen?
Gevunded mit die zelbe vofen?
(Hath not a Jew hands, dimensions, senses, affections, passions?
Fed with the same food
Hurt with the same weapons?)

Krigt die zelbe Krankheiten?
Gehaylt mit die zelbe mittlen?
(Subject to the same diseases,
healed by the same means?)

Gevarmt un gekelt durch die zelbe zumer un vinter
vie a Krist?
(Warmed and cooled by the same winter and summer
as a Christian is?)

Aib du shtecht unz,
blutchken mir nisht?
(If you prick us,
do we not bleed?)

And to audiences on Second Avenue, one of the most familiar lines was:

Tsu zayn oder nisht tsu zayn.
"To be, or not be."

Yiddish onstage aspired to more—and less—than high art.
What paid the Yiddish theaters' bills were melodramas bursting
with overemotion that brought tears, laughter, or just plain relief to the simplest eighteen-hour-a-day sweatshop slave.

Consider Maurice Schwartz (1888–1960), one of the top three
or four Yiddish actors ever to tread boards on Second Avenue,
a.k.a. "Knish Alley." Schwartz was an actor of such histrionic
movement and language that his acting bordered on mania. Still,
a *New York Times* theater critic was generous, telling his discern-
ing readers that when you went to see Schwartz in Yiddish, "you
always know that you are not in a library."

A contemporary account of Schwartz's technique described his
sui generis style. It too is the sound of Yiddish, specifically, panic:

One of the most marvelous sights to behold in all the world
is a death scene in the Yiddish theater. There is Maurice

Schwartz, or some other great Yiddish actor, and he has just discovered his wife in bed with another man, and he has a heart attack, and it is the end of him.

But he doesn't die just like that. First he screams, *"I am having a heart attack! I am dying!"*

Then he falls, and the fall itself takes a full minute onto the sofa, then he moans and groans; then he rises and stumbles across the room, knocking over furniture and all the while yelling, *"I am dying! I am dying! Oh, God, I am dying!"*

Then he stumbles offstage, wailing and moaning; then he stumbles back onstage and clutches at the draperies and sinks to the floor. And by now the whole family is standing there watching all this, crying and shrieking, *"My God he is dying!"*

And when he finally lands on the floor, he writhes painfully and he makes a speech, gasping out each word. And this speech includes all the philosophical Talmud learnings of his life, and it is chock-full of advice to his sons and farewells to his daughters and his wife, and this speech alone takes six minutes. And then at long last he gives one more great effort to get up again, and he almost makes it, but just when you think he's going to be all right, he lets out this horrible, croaking groan and stumbles over the entire stage again, knocking over what's left of the furniture and the family, and finally he dies. If the play is a musical, it is exactly the same, except with singing and dancing and very melancholy music underscoring the whole thing.

And the audience, which is composed of Jewish people who have troubles of their own, feel this man's great pain, and *they* moan and groan and weep, and when he is finally dead, they sigh with relief and they feel this wonderful sense of total satisfaction.

Schwartz was a *bulvon*, a *shmuck*. Who else could opine: "Any writing about the Yiddish art theater movement is about Maurice Schwartz, because the Yiddish art theater is Maurice Schwartz, and Maurice Schwartz is Yiddish art theater."

Putz.

SO THE JEWS invented Yiddish, piece by piece, century by century, wandering from country to country, despised like Shylock by their grudging—and always temporary—hosts. Along the way, though, the Yiddish language gave an ironic *zetz* (needle) to the very people who formed the tongue with a recipe of one part irony, stirred in with one part tragedy, and seasoned with joy and laughter to taste.

The language's joke on its own people is that no matter how expansive and expressive Yiddish is, there still isn't a word or phrase to explain what it actually *sounds* like. Yiddish is first of all not German. German is guttural, while Yiddish is from the guts. Still, Yiddish, cruelly and badly understood, is most often—and always wrongly—considered a dialect of German. It is not.

And what *is* a dialect, anyway? On that question, there was little doubt in the mind of the late, great, Max Weinreich. Weinreich was director of the world's Yiddish research institute (YIVO) in Warsaw before World War II, and in the new YIVO in New York after the war. In 1952, he was also the recipient of an endowed chair as Columbia's Professor of Yiddish Studies.

"A language," Weinreich said, "is a dialect with an army and a navy."

For others, however, Yiddish bears the sound of embarrassment. From roughly 1880 to 1920, the ones who were the most embarrassed by those sounds in America were the prosperous, assimilated German Jews living on or adjacent to New York's Central Park West. These Jews, with names like Guggenheim and Schiff, were horrified by the bad manners evinced by "them."

"Them" were the millions of Eastern European peasant immigrants right off the boat, and the uneducated prisoners of Lower East Side tenements who only spoke Yiddish.

German Jews hadn't understood that Yiddish babble since the eighteenth-century Western European Enlightenment. So, it was understood uptown that their downtown brethren who spoke only Yiddish, and upon whom the Enlightenment never shone in their part of the Diaspora, weren't "good" Jews. Those Jews embarrassed the "good" Jews, like themselves, in the eyes of the Gentiles. So they took out their embarrassment by blaming the peasants' language.

English-Jewish papers, with names like the *American Hebrew*, most typically called it "piggish."

Saul Bellow knew about pigs and Yiddish: in *Him With His Foot in His Mouth* he writes:

> You may have heard charming, appealing, sentimental things about Yiddish, but Yiddish is a hard language, Miss Rose. Yiddish is severe and bears down without mercy. Yes, it is often delicate, lovely but it can be explosive as well. "A face like a slop jar," "a face like a bucket of swill." (Pig connotations give special force to Yiddish epithets.) If there is a demiurge who inspires me to speak wildly, he may have been attracted to me by this violent unsparing language.

And it is a symphony.
And a poem.

A Yiddish Poet

BY MENKE KATZ (1965)

My mother tongue is unpolished as a wound, a laughter, a love-
   starved kiss.
Yearnful as a martyr's last glance at a passing bird.
Taste a word, curse and merciless as a tear.
Hear a word, terse and bruised as a tear.
See a word, light and lucent, joy rapt as a ray.
Climb a word—rough and powerful as a crag.
Ride a word—free and rhymeless as a tempest.

This is but one example where Menke Katz showed his Yiddish poet's soul. Tragically, Katz, an artist in Yiddish, had to ultimately compose these lines in English, not his *mamme-loshn*, if
he ever wanted anyone on the globe to be able to read him.

Then there is S. H. Chang, China's only Yiddish philologist.
A professor at Taiwan's Wenzao Ursuline College of Languages,
she reads and speaks Yiddish, the latter a skill not shared by
many of her American peers.

Still in her early thirties, she began studying Yiddish after
receiving a Ph.D. in German from Germany's Trier University.
"When I set about learning Yiddish, I was merely opening up a
new door for myself," she said, viewing the language only as
a way to bolster her employment chances. Now she is also a
world-renowned scholar of Jewish literature, while her newest
project is a nonacademic book written in Chinese "explaining
the nuances of Yiddishkeit and the history of the Jewish
Diaspora—and the meaning of such words as *kvell, chutzpah,*
and *nachas.*"

Yiddish is also the sound of one eyebrow rising; two palms
turned inside out, as if to say "whaddya gonna do"; one finger

being jabbed into your chest as you get unasked-for advice from somebody's demented uncle; the rustle of a peasant family trying to pack as much as they can in five minutes, hit the road, fast, and get as far away as possible from what used to be home.

Acting coach Lewis Herman had another way of looking at Yiddish. In a 1943 handbook addressing stage performers, he wrote a score of pages on how to "sound Jewish." The book is legitimate: Playwright Garson Kanin wrote the introduction.

Herman wrote:

In general, it is best, when simulating the Yiddish lilt, to sound the keynote of the sentence about three or four notes above the American and sing the first few syllables on the same note. Then, on the stressed keynote, make a sudden rising or falling inflection on the balance of the syllable. This will endow your dialect with the Yiddish lilt. But remember that the word meaning which affects the lilt and is changed by a combination of stressed and tonal emphasis can change the speech pattern.

Herman's handbook also gave practice sentences. To say "even by my worst enemy it shouldn't happen," students are instructed to sound out "iv'n bAHin vUHst AnAmi Eet shood'n hEHp'n." Baggage should be pronounced, the text goes on, "bE-Hgitch," and steam heat should emerge as "stim'it."

So what makes Yiddish such a different language from any other? Is it its musical scale, jumping up an octave in the perpetual asking of questions, or alternately dipping down in certainty, dread, or while telling the punch line of a dirty joke.

Whatever it was, Yiddish was always *alive*. Dr. Samuel Johnson wrote in the preface to his 1755 masterpiece, *A Dictionary of the English Language*:

> When we see men grow old and die at a certain time one
> after another, from century to century, we laugh at the
> elixir that promises to prolong life to a thousand years; and
> with equal justice may the lexicographer be derided, who,
> being able to produce no example of a nation that has pre-
> served their words and phrases from mutability, shall imag-
> ine that his dictionary can embalm his language, and secure
> it from corruption or decay.

Judaism would have disintegrated without Yiddish to communicate and keep the tribe connected. Yiddish crossed all borders all the way to Shanghai, kept Judaism from shrinking into
dozens of disparate tribes with different rules. These disunited
population slivers would have disappeared into assimilated
somethings, and Judaism and Jews would be gone, like the Babylonians, Moabites, and Hittites.

Jews around the world would have disappeared into their
own ingrained habits and rituals. Each region would have its
own interpretations of how to practice Judaism, live by the Torah, and obey its 613 commandments.

In medieval China, Yiddish-speaking rabbinical authorities
may have decided that in prayer, Jews should face away from Jerusalem's Wailing, or Western, Wall, the last remaining sign of
the Jews' Second Temple, and the beginning of the Jews' wandering. In every other synagogue, you face forward.

In medieval France, Jews might have decided that shellfish is
kosher. And in the Rhineland, it could have been ruled that Hanukkah shouldn't even be considered worthy of a holiday, and
eliminated.

That, indeed, is what happened. Anarchy reigned among different Jewish communities around the world. By the fifteenth
century, Judaism itself seemed fractured. Then, stepping into

the breach like the Mounties, came Joseph Karo, a passionate genius about all matters Torah and Talmudic.

Sensing the threats to Judaism from within, Karo wrote up a new rulebook, just about in time for the invention of the printing press. Ultimately, his writings became what he termed the *Shulchan Aruch*, literally, the "set table." Karo's book codified all the laws of the Torah in detail; every Jew would be playing by the same rules. A miracle: The *Shulchan Aruch* was accepted around most of the Jewish world as definitive.

So, for instance, Karo analyzed each of the Ten Commandments, and deciphered for all Jewry how those commandments should be practiced. For "Honor thy Mother and Father," he wrote a score of scenarios of how exactly to deal with this law. So, went the rules by Karo, *honoring* one's parents didn't mean you also had to *love* them. He decided when you had to, and when you shouldn't lend money to your parents. Show your respect by helping your parents with their chores. Make life easier for them, he wrote. Unless they're crazy, in which case Karo laid out a whole new set of rules.

Oy, the therapy bills that could be saved if the *Shulchan Aruch* were consulted more often than the DSM-IV. *That* would be Yiddishkeit!

CHAPTER 6

שרײַבֿן דעם שלאָסל שרײַבֿן דעם שלאָסל

The Secrets of Yiddish

Dray kenen haltn a sod az tsvey zaynen meysim.
"Three can keep a secret if two of them are corpses."

It is a virtual secret among the public that is not part of the subculture of Yiddishists, meaning it is a virtual secret of the planet. Oddly, the *Village Voice* wrote about the movement in 1996, claiming it was already ten years old.

"Queer Yiddishkeit."

"Gay Yiddishkeit."

It's everywhere you wouldn't think, which could be anywhere in the Yiddish world. Take the National Yiddish Book Center, founded by the heroic Aaron Lansky in 1980 in an effort to save the precious legacy of books that had been written in, or translated into, the *mamme-loshn.*

Before Lansky, hundreds of thousands of volumes were being tossed into Dumpsters across the country, their words and authors lost. The tossers weren't uncaring clods, just unknowing. After all, what do one's relatives *do* with the personal libraries of Yiddish-speaking-and-reading elders after they died? What else *could* be done but dispose of those books, even most

ungraciously into public trash bins, by grandchildren more concerned with quickly emptying *zayde's* apartment while they
looked for his stamp collection?

According to Adrienne Cooper, director of program development at the Yiddish-based Workmen's Circle and a Yiddish per-
former in her own right, the original board of the Yiddish Book
Center was composed of "Aaron Lansky and five lesbians."

It makes sense.

Yiddish has always been marginalized and ridiculed historically, an embarrassment even to the parents who bore and
raised what they had created. Homosexuals have also always
been marginalized, not only by their enemies, but also by parents eager to entirely disown their own children. As Gore Vidal
put it, "Homophobia is the last socially acceptable form of rac-
ism."

There is more to the equation than that both Yiddish and
gay culture have usually been marginalized on the edges of "acceptable" Jewish society, as well as the mainstream heterosexual
world. Historically, the same dynamic has existed of marginal-
izing those who marry *shiksas* or, in the larger world, engage in
Olympic male ice dancing.

And yet . . .

Progressive politics is one area where Yiddishkeit and gay
activism seem to share a Venn diagram. Take the slice of young
Jewish immigrants and first-generation Americans who devoted
themselves to the flourishing leftist movement during the time
roughly framed by the repressive Russian "May Day Laws" of
1882, and the United States Congress of 1920 turning the tap to
dribble level for would-be Eastern Europe immigrants—that is,
Jews.

Often, the most strident political sharpshooting among the
Jewish activists was aimed at each other. The Labor Bundists

rallied against the Socialists, who wrote back heated editorials in the *Forverts*, who in turn were vilified as the bourgeoisie by the trade unionists, anarchists, Trotskyites, and Mensheviks.

None could stand each other, it appeared, especially amid those battling for leadership positions in their own political camps. Only one issue seemed to join all the warring and far-left-of-center groups: Yiddish.

In the streets, it was the language of debate as well as the holy secularist tongue of the urban masses. At home, the language of an intergenerational war, as religious parents evinced an almost total lack of understanding of their atheistic, political, agitating children.

They were the elders who thought and lived in Yiddish, whether they were buying a paper-thin tablecloth for *Shabbos* dinner from a pushcart *shmatte* salesman (rag seller), or purchasing a thick Yiddish newspaper filled with ads for items such as Schapiro's kosher wine—"the wine so thick you can almost cut it with a knife."

Urban secularism, the embarrassment of parents over their children's choice to use their beloved *mamme-loshn* to stir up trouble with strangers, Jewish and Gentile society's scorn . . . add them together, divide by history, and one comes up with:

"Queer Yiddishkeit."

"Queer Yiddishkeit gives permission to go to the world of my grandparents without leaving myself behind," Sara Felder was quoted in late February 2007, when the English-language *Forward* finally took on the issue.

"It's about alienation from the Jewish religious establishment," said Alissa Solomon, the former *Village Voice* writer whose 1997 piece on the movement in the magazine *Davka* is considered one of the key texts of Queer Yiddishkeit. "There's a kind of analogy people make with the marginalized status of Yiddish itself," Solomon continued. "It's an outsider stance."

Queer Yiddishkeit has plenty of detractors, most of whom stay as underground and unquotable as movement members themselves were for the last few decades. One who has spoken out against Queer Yiddishkeit is Ruth Wisse, the esteemed Harvard Yiddishist and author of *The Shlemiel as Modern Hero*.

Wisse wrote a 1987 piece for *Commentary* in which she chided gay activists centered around Yiddishkeit who "freely identify their sense of personal injury with the cause of Yiddish."

It was a "double fault," she wrote. Gabriel Sanders quoted Wisse in the *Forward*, interpreting the professor's words as a claim that Queer Yiddishkeit's philosophy "distort[s] the past and call[s] into question the Jewish future."

According to Faith Jones, many Yiddish scholars like Wisse, as well as traditional *mamme-loshn* and Yiddishkeit lovers, are appalled by the movement. Jones, a librarian at New York's mid-Manhattan branch, was a panelist in January 2007 for a forum sponsored by Yugntruf, a New York organization dedicated to furthering the cause of Yiddish.

Jones declared the traditionalists were afraid that their beloved language would be hijacked by soldiers of Queer Yiddishkeit. And Professor Wisse, she told Gabriel Ganders, was missing the point that "they [gay Yiddishkeit adherents] are her own students she's writing [negatively] about." Analyzing Wisse's statement, Jones said, "Her response is that it would be better for the language to die. That kind of thing is very hurtful."

THE MERE WORDS "Queer Yiddishkeit" are enough to curl the remaining hairs of one's eighty-five-year-old *bubbe* and *zayde*.

Those universal grandparents are almost always horrified at the mere notion of such a thing, as are their fellow members of most any local Jewish community center's monthly Sunday morning Yiddish Club, median age usually around, well, eighty, prune Danish and coffee available afterward.

The elders' vehemence (and private disappointment) with the rise of the Queer Yiddishkeit movement echoes their ancestors, the *mitnaggdim*, the "againsters" who tried to stamp out Chasidism in Eastern Europe centuries ago and were so single-minded that one needn't even ask what or whom they were against.

Even today, almost none of the casual old-time Yiddish speakers are even aware of Queer Yiddishkeit, unless they subscribe to the English-language *Forward*, and happened upon these few articles over the last months. (Most turn right to *Forward* columnist "Philologos," the language *maven* and the Yiddish equivalent of William Safire. Each week, "Philologos" parses questions about the *mamme-loshn* (and sometimes Hebrew) for his devoted readership grateful that *someone* out there is serving as sheriff of Yiddishville.

Even the *zaydes* in the Yiddish clubs with gay grandchildren say Queer Yiddishkeit is a *shanda* to the *mamme-loshen*, a disgrace to the mother tongue. Even the *zaydes* who've been gay themselves ever since they were cleaning out stables in their own *zayde's shtetl* stable heave a mighty *feh!* when confronted with the issue.

Yiddish, their Yiddish?

In the hands of young *fay-gell-ahs?*

Despite their apparent bias against gays, it is highly comforting that these octogenarians who learned Yiddish from their parents, and not a college textbook, still care about the language. Yes, they're still out there, in sadly, quickly dwindling numbers.

Almost all are very nice people, and represent a small army of civilians and intuitive Yiddishists who have helped save the language over the last fifty years. Actually speaking Yiddish, they have tenuously bridged the generations spanning the Nazis' virtual destruction of Yiddish-speaking European Jewry, the establishment of an endowed chair of Yiddish studies at Oxford, and the surge in Yiddish-based fervor from young secularists.

Today, these elders' perfect Yiddish, learned in kitchens generations ago, is most often utilized for those Sunday-morning J.C.C. programs that feature club members taking turns giving innocent preprepared talks about what Galician Yiddish-speaking Jews traditionally have thought of their neighbors, the Lithuanian Yiddish-speaking Jews, and vice versa.

(The Galicians, Galitzianers, have always believed the Lithuanians, Litvaks, are coldly unemotional, overly academic, and conservative stuffed shirts. Conversely, the Litvaks have long held that the Galicians are *gonifs* [thieves].)

Yet here comes Queer Yiddishkeit, and as the older Yiddish speakers learn of the movement, the shock grows.

"Too baddd," as the policeman in Rome says when he learns that the traveler's checks just lost by the distraught Jane and John Doe tourists before him weren't American Express—"too badddd."

Yiddish, to survive beyond the world of the academic footnotes, needs new blood to replace the old.

Yet is referring to the movement as "Queer Yiddishkeit" even *kosher*?

Yes. If you're gay, or on their side.

Of course, one has no more need to be young and gay to take

part in the language's revival than one has to be at a second-grade reading level to laugh and learn from Ellis Weiner and Barbara Davidman's *Yiddish with Dick and Jane*. Nor does one need a Ph.D. in linguistics to marvel at Professor Dovid Katz's *Words on Fire*, the crowning work of Yiddish history and theory by Oxford's first endowed chair of Yiddish studies.

The kind of verbal turnaround involved in making Queer Yiddishkeit not a *trayf* (nonkosher) slur is in itself part of the historic Yiddish soul, though heretofore not in sexual matters. Take the word *chochem*, Yiddish for a very intelligent person: Lift one's eyebrow while saying it, however, and the word means a complete idiot.

Similarly, a *macher* is a big shot; hunch one shoulder for a second and it means an impotent nitwit pretending he actually has weight to throw around. Say "Queer Yiddishkeit" one way and it's positive; say it another and it's a slur.

One area in which Queer Yiddishkeit has particularly resuscitated the *mamme-loshn* is *klezmer* music. Originally played by wandering Eastern European Jewish troubadours in the fifteenth century, *klezmer* provided the soundtrack for the old-world *shtetl*, with songs in the minor key of life.

Joyous and mournful, like Yiddish itself, *klezmer* can be both a despairing mournful weep or a sprightly joyful noise. Over the last two decades, *klezmer* has alchemized into a slowly but ever-increasingly popular cross-over success: *Gott in himmel* (God in heaven), The Klezmatics have won a Grammy, and there are now thriving groups with names such as The Isle of Klezbos and Gay Iz Mir.

As it was centuries ago, a strolling *klezmer* group usually features an assortment of trumpets, clarinets, fiddles, cymbals, drums, and whatever is handy in the way of other woodwinds and brass (when an ensemble is seated, throw in a piano and stand-up bass).

And then there is the ever-present *klezmer* accordion, made to sing as if it's from another galaxy of instruments than the candy-ass squeeze box utilized by the likes of the *goyishe* Whoopie John Wilfahrt polka band. Those polka ensembles are usually from Poland—*feh!*—a country so historically anti-Semitic they slaughtered Jews who'd somehow survived the concentration camps and wandered home *after* World War II was over.

To those unfortunates who haven't sampled the music—on you, *a shanda und a kharpe!* ("a shame and a disgrace!"). You don't have to be gay to soak in the music's unique brand of, well, Yiddishkeit emotions.

A great *klezmer* group sounds and feels most akin to an appropriately mournful New Orleans funeral band on the way to the cemetery. The original *klezmer* ensembles, so lovingly recreated today, could travel in one direction across sad and bloody Jewish land beyond the Pale of Settlement, playing the kind of minor-key jazz dirge cried out behind a crawling Crescent City hearse, its notes soft tears played with bowed heads. Afterward, headed in a happier direction, *klezmer*, like that jazz band, struts its brass with life reaffirmed, its trumpets and trombones held high, blaring hope and dance.

So, take an all-encompassing love of modern Yiddish and its crescendoing sentences always seeming to end with the sound of a question mark. Add devotion to *klezmer*, the *mamme-loshn*'s centuries-old soundtrack.

Put in a heavy dose of traditional American Jewish leftist politics, proudly Yiddish-centric and progressive. Nothing new there—it's just like the Yiddish unions of the early 1900s marching in protest to the site of the Triangle Shirt Waist fire; or the

red-diaper babies brought to New York's Union Square on Fourteenth Street in the 1950s to demand a permanent stay of execution for Julius and Ethel Rosenberg.

And there's Queer Yiddishkeit.

Members of the movement using the word "queer" are seizing the slurs of society's oppressors, like Shylock, proud and de-
fiant, declaring unashamedly, *"Ich bin ein Yid."* in *The Merchant of
Venice* to a crowd of merciless Gentiles for whom the word "Jew"
is slander in itself.

Yiddish is a queer tongue indeed, in the oldest, nonhomopho-
bic sense of queer. What other language could be so diverse, able
not only to withstand but flower under Charles Rappaport's truism that he could speak almost a dozen languages, all of them
Yiddish?

YIDDISH FIRST FLASHED on the radar of my mostly vacant
prepubescent brain as, I believed, a devious linguistic plot to
exclude me from learning the real *shmutz* (dirt) of life. This "Yiddish" was a frustrating, maddening, conspiracy of adults.

I wanted simply to know what mysteries were in Yiddish,
that unknowable, peculiarly pronounced tongue. I was sure my
parents were talking nasty truths when they lapsed into Yiddish. Why else would they want to be incomprehensible?

After speaking in their Yiddish code for a while, my parents
would revert to English—and conversation that was hell-with-
the-lid-off boring to a ten-year-old. So, like many hundreds of
thousands of Jews who grew up over the last half-century, I
heard my first Yiddish as a child being shut out of no-doubt-
unspeakable naughty bits and highly classified information unfit for the three kids in the family. Yiddish was a secret language
seemingly invented to keep the children ignorant of good *drek*.

Philip Roth remembered in a 1966 interview that as a child in Newark, the *mamme-loshn* was a question mark he never was interested in answering.

"Very little Yiddish was spoken [in our house]," Roth said, continuing:

> When Yiddish was spoken, it was not spoken so that I would understand, but so that I *wouldn't* understand. That is, it was the language of secrecy, the language of surprise and chagrin. So I learned very little; I didn't pay much attention to it.

So said the literary *provocateur* who, three years later, would publish *Portnoy's Complaint*. With the tale of tortured Alexander Portnoy, Roth took the stereotype of the suffocating Jewish mother and neurotic Jewish son to rarefied, noxious, yet liberating Everest-ian heights. Even though Roth is a genius, he has long been considered a disgraceful *shanda fur di goyim* by the Jewish establishment. Why, they wondered, would a Jew want Gentiles to read a make-believe story about a teenaged Portnoy performing Onan's crime into a large lump of liver?

Both my parents were fluent in Yiddish and despised Roth's casual desecration of the *mamme-loshn*. My mother came from a bilingual home, while my father's father and mother never bothered to learn English. They'd been the only ones in their extended families to escape the Nazis' death pit in Slutsk. Both my grandparents had decided they would continue to live their lives as best as they could in the best approximation they could make of their old *shtetl*.

So, English wasn't deemed necessary as my grandparents began trying to etch new lives in the new world. So, raised in a monolingual household, my father had no choice but to learn fluent Yiddish if he wished to simply ask his parents, "Can I eat the *pupik* [gizzard]?" or explain to them that "I'm bleeding because some *shtarker* [mindless tough guy] threw an ice ball at my head."

He learned and played in English in public school and the streets. And he either must learn Yiddish, or he would literally be unable to communicate with his parents in his own house.

Drops of Yiddish were handed down to me. Painful circumstances—being tortured by my older siblings—ensured that I would have no entertainment alternative as a boy but to spy on my parents speaking Yiddish. My Yiddish 101 was held in painfully close quarters, for dozens of hours every summer. And the tutors didn't even know they were teaching.

My parents, like Philip Roth's folks and almost every one of my Jewish friends' *tateh* and *mamme*, lapsed into Yiddish in our house as a matter of course during the whole year. The reasons were the same for everybody: At home, my parents didn't want me and my two siblings to understand what they were saying.

However, the isolated stray phrases and sentences I heard at home stumped me for both meaning and nuance. So, my real Yiddish education began in an ad hoc language-immersion program that my parents unknowingly offered during that torturous annual ritual of Midwest families—the never-ending car trip of the kind seen in Chevy Chase's *National Lampoon's Vacation*.

Every summer, we'd drive to Chicago to see my mother's relatives; during other years we drove on family sightseeing trips to New York, Boston, Washington, Mount Rushmore, or the Wisconsin Dells. There was nothing to look at except an occasional cow during the eight-hour ride.

After crossing our Minnesota border, Wisconsin was as nonstop horizontal as the Bonneville Salt Flats, and Illinois wasn't much better until you hit the Second City. And as the youngest of three siblings, I was always the one elbowed into the middle of the backseat, the worst ride in the ride. My older brother and sister could look out their windows, contemplate their adolescent beings, consider the nothingness of what my father's Mercury was speeding past, vainly look for cheese factories that offered free tours and samples, announce the mileage signs indicating how far we were from Milwaukee, stretch their arms, or give me backseat wedgies.

I, meantime, was so shoehorned into the middle of the seating arrangements that my only available entertainment was listening in on my parents' conversation in the front seat. Those dialogues, with my father driving eighty and my mother co-piloting with the maps, were stultifying dull.

Stultifying dull, that is, when they were speaking English. My parents, apparently, were just as bored with what they were talking about in America's *mamme-loshn* that they'd spend full half-hour intervals conversing in this bizarre language I didn't know.

I don't why I had this hunch, but Yiddish sounded incredibly filthy. Then again, I thought everything foreign was libidinal in nature, and incomprehensible.

I'd discovered girls in the months before I turned eleven.

Eavesdropping on my parents was crazy-making at first: As always, just when conversation in English in the front seat sounded like it was beginning to get interesting, they'd switch for those extended periods into that enticing, incomprehensible tongue. Suddenly, once again, just as things started to get good, came Yiddish. With it came hushed voices, sighs, belly laughs— all in some other language that sounded like gibberish divided by Esperanto.

"What language is that?" I'd plead with them.

"Jewish," one of them would say, then go back to their unintelligible conversation with the other.

After years of internment in the backseat, I realized I had nothing to do but go mad, or continue listening in on my parents' conversation. And after a couple of trips I deduced that words beginning with "sh" sounded the best. Even if I didn't know what the words meant, they were somehow my favorites.

Shmuck. Shmeckel. Shlemiel. Shlimazel. Shmatte. Shmendrick. Shmeggege. Shlock. Shlockmeister. Shmo. Shtup. Shmutz. Shnook. Shnoz. Shlep. Shlepper. Shiksa. Shagetz. Sha! Shabbos goy. Shamus. Shloomp. Shmaltz. Shlub. Shmeer. Shnapps. Shtunk. Shtick. Shvitzer. Shanda. Shvantz. Shmooze. Shikker.

Oh, I could tell that a *shikker* was serious, dangerous, a lost soul. After my parents whispered that one word—*shikker*—they'd immediately raise their voices to a normal volume. It was the same way they would refer to my great-uncle Augie, who used to own a strip club in downtown Minneapolis, married four *shiksa* strippers, and was, my grandmother would whisper, "a *genghstah*." He wasn't, but marrying four non-Jews made him a *shanda* to the infinite power.

Yiddish had innumerable words to delineate exactly what kind, and how big, a generic *putz* someone was. A *shlemiel*, for example, was someone who is always spilling their milk; a *shlimazel* is one who was always having milk spilled on them.

The most expressive Yiddish words, I deduced, seemed to begin with "sh," even if I had no idea what these vaguely obscene-sounding "sh" words meant. So, I had to wait in the backseat for more data and then I would be rewarded from the front seat when my parents would say a few words in English, then end their sentence with a "sh."

A police car would show up in the side-view mirror, and my mother would say, "Slow down watch out, there's the *shamus* [the police]."

Or, "That Lenny Raskas, I saw him drink seven *shnapps* at the Cohn Bar Mitzvah, he's a real *shikker*."

Or, "Irv Rotblatt, that *shmuck*, can't keep his zipper zipped and his *shvantz* in his pants. Can you believe he left Adele for that blondie *shiksa* secretary of his? She's so Catholic *they got married in a church*! His parents were so *verklempt* they were ready to *plotz*! It's a *shanda*, I tell you, a *shanda fur di goyim*!"

Sometimes I'd get confused; some of the "sh" words weren't ribald or profane, but Jewish holy days. Even if I hadn't been so ignorant, confusion was endemic to most people who didn't grow up speaking Yiddish.

Shmini Atzerot: I still have no idea what this holiday is, but as an adult one will never *not* get a laugh by telling another Jew, "I haven't seen you since Sh-mee-nee-atz-erot."

There is Shavuos, pronounced Sha-voo-es, that occurs seven weeks after Passover; it took Moses a month and three weeks to move his army of wanderers out of Egypt and through the desert before he could ascend Mount Sinai. There he took dictation from God of the Torah, sealing the deal between God and the Jews that they got to be the Chosen.

Shavuos, unlike Shmini Atzerot, is a major holiday.

Yet with virtually anyone, ranging from scholarly rabbis to supreme God, Yiddish makes fun.

Ah-tah bekh-ar-taynu me-kol ha'amim—vos hast'- zoo zeech
　　on-ge-zest' oyf und?
"Thou hast chosen us from among the nations—what,
　　O Lord, did you have against us?"

Or,

Got veyst shoyn oykh nit vos er tut.

"God Himself doesn't even know what He does."

Mocking the momentous event when the Jews got their Torah and were made God's first-draft pick for Chosenness was a centuries-old tradition. Eventually, it traveled across the ocean and time into the new world.

Said Henny Youngman: "Moses went up to Mount Sinai and said, 'This would be a good place for a hospital.'"

SITTING IN THE backseat on those interminable family drives, I began testing Yiddish's rhythms. It was a potpourri of words whose meanings were incomprehensible to me.

Daven dreidel drek.

Ganef gelt goy gefilte fish.

The "ems" were dynamite: *maven, mentsh, meshugga, mishpocha.*

Understanding much of Yiddish meant being aware of context and body language, and simply paying attention. One needn't even understand Yiddish to understand Yiddish.

In 1934, the *New York Times* drama critic, who did not speak Yiddish, could barely find enough words to gush with upon seeing the Yiddish proletarian theater production of *Rekrutn,* an adaptation of Israel Akseford's *The First Jewish Recruit in Russia.*

"The Provincetown Players have come to life again. In their reincarnation they speak Yiddish," the *Times* critic said. That was just the beginning for the Yiddish play; it also earned raves from non-Yiddish-speaking critics at the *New York World-Telegram,* the *New York Post,* the *New York Herald,* and the *New York Daily Mirror.*

So who needed to know Yiddish, if you could *feel* what it meant? Before I was a teenager, I couldn't feel what my parents were discussing, but I did pick up enough in the backseat to amuse my classmates during recess at elementary school about who in the neighborhood was an always drunk *shikker,* or a *gonif* of a lawyer with the heart of a thief.

Rutgers' Jeffrey Shandler is one of the most interesting and provocative Yiddishists alive. His book *Adventures in Yiddishland: Post-Vernacular Language and Culture* (2005) is destined to be a classic of modern Yiddish scholarship. Still, Shandler admits, he is only "a native listener to Yiddish."

Jargon is in the eye of the beholder, and the constant influx and reshaping of other people's words often remade Yiddish's borrowed vocabulary into a lexicon that had nothing to do with the original meanings of the words they'd borrowed. Almost as soon as it began to develop in the eleventh century, Yiddish could not truly be understood by anyone but those who knew that the key to the language's usefulness was its mongrelized malleability. Like the Jews, the *mamme-loshn* of the Diaspora had to be ready to get up on a second's notice and run to the next port of exile—where it would then pick up even more vocabulary.

The language was more than alive; it was crackling. "A living language," wrote H. L. Mencken, linguist (and casual, caustic anti-Semite):

is like a man suffering incessantly from small haemorrhages [*sic*], and what it needs above all else is constant transactions of new blood from other tongues. The day the gates go up, that day it begins to die.

Despite the seeming universality of Yiddish, it still, in essence, was a way to forever communicate to other Jews without fear of misinterpretation by non-Jews. Or even interpretation itself.

In the late 1940s, for example, the Minneapolis Lakers professional basketball team (stolen in the early 1960s by Los Angeles) drafted the enormously gifted George Mikan out of DePaul University. Mikan came to Minneapolis for a day just to hear out the Lakers' pleas for him to sign.

Mikan had no intention of playing professional ball; he was planning on going to law school. Finally, he said he was going home to Chicago—he just wasn't going to turn professional with Minneapolis.

"Don't let him get on that airplane, get lost on the way," Laker owner Max Winter told Sid Hartman, the team's general manager, in Yiddish. So, Hartman purposely drove around in circles until Mikan's plane had safely taken off and the ballplayer was forced to stay in Minneapolis another day.

Mikan was subjected the next morning to a basketball team owner reloaded with arguments. Mikan changed his mind, signed, led Minneapolis to five straight championships, and in 1950 was named by the Associated Press as the greatest athlete of the first half of the twentieth century. Thank God, they still say in Minneapolis, that the Catholic Mikan didn't know Yiddish.

THE LANGUAGE CAN be seditious, and profane, protectively wrapped fully in its own secrecy. As the Three Stooges said onscreen in 1990:

> *"Alle menschen muss zu machen, jeden tug a gentzen kachen?"*
> "Who do you have to fuck to get a break in this town?"

Mel Brooks paid proud homage to the Stooges' secret effrontery half a century before on behalf of Yiddishkeit. It came in a song Brooks wrote for the theater version of *The Producers*. Midway into the tune called "The King of Broadway," he wrote in the same line the Stooges asked in Yiddish in *You Nazty Spy*.

Then Brooks, for the benefit of a nun in the cast, went on to translate the offending phrase into English. At the last second before *The Producers* premiere, the song was cut from the play. "The King of Broadway," however, made it in its entirety as the first song on the cast recording. From the song's perspective, Yiddish's adherence to superstition was well founded.

Azdos mazl is kleyn helft nit keyn gevehn.
"If your luck is small it won't help to bawl."

On the other hand, for those so blessed:

Er shloft un zayn mazl ligt oyf.
"He sleeps, yet his luck remains awake."

Luckily, Yiddish studies has today found a foothold in academe as a dynamic and relatively fresh field of study. Much of the credit must go to linguists who are continually adding new proof that the language is indeed a language and not some mongrel dialect. Now, with the preparation of college-level textbooks and a proper dictionary, Yiddish scholars over the last half-century have managed to squeeze themselves and their scholarship into academe as a true discipline.

Loz mikh nor arayn, gefinen vel ikh shoyn an ort.
"Just let me in and I'll find a place."

And yet, spoken *Yiddish*, used now mainly by people in their seventies through nineties, can resonate as a death rattle. Can Yiddish be so bound up in another time and place that few modern professional experts of the *mamme-loshn* have ever actually thought they needed to *speak* it?

How ironic for this irony-bound language. Since its beginning, Yiddish, the *mamme-loshn*, has been a *talking* language. This is part of the reason Yiddish has remained such a particularly alive language, seeming to breathe most hardily during centuries when scholarly or secular Jews, or genocidal Gentiles, have tried to stomp it out and declare Yiddish, Yiddish culture, and Yiddishkeit dead.

Hebrew always stayed holy, but its attitudes, vocabulary, and means of expression had been entombed in time. When spoken aloud, it sounded, as it should, like Cecil B. De Mille booming with Divine authority as the voice of God in *The Ten Commandments*.

Yiddish was completely different, Isaac Singer said, midway into his speech while accepting his Nobel Prize in Literature in 1978.

> The Yiddish mentality is not haughty. It does not take victory for granted. It does not demand and command, but it muddles through, sneaks by, smuggles itself amidst the powers of destruction, knowing somewhere that God's plan for Creation is still at the very beginning. . . . In a figurative way, Yiddish is the wise and humble language of us all, the idiom of frightened and hopeful Humanity.

And then, just as soon as Yiddish is legitimized—taught at the college level with weekend-long conferences and endowed chairs—nobody seems to be able to speak it. *Especially* the professional smarty-pants.

"If Yiddish has a future on college campuses, it may literally go unspoken," Anthony Weiss wrote in the lead sentence of a 2006 article for the English-language *Forward*. (The *Forward* still runs off a weekly one-page edition in Yiddish for the stalwarts who remember when the paper was a daily and called the *Forverts*.)

"In Yiddish studies programs across the country," Weiss continued, "a new generation of scholars are learning Yiddish as a language of scholarship, but many of them never master Yiddish as a language of conversation."

Beyond irony, is there any lesson in fact that the academic Yiddishists slaving away in the carrels of the ivory tower can rarely actually speak the language upon which they've centered their microscopes of scholarship? Bent over Yiddish texts from the past, and writing up their own linguistic excavations of the language, these academics ensure that Yiddish these days is largely seen but not heard.

Academic writing concerning the *mamme-loshn* is probably more plentiful than the number of people who can actually speak the words the scholars dissect. Though the language itself is difficult to understand by those who didn't grow up with it in their homes, what to make of the supposition of one prominent linguist, whose book on Yiddish has gone through several printings, that "each word [in Yiddish] has an aura of connotations derived from its multidirectional and codified relations not just within a semantic paradigm, as in other languages, but to parallel words in other source languages, to an active stock of proverbs and idioms, and to a typical situational cluster."?

But what other language, including the truly dead specimens of Latin and ancient Greek, MUST be heard to be truly understood? Inside Yiddish's letters there is more than a language, but Yiddishkeit itself, what Jewishness, and being a Jew, means.

One reads the word *oy*, and it is a language unto itself, with thousands of meanings, definitions, and uses, from horror to exultation to the moans of making love. There is the late singer-comedian Allan Sherman using dozens of enunciations of *oy* to circle the globe of human emotion in his song *Oh Boy*. Or Al Franken, whose daily radio show had a weekly feature called "The Oy Yoy Yoy Show," where he played an ancient Jew named "Uncle Al," who responded to the most depressing news items of the week with a heartfelt *"oy."*

Even a few academics have noticed the power of Yiddish talk over Yiddish reading. Among them are Benjamin Harshav, the Jacob and Hilda Blaustein Professor of Hebrew and Comparative Literature at Yale, as well as the author of a scholarly, yet mostly readable, volume of linguistic razzamatazz known as *The Meaning of Yiddish*. Professor Harshav took note of what was happening to the sound of Yiddish in academe in a chapter called "Semiotics of Yiddish Communication." According to Harshav, "Several basic conditions of [Yiddish's] history have influenced the nature of Yiddish discourse."

He continues that one essential fact about the language is that in a book-oriented society like the Jews, Yiddish was primarily a language of conversation, and, he wrote, "Yiddish sentences are replete with gestures of a speech situation."

Unfortunately, some of Yiddish's spoken nuances were more or less forgotten in February 2006, when New York University held a two-day conference on Yiddish. All the experts spoke in English, including the esteemed professors who offered hagiographical addresses about the glories of Yiddish and the serious graduate students presenting papers and headed for Ph.D.s in Yiddish at one of the thirteen Yiddish studies programs in North America that offer terminal degrees in this seemingly terminal language.

At breaks, not a word of the *mamme-loshn* could be heard above the shoptalk in English.

"Keeping alive a dead language has become an academic field," Lawrence H. Schiffman, chairman of NYU's Skirball Department of Hebrew and Judaic Studies, the sponsor of the conference, told the *Forward* in 2006.

And academe, he went on, is not a place where a language can be resuscitated in all its glory from a moribund state.

Where did it go?

As they say in the *mamme-loshn*:

Yidishe ashires iz vi shney in marts.
"Jewish wealth is like snow in March."

CHAPTER 7

שמאָלץ וווּנדערבאַר שמאָלץ וווּנדערבאַר

More Questions, Questions, Questions!
Or
More Questions, Questions, Questions?

Question 1
Why would Steve McQueen know Yiddish? That *hoo-hah* superstar movie hunk who specialized in roles filled with such *goyishe nachas* as driving motorcycles, cars, and airplanes too fast?

Answer
Why? As is said every time "why?" is asked in Yiddish: "Why not?"

The first lines McQueen ever spoke professionally came in an all-Yiddish production of *Molly Picon,* a bioplay of the beloved actress who was simultaneously the Sarah Bernhardt of the Yiddish theater, as well as the Clara Bow of the once-vibrant *mamme-loshn* movie business.

The four lines McQueen uttered in his walk-on part fully embodied the tragic side of Yiddish's temperament: the sense of impending catastrophe, well earned over the millennia by Jews wandering in the Diaspora.

"Alles iz forloren!," he declaimed.

"All is lost."

Another quarter of McQueen's allotted lines:

"Es vet gornisht helfen."

"Nothing will help!"

Despite McQueen's later reputation as a hardy individualist, he earned his professional debut by being an overt *tuchus lekher* (ass kisser) when he was studying under Sanford Meisner, the world-renowned acting teacher-tyrant and founding member of the Group Theater, a leftist, Yiddish-inflected proletarian repertory company that included John Garfield, Clifford Odets, and Harold Clurman.

McQueen was fired after four performances of *Molly Picon*, produced by Meisner's Neighborhood Playhouse. Despite his attempted sycophancy, McQueen later said ruefully, "I guess I just didn't know Yiddish well enough."

Question 2

Isn't Yiddish just a bastardized dialect of medieval German?

Answer

Feh! Oy! Oy gevalt!

As for what language came first:

Deutsch meynt az drek iz znyn feter!

"German thinks it's king shit!"

Yet modern Yiddish was born before modern German. Technically, for ease in roping in this mustang of a language (good luck!), Yiddish is divided into four 250-year quadrants from its supposed birthday in 1069. There is "Initial Yiddish," "Old Yiddish," "Medieval Yiddish," and "Modern Yiddish."

However, according to a new line of scholarship, that old line of scholarship is *fartoost* (mixed up). Yiddish, goes the new theory, developed centuries before Jesus, even before Hebrew.

The first written Yiddish accompanied by a date came in 1272, when this one sentence was found written in a *machzor*, the Passover prayer book, in Worms, Germany.

"May a good day come upon him who will carry this *machzor* into the synagogue."

Meantime, Modern German is usually dated to Martin Luther's sixteenth-century translation of the Bible. (Luther's next book, *On the Jews and Their Lies*, came in 1543. In its pages, he argued that Jews' synagogues and schools should be put to the torch; and they should not be allowed to pray, teach, or say the name of God. Ultimately, he wrote, society must be rid of the *yidn*.)

> *Ale tseyn zoln im aroysfaln, nor eyner zol im blaybn oyf tsonveytik!*
> "May all his teeth fall out and only one remain for a toothache!"

Erica Jong is best known as the author of *Fear of Flying*, where she fictionally investigated the sensual possibilities in a zipperless world in the sky. Yet the smartest observation of her notable career was firmly grounded in putting *tuchus offn tish,* stapling her "ass on the table," i.e., getting down to brass tacks, about the meaning of Yiddish.

"Yiddish wasn't just words," Jong said of the *mamme-loshn* when it was most vital. "It was an attitude. It was sweet and sour. It was a shrug and a kiss. It was humility and defiance all in one."

Once again that attitude, so different from German, can be seen in the utter opposition of metaphor and humor behind the two cultures' phrasing of "she is good in bed."

In Yiddish, as Dr. Levitz taught me, one might say:

Zi veys take vi tsu tantsn matratsn-polke.

"She really knows how to dance the mattress polka."

In German, the same phrase would simply be:

Sie ist gut im bett.

"She is good in bed."

So which language is better? Case closed.

BACK SEVERAL CENTURIES, German Jews were segregated in the *Judengasse* ghetto, the "Jewish streets." At that time, the only place Jews and Gentiles could freely commingle was in the criminal underworld. There, the Germans picked up such Yiddishisms as *gonif* (thief) and *fin* or *finif* (five), which is still commonly used by gamblers and hustlers of all denominations to indicate half a sawbuck.

A *zetz*, meantime, which in Yiddish means giving someone the verbal needle, came to denote for German hitmen an assigned murder. *Drek* was borrowed by Christian German *gonifs* to call the paste they'd heisted that they'd thought were pearls.

In old Poland also, Jews often were only able to hang with Gentiles in gangsterville. There, Polish criminals began using the word *trayf*, Yiddish for not kosher, to describe a planned robbery, kidnapping, or murder that had to be called off because there were too many police around.

And while it is true that perhaps 80 percent of Yiddish's vocabulary has some variation of a medieval German root, that means nothing. While Yiddish speakers are almost uniformly able to speak German, few Germans can understand Yiddish.

War criminal Adolf Eichmann tried to learn Yiddish in order to know thine enemy, but gave up knowing only a smattering of words. And in *The Dance of Genghis Cohen*, Romain Gary's transcendent Holocaust novel, the title character flashes his ass and screams at the S.S. officer about to machine-gun him:

> *"Koosh mir in tuchus!"*
> "Kiss my ass!"

Though the phrase is widely understood today, the haunted German Nazi officer who killed Cohen spent three weeks traveling to concentration camps trying to find out the meaning of *koosh mir in tuchus.*

Question 3:
So what *is* Barbra Streisand's thing about *shtetls* and paying homage to Yiddish culture?

Answer
Who really ever knows with Barbra?
Yet the clues are many. She made a dumb film of *Yentl*, Isaac Bashevis Singer's gold-standard short story—and refused to let Singer, the literary Nobelist, even read the final screenplay.
Yet when Barbra Streisand's like-buttah voice is finally stilled, and the last *verklempt* (overcome) fan has paid their respects, her mortal remains will be placed in a spacious, already built mausoleum marked STREISAND. Located in the Jewish Mt. Hebron Cemetery in Flushing, Queens, Barbra's mausoleum is in section 104, near the road.
Her charnel house is not far from La Guardia Airport. And Streisand's decision to eventually rest there is actually a magnificent nod to her Yiddish theatrical forebears in New

York, who not so long ago entertained their fans with song and dance delivered in the *mamme-loshn*.

Since its opening in 1909, Mt. Hebron has been a bastion of Yiddishkeit. Inside the whole cemetery are buried luminaries ranging from the most noble thespians to the biggest gangsters-cum-avengers against anti-Semites. The then-thriving Yiddish Theatre Alliance bought a section of the graveyard for the benefit and burial of its membership. There, almost the entire pantheon of Yiddish stage immortals are buried. Sadly, virtually every name is now forgotten.

Here, among the graves are not only Steve McQueen's Molly Picon, but such forgotten unforgettables as Celia Adler of the famed theatrical family, who also acted in English in both the film and TV versions of *The Naked City*. Nearby are both Ida Kaminska and Boris Thomashefsky, the driving forces behind the entire Yiddish acting world (perhaps Thomashefsky's greatest success as a producer came with the always popular *Shmendrik and the Fanatic*).

Also buried in Mt. Hebron are Jack Gilford, né Jacob Aaron Gellman, the Crackerjack man; Allan King, born Irwin Alan Kniberg, comedian and Abbot of the New York Friars Club; Alfred Eisenstadt, the best photographer *Life* magazine ever had; and a who's who of Jewish gangsters from the first third of the twentieth century, including Lepke Buchalter, Martin "Buggsy" Goldsteinberg, and Irving Wexler, better known as "Waxey Gordon" to his Philadephia Jewish gangster associates Boo-Boo Hoff and Nig Rosen.

And yet one must always return again to Barbra Streisand's cemetery mansion on the hill. Even without directions one can't miss the only mausoleum on the block. Her building is so *Barbra*, proof, once again, that she is operating from her delusion of grandeur that she is, in fact, Barbra Streisand.

Always making *tsoris* (trouble) that Barbra, because she is a *ganze macher*, a very big shot, and she can. After all, the first commandment of Jewish show business is "the star is always right."

(The second law is "know your room," while the last is in pure Yiddish. *"Nem di gelt,"* vaudevillians would say—literally "take the money." This Yiddishism is actually used by entertainers to mean "get the money." In other words, do *not* leave the theater before collecting for your performance from suddenly evaporating stage managers. Nowadays, civilians who want to get out of a social engagement can best word an excuse by saying they are buried at the office trying to *nem di gelt*—"earn the money.")

But the golden rule of show business will always be the star is always right, be it Barbra Streisand or Boris Thomashevsky. At least Boris had the good sense to be buried in the dirt. Streisand, by building herself a mausoleum, thumbed her nose at the conventional Jewish wisdom that such aboveground graves are an automatic go-directly-to-hell card. If you want to be interred in a mausoleum, goes the tradition, forget being *plotzed* in any kind of Jewish cemetery plot.

Barbra's *chutzpah* in building a mausoleum for herself is astounding: The underground tradition has always been more than a habit. For centuries, Jewish religious authorities have put the official *kibosh*—Yiddish for a Brooklyn-style fuhgeddaboutit—concerning burial bungalows. The commandment is right there in the parchment of the Torah, Genesis 3:19. In that sentence, God commands that the dead should be buried in the earth, as in the dirt *below*, not the cement above.

"For dust you are and to dust you shall return," says the Torah—even if the Divine Barbra Streisand has *already* built a mausoleum for herself in a Jewish cemetery. Had she perhaps just been a dope? After all, while hosting a benefit for leftist Nicaraguan rebels in the 1980s, Streisand ventured to ask, "Where *is* Sandinista?"

In Jewish law, however, dopiness is not an out. Rules, rules, rules!

To take the harshest example, a *shtetl* suicide had to be buried just outside hallowed cemetery ground. This Yiddishkeit dishonor bestowed on Jews who killed themselves was roughly akin to the Sicilian tradition of burying self-killers under unmarked crossroads. There, those who dared take their own souls would be unknowingly trod upon by the living who had somehow found the strength to carry on with existence.

But hundreds of years after the Sicilians stopped performing *that* ritual, the old-world *shtetl* remained as strict as ever about certain ghoulish matters. If one's child married a non-Jew— *sha!*—the parents were ordered into actually mourning. They rended their clothes in grief, sat *shiva*, and lit memorial candles, just as if the bad seed were actually dead.

As time passed for Jewish immigrants in America, however, Yiddishkeit bent with growing mercy to self-annihilators. Their graves came closer and closer to hallowed ground. Until only a generation or two ago, suicides were buried inside the cemetery but against a fence, which was technically declared outside the graveyard boundary.

Though these unfortunate souls had gotten inside the cemetery, their plots were so far removed from the resting spots for the truly righteous that shame virtually radiated around their fence. Now, killing yourself is viewed as a mental illness, a sickness as blameless as typhoid fever—and such tortured souls can at least be buried with the rest of their families.

But with her mausoleum, Barbra was in trouble. In 1983, the Committee on Jewish Law and Standards of the Rabbinical Assembly (the official mouthpiece of the Conservative movement) voted 11–0 in favor of the continued outlawing of aboveground burials for Jews. Once again, Genesis's dust-to dust commandment was cited.

That was the first page of the report. Yet the committee, the report went on, could not stop arguing about the meaning of that phrase concerning dust-to-dust in the first book of the Bible. Endlessly, the rabbis interpreted and reinvestigated every what-if and howz-about in their analysis of mausoleums through the prism of the Jewish religious canon.

Indeed, the rabbis peeked at the issue from so many angles that their final paper was like an old-fashioned *shtetl pilpul*. The *pilpul*—academic arguments between scholars and scholars, and rabbis and their *yeshiva bochers* (young rabbis in training)—went on in the old country for hours as every facet of an ancient Hebrew word, sentence, or page was aridly, insanely analyzed.

Still, it seemed at first like the mausoleum rabbis got right to the point. No way can you be buried in an aboveground house, and that would include you, Miss fancy-shmancy Barbra Streisand.

The first page of the rabbis' finding stated categorically that:

Our present tradition of burying the dead in a casket placed in a grave belowground is so universally recognized that it has become virtually inconceivable to even suggest that other methods were ever employed or may be employed today.

And yet, after pages and pages of Talmudic boilerplate, the rabbis suddenly reversed themselves in their conclusion. Barbra, when she sings no more, is safe, her kind of graveyard Yiddishkeit not lauded but allowed.

The rabbis wrote:

Although there does not seem to be any impediment in Jewish law to using a mausoleum for burial, it should not be encouraged. Indeed, it should be actively discouraged since it is an obvious change from methods universally accepted today and its general publicized approval may create confusion. While it should be discouraged, we must recognize that it is permitted [by Jewish law] and that a rabbi may therefore officiate at an interment in a mausoleum.

They continued:

Although a mausoleum is permissible [according to Jewish law], certain restrictions should be applied. The mausoleum should be used exclusively for those of the Jewish faith. If a non-sectarian mausoleum is used, definite and easily recognizable demarcations should be imposed, such as its own central hall and entrance, clearly [stating] its Jewish nature.

Perhaps because of Streisand's healthy ego, she built the huge structure for herself because she didn't want to be ultimately unremembered, like almost all of the once-famous Yiddish theatrical stars buried so near. Maybe she had to be aboveground because, as Yiddish states:

Vos di erd dekt tsu muz fargesn vern.
"What the earth covers must be forgotten."

Or maybe her mausoleum is beyond ego; maybe she simply wants to rest with her father who died at fifty-five, when Barbra was fifteen months old. At the moment Emanuel Streisand is buried in Mt. Hebron underneath a simple granite marker, against which his daughter was once photographed standing with the saddest expression perhaps ever seen on her face. If he is to join her, he'd have to be disinterred in order to be put in Streisand's barely legal mausoleum.

If Streisand wants her father near her, it would be an act of Yiddishkeit, just like her desire to be buried near the greats of the Yiddish theater. It would bring *koved* (deep honor) to her immediate *mishpocha*—one of the largest components of Yiddish grace.

Question 4

Which is the correct pronunciation—*mish-mash* or *mish-mosh*—for the Yiddish word relating to any human endeavor or crazy-quilt project into which every conceivable item has been thrown in, *sans* perhaps the infamous kitchen sink?

Answer

As often happens in Yiddish, there is a simple answer. But as per Yiddishkeit, why not wrap that answer in an illustrative story recalling the deeds of a venerated ancestor or religious hero? Unless you were involved in an annoyingly long and meaningless *pilpul*, who didn't have time in the *shtetl* to hear a Yiddish tale?

One very true case involving this pronunciation issue occurred when an aristocratic Protestant congressman appeared on Groucho Marx's *You Bet Your Life* television quiz show in the 1950s. In the brief who-are-you segment preceding the quiz, the legislator described a bevy of interests indicating he had a mind as curious and creative as Thomas Jefferson.

The congressman finally wrapped things up by saying his catholic tastes were the usual "mish-mash."

Groucho looked at the congressman, raised an eyebrow, and

said with a Yiddish-inflected retort: "You'll never get any votes in Brooklyn if you pronounce it that way again."

It's *mish-mosh*.

Question 5

What's with all these Yiddish questions, questions, questions, when a simple answer would do?

Answer

Vy not? You in a hurry mebbe, Joe College?

In Yiddish, a good question is often considered better than a good answer. In the generally upward-lilting flow of Yiddish, the question mark is a natural rhythm. It can also be a code turning the meaning of sentences completely upside down. For instance:

> Standing on Lenin's Tomb in the Red Square, Stalin was acknowledging the acclamations of the masses. Suddenly he raised his hands to silence the crowd.
>
> "Comrades!" he cried. "A most historic event! A telegram of congratulations from Leon Trotsky!"
>
> The crowd could hardly believe its ears. It waited in hushed anticipation.
>
> "'Joseph Stalin,'" read Stalin. "'The Kremlin. Moscow. You were right and I was wrong. You are the true heir of Lenin. I should apologize. Trotsky.'"
>
> A roar erupted from the crowd.
>
> But in the front row, a little Jewish tailor gestured frantically to Stalin. "Psst!" he cried. "Comrade Stalin!"
>
> Stalin leaned over to hear what he had to say.
>
> "Such a message! But you read it without the right feeling."

Stalin once again raised his hands to still the excited crowd. "Comrades!" he announced. "Here is a simple worker, a Communist, who says that I did not read Trotsky's message with the right feeling. I ask that worker to come up onto the podium himself to read Trotsky's telegram."

The tailor jumped up onto the podium and took the telegram into his hands. He read:

"'Joseph Stalin. The Kremlin. Moscow.'" Then he cleared his throat and sang out:

"'You were right and I was wrong? You are the true heir of Lenin? I should apologize?'"

Frequently, the Yiddish-style question as answer is heard being offered by patients visiting their doctor's office.

"How do you feel?" asks the doctor.
"How should I feel?" says the patient.

"What hurts you?" asks the doctor.
"What doesn't hurt me?" says the patient.

"When do you feel bad?"
"When don't I feel bad?"

"When did it start?"
"When will it end?"

SOMEHOW, THE EVER-MORPHING story of Yiddish language and life explained for most of the world's Jews why, if they were so Chosen, they had been blessed over the past three thousand years as a mostly mangled and marginalized people, loathed by virtually the rest of the world.

For most of its millennium existence, talking, living, thinking, and feeling in Yiddish gave Jews a believable enough explanation for why God made the world this *verkokte*. It lent an army of words—for times good and usually bad, for centuries of hilarity and calamity—to explain what made their generally horrific lives worth the hassle.

That code of "keep going" would be Yiddishkeit—the same impulse that informs the modern decisions of individual Jews whether or not to order a surely tasty McDonald's McHamwich. A good Jew is expected to still do the right thing, even when nobody can see you at the drive-thru.

Then again, as Chasidic rabbi and Yiddish scholar Manis Friedman says, "It doesn't matter if you're a good Jew or a bad Jew, you're a Jew and we're stuck with you."

THE STORY OF Yiddish is partly about how Jews came to describe their lives to themselves amid other Jews and the not always so nice Gentiles. Yiddish also carries high praise for the very nice non-Jews blessed with the true and pure soul that even many Jews are missing.

There are Yiddish words for other worlds that have come to respect, like, and endorse the Jewish people, as well as secret *mamme-loshn* reserved for stone-cold anti-Semites who over the centuries have grudgingly put up with or just slaughtered these wandering Jews.

The story of Yiddish also explains to *yid* and *goy* who have at least always wondered what makes the Jews so . . . Jewish. (And that's a compliment. My father is going to be reading this book!)

Some of the story takes place in *shtetls* segregated by official decree. There, for centuries, synagogues were rickety shacks usually consisting of a couple of dozen warped planks haphazardly nailed together. Inside, studying sixteen hours a day, were the *yeshiva bochers*, the young Torah scholars and the next rabbis, their faces pale because the synagogue had no windows. As the Jewish Russian writer Isaac Babel described them, they wore "spectacles on their noses and autumn in their hearts."

Among Jews, Yiddish was the language of debate, argument, washtub wisdom, stable lore, and muddy love. It was the language of *rachmones*, profound and true empathy, and cause in itself for always rooting for the underdog, for having one's throat slit in Mississippi because you were outside agitators trying to get blacks to be allowed to vote.

Yiddish meant survival for a people with no armaments, or any inclination to learn how to use them if they did. The language was their army. As is said:

Got zol op opheaten fun goyishe hent un yidishe reyd.
"God protect us from Gentile hands and from Jewish
   tongues."

Yiddish could be used as a sonnet, or a slingshot; juicy gossip, or joyous dancing in the face of a world usually nasty, brutish, mean, and *kelt* (cold). There is no conventional wisdom: This Yiddishist from Oxford says the language started during *this* time frame in *this* place, while that Yiddishist from Berkeley says the Jewish Diaspora's *lingua franca* started centuries later, way over *there*.

Meantime, the Kibitzer from Maryland, Yosl Alpert, says all the professors are wrong. What also is *farshtinkener* (stinks), he writes on his website, is the standard Yiddish-English dictionary, first printed in 1968, and among the few books thought to have saved Yiddish from having its plug pulled over the last generation.

The Kibitzer raves on on his website. The "Yiddish Mafia" that putatively controls the Yiddish dictionary, he says, are probably, clinically, *meshugge*. That cabal, he says, has invented Yiddish words out of thin air, and the dictionary is woefully prudish.

The Kibitzer logically writes, "Now, honestly can you trust a Yiddish dictionary that doesn't have a **tokhes**???"

No one is arguing about a few sad facts. According to the Yiddish Book Center in Amherst, Massachusetts, eleven million people, 75 percent of the world's Jewish population, spoke Yiddish as a first or only language in 1939. Hitler took half of them; Stalin, American assimilation, and the Israelis' loathing of Yiddish in favor of an updated modern Hebrew took most of the rest.

To the question of how many people speak Yiddish today, the book center's fact sheet answers in a most Yiddish way with "?."

Question 6

Do I have to be Jewish to know or appreciate Yiddish?

Answer

No.

Leo Rosten himself said, "It is a remarkable fact that never in its history has Yiddish been so influential—among Gentiles. (Among Jews, alas, the tongue is running dry.)"

Indeed, what is not understandable to all English speakers in the following diatribe attributed to Jackie Mason?

We must preserve the exclusivity and, above all, the purity of English by excluding all foreign speech that might make its way into our language.

To all the *shlemiels, shlemazels, nebbishes, nudniks, klutzes, putzes, shlubs, shmoes, shmucks, no-goodniks,* and *momzers* out there, I just want to say that I, for one, believe that English and only English deserves linguistic prominence in our American culture.

"To tell the truth, it takes me so *farklempt,* I'm fit to *plotz.* This whole *schmeer* gives me *broyges,* especially when I hear these erstwhile *mavens* and *luftmenshen kvetching* about how we in the United States need to allow the languages of new immigrants to be used in schools, and even letting parts of those languages seep into English. What *chutzpah!* These *shmegegges* can tout their *shlock* about the cultural and linguistic diversity of our country, but I, for one, am not buying their *shtick.* It's all so much *dreck,* as far as I'm concerned. I exhort you all to be *menshen* about this and stand up to their *fardrayte* arguments and *meshugganah, farshtunkene* assertions. It wouldn't be *kosher* to do anything else.

Remember, when all is said and done, we have English and they've got *bubkes!* The whole *myseh* is a pain in my *tuchas!*

So no, again, no. You don't need to be Jewish to understand the language or, more important, its essence.

And one certainly need not be a fluent Yiddishist to understand the all-important tenets of Yiddishkeit.

Did Charlie Parker have to know how to read music to make magic come out of his famous plastic saxophone?

Do you need to be Jewish to understand under the skin a Yiddish-based joke? What, so you don't know how to laugh?

Take the famous tale of the elderly Jewish woman walking on Fourteenth Street, the longest byway in Manhattan, near the Lower East Side.

"Excuse me, mister," she asks a stranger, "do you know Yiddish?"

The man says no, and the woman moves on.

"Excuse me, Miss Blondie," she then asks a fashionably dressed woman, "do you speak Yiddish?"

The fashion plate shakes her head.

Another man walks by, and the elderly woman asks, "Excuse me, mister, do you know Yiddish?"

The man stops, nods his head, and tells her he does.

"So," she asks her fellow Yiddish speaker, "vat time it is?"

That joke is the universal Yiddish heart that has everything—and nothing—to do with being Jewish. Yiddish is the laugh atop the desperate human longing to belong, to find a recognizable face, home, or feeling amid the unfriendly masses bumping past you in Minsk, on Fourteenth Street, or in an anonymously unhappy airport bar.

You don't need to *know* Yiddish to *feel* Yiddish.

You just need a stranger to tell you vat time it is.

Question 7
So, Yiddish *does* have filthy words*!?*

Answer
Yes. No. Maybe.

It's hard to tell sometimes if Yiddish has volumes of dirty phrases, or is instead so shy that it relies on filthy interpretations of metaphors, if you lean that way. *Tuchus* isn't literally "ass"; its etymology is from the Hebrew word *tach-at,* meaning "underneath."

Or take the mouth of Lenny Bruce, whose *shpritz* combined Yiddish and jazz argot into manically profane stream-of-consciousness monologues that got him busted so many times that his stage act eventually became a pathetic monologue about getting busted so many times. Once, at the Troubadour Theater in Los Angeles, the vice squad sent a Yiddish-speaking policeman to monitor Bruce's show to see if he was hiding behind the language to spout obscenities.

As they say in Yiddish, send a Jew to get a Jew—and they got him. In the arrest report, recalled Bruce from the stage, it said he'd used the phrase *"fressing the maid."*

Describing the event, the comedian explained that:

> *"Fressing"* is Yiddish; it means eating. "Eating," in English, is an act of oral copulation. So I'm putting on an obscene show. How is that for Tinker to Evers to Chance? But [the report] ought to continue [that] oral copulation is *goyish.*
>
> Because there is no word in Yiddish that describes oral copulation. In fact, there are no gutter phrases in Yiddish. It's amazing. *Emmis* [Yiddish for "no bullshit, it's true"]. There are no words that describe any sexual act, *emmis,* or parts, or lusts.
>
> Dig: *shmuck* is a German word. In the official Yiddish dictionary, *shmuck* is a yard or a fool. So dig what happens. The Jews take it humorously, make a colloquialism out of a literal word—and some *putz* who doesn't understand what we're talking about busts you for obscenity.

Question 8

I still don't get the difference between Yiddish and Hebrew.

Answer

That's not a question, but Yiddish likes to be repetitive, so let's try once more.

Though both languages are written in Hebrew script, they are as comparable as Doris Day and Billie Holiday. Yiddish is Judaism's dripping mutt, its bastard language with a forever-molting vocabulary sponged from friends and enemies. Hebrew was for reverent prayer; Yiddish was meant to be spoken while cleaning out stables or gossiping about one's neighbors.

While you could describe today's weather in Yiddish, holy Hebrew became mummified, entombed in its own antiquity, as inviolable to change as ancient Latin. There was no Hebrew word for "popsicle" or "atomic bomb," nor could one ever be invented.

Yiddish, meantime, lived to adapt to real life. In America, Jewish immigrants at the turn of the century turned such words as "window" and "payday" into Yiddish equivalents like *"vin-deh"* and *"peh-dey,"* the latter coming literally to mean the enve-lope that held the weekly wage of Jewish laborers.

It also became the *lingua franca* of a country with no borders, the record of a people simultaneously blessed and fucked.

Question 9
Why should we care?

Answer

We should care because to understand Yiddish, and Yiddishkeit, means more than understanding Jews as best as they can be un-derstood by anyone, especially by themselves. It means striving to be a *mentsh*, a human being, in a world where:

"People are people, and sometimes not even that."

Question 10

Who is this Sholom Aleichem? I know Jerry Bock wrote the music for *Fiddler on the Roof* and Joseph Stein is credited with the book. Was this Aleichem fellow perhaps the lyricist?

Answer

No. Sheldon Harnick wrote the words to such historic Broadway toe-tappers as "Tradition," "Sunrise, Sunset," and "If I Were a Rich Man."

Sholom Aleichem wrote the real, actual story about the travails of Tevye, his family, et al. Aleichem is ranked among the very top Yiddish writers of all time; these days he is best remembered as the scrivener whose sardonic, often tragically comic portrayals of *shtetl* life were bowdlerized into *Fiddler on the Roof.*

Ironically, when Aleichem came to New York at the beginning of the twentieth century, two of his own Yiddish plays bombed. Yet he already was an international hero who never stopped fighting to make Yiddish the official Jewish language. (He wrote over forty volumes of Yiddish prose, poetry, and drama; his first book was composed when he was fifteen. It was an alphabetical vocabulary of the Yiddish epithets his stepmother liked to hurl.)

Aleichem arrived in America from Russia in the wake of the 1905 pogroms, and died in the Bronx on March 13, 1916, at age fifty-nine. Many said the cause of Aleichem's death was grief over his son Misha, who had died in Europe of tuberculosis the year before, separated from his father in order to receive medical treatment. Beyond a broken heart, other biographers have diagnosed his death as a case of nervous exhaustion brought on by the prodigious amount of material he had to produce, and the harried cross-country lecture schedules he had to obey in order to keep his family eating.

His death marked an almost unheard-of ceasefire among all the warring factions of Yiddish politics and letters; an estimated 100,000 to 300,000 people followed his funeral procession, arguably the largest such crowd in New York until that time. His tombstone was a humble paean to the *mammeloshn*.

His will appeared on the front page of the *New York Times*, and was read into the Congressional Record. Aleichem's final testament wasn't about the disbursement of money; he had virtually nothing. Rather, he left instructions that "my name be recalled with laughter, or not at all."

Each year on his *yahrzeit*, the ritually observed anniversary of a Jew's death, he asked that his friends join together and "select one of my stories, one of the very merry ones, and recite it in whatever language is most intelligible."

Perhaps Aleichem's most remembered line was, "You can take the Jew out of the *shtetl*, but you can't take the *shtetl* out of the Jew."

For a master of prose who concentrated not so much on words but weaving magical stories, Aleichem was remarkably quotable in suitably Yiddish-style one-liners:

"A bachelor is a man who comes to work each morning from a different direction."

"Gossip is nature's telephone."

"Life is a dream for the wise, a game for the fool, a comedy for the rich, a tragedy for the poor."

"No matter how bad things get, you got to go on living, even if it kills you."

"The rich swell up with pride, the poor from hunger."

Yet his style is what ultimately will resonate forever, never mind *Fiddler on the Roof.*

From "An Early Passover":

Pinhas Pincus is of less than normal height, with one small eye and one bigger eye. When he talks, it seems as if the eyes talk to each other; the smaller eye asks for and seeks approval from the bigger eye; and the bigger eye gives its approval of every plan or undertaking. When he first came to Nuremberg, there was no limit to his sufferings; he had to endure starvation, misery and personal insults from his German brethren. In Nuremberg he was protected from massacres, but was not protected from starvation.

IT IS EASY for Yiddishists to dismiss *Fiddler on the Roof* as mal-adapted *shlock*. Yet the musical ignited a worthy nostalgia for a never-known world of Yiddish and Yiddishkeit in the 1960s, when a majority of *yidn* had seemingly abandoned all Jewish traditions except for a love of Chinese food on Christmas.

Still, *Fiddler on the Roof*, dripping in sentiment, has been hammered unrelentingly as an unworthy philistine work. If one hadn't seen the play, but only intellectuals' critiques concerning *Fiddler*'s alleged fakery, one could guess it might better have been called "Art Linkletter's Lighter Side of Pogroms."

Not fair.

Yet even in the translated fictional letters he composed in his stories, Aleichem's actual work expels a power unknown in Broadway's *Fiddler*. The words he puts in a missive sent by one of his *shtetl shlubs* to a relative who'd fled for America, *sound* Yiddish, even when rendered in the King's English.

The infamous massacre of Russian Jews in Kishinev in 1903 had just occurred, prompting several hundred thousand Jews to hike across Europe and sail away to America.

"Dear Yankel," the letter in Aleichem's short story began.

You asked me to write at length, and I would like to oblige, but there is really nothing to write about. The rich are still rich, and the poor are dying of hunger, as they always do. What's new about that? And as far as pogroms are concerned, thank God we have nothing more to fear as we've already had our two of them and a third wouldn't be worthwhile.

All our family got through it safely, except for Kippi, who was killed with two of his sons, Noah and Mordecai; first class artisans, all three of them. . . . Perel was found dead in the cellar together with the baby at her breast. But as Getzi used to say: "It might have been worse; don't think of the better because there's no limit to that."

You asked about Heshel. He's been out of work now for over a year. The fact is they won't let him work in prison. Mendel did a clever thing: he upped and died, some say of consumption, others of hunger. Personally, I think he died of both. I really don't know what else to write about, except for the cholera, which is going great guns.

CHAPTER 8

ש שׁכבנרבֿךכברבנבֿשׁכבבֿרבברבֿ

Yiddish; More Yiddishkeit; Bob Dylan; Sandy Koufax; Fergie, Duchess of York; and Woody Guthrie

iddish and Yiddishkeit, Yiddishkeit, Yiddishkeit.

What is it?

Can late Jewish gangsters (there haven't been any for decades, except for the likes of Bruce Cutler, John Gotti's attorney) be purveyors of true Yiddishkeit?

Yes. Ask Meyer Lansky or Mickey Cohen. If only, unlike Jesus, as Yiddish declared, they could *geshtoygen und gefloygen,* rise from the dead and fly.

Lansky, Cohen, Dave "the Jew" Berman, and most of their *yidn* criminal cohorts spent much of their off hours working on Jewish causes after inventing Las Vegas, the casino "skim," money laundering, and honest gaming tables. Historically verified fact shows Lansky, Cohen, even Bugsy Siegel, et al., spending their time eating dinner with their families and never discussing business at the table; humiliating anti-Semites; and actively fighting for European Jews trapped behind enemy lines while official American-Jewish leaders kept their thumbs up their asses for fear of offending the Gentiles.

In 1948, Harry Truman privately slurred the *yidn* and Zionists, finally agreeing to recognize the imminent state of Israel because he didn't want the Russians to do it first. He'd recognize the partition, but as per his personal feelings and those of General George Marshall, he wouldn't provide Israel one bullet lest the United States offend their Arab oil providers.

So, the likes of Lansky began ordering the hijacking of weapons on the New York docks headed for the Arabs; while young Jews like Hank Greenspun, briefly Bugsy Siegel's P.R. man at the Flamingo Hotel, started personally running guns by speedboat to Israel. (Later, Greenspun started the *Las Vegas Sun*, and in a profound act of Yiddishkeit, became the only publisher in the nation to condemn from the beginning Senator Joseph McCarthy and his witch hunt for Communists.)

And so, even if Jewish gangsters lived by the rules of the street, most also lived by or amid the rules of Yiddishkeit. Take what happened to Sam "Killer" Kaplan, an active member of Murder, Inc., the Jewish homicides-for-hire organization efficiently run in Brooklyn for the benefit and *gelt* of Italian mafiosi with disorganized *goyishe kopfs* across the country.

IF ITALIAN SHMEGEGGES bothered the Mafia in the 1920s and 1930s, Lucky Luciano, the national *capo di tutti capi*, boss of bosses, would contact Murder, Inc., which offered no mess, no fuss, no cops, and the kind of motiveless protection afforded paid *zetz*-men, those who have no idea who they are *zetzing*.

Murder, Inc., provided the kind of efficiency of Harvey Keitel, *Pulp Fiction*'s Winston Wolf, who could eliminate all signs of a gruesome murder committed by others with a cup of black coffee and three-quarters of an hour. Keitel, as Mr. Wolf, a Jew in real life, also offered the following piece of Yiddishkeit: "Just because you're a character doesn't mean you *have* character."

And so, on the farthest extremes of society, the spirit of Yiddishkeit could be found—even in the dying happenstances of Sam "Killer" Kaplan. Kaplan was a valued Murder, Inc., hit man for any crime family who wanted to leave no fingerprints.

One afternoon, Killer Kaplan was on his way to visit his mother near Murder Inc.'s headquarters. Coming to his *mammele's* apartment, Kaplan walked into the crossfire between members of Murder, Inc., and some local *pishers*.

Luckily for the grievously wounded Kaplan, his loving and all-forgiving *Yiddishe mamme* lived on the same block as the shoot-out. Barely able to climb the steps, the bloody Kaplan could hardly summon the strength to bang on his mother's door.

"Mama," he cried out. "It's me, Sammy. I'm hurt bad."

"Sit down and eat," his mother said, opening the door. "Later, we'll talk.

AND WHAT DOES Yiddishkeit have to do with fallen, then arisen Bar Mitzvah boy Bob Dylan (whose conversion to Yiddish-based Orthodox Judaism inspired Adam Sandler's "Chanukah Song" (itself a modern testament to Yiddishkeit), where Dylan was lauded for being "Jewish/then he wasn't/but now he's back"?

And what does Yiddish have to do with the poetry of Woody Guthrie, Dylan's long-dead Okie superhero? Or Sandy Koufax, the World's Nicest Jewish Boy, and the greatest source of *Yiddishe nachas* (Jewish pride) since Maimonides?

Or Yiddish and Yiddishkeit and Sarah Ferguson, still on the world's short list of leading *shiksas*? Fergie, for *HaShem's* sake!?

Fergie? From the country that gave the *yidn* Shylock in the originally titled *The Jew of Venice*? Why was Fergie learning Yiddishkeit with an ultra-religious Chasidic rabbi after she adulterously *shtupped* a playboy *shagetz* (non-Jewish male) who, unlike Bob Dylan, no doubt hadn't even had a *bris*? *"Feh!"* says Yiddishkeit to such uncircumcised *shlongs*!

Fergie, discussing the meaning of *tzedaka*, Yiddish for the all-critical Yiddishkeit demand to give "charity," with chasidic rabbi Manis Friedman? When she could have had so much to give before she gave up her duchess-ship because, "she danced the mattress polka"?

Sex, having it or not, is in itself an important precept of Yiddish and Yiddishkeit. Now, assimilated Jews seemed to stop at 2.2 babies.

But in the old days, as is said in the *mamme-loshn*:

> *Yidn zaynen geven tsu farnumen kinder hobn tsu zorgn zikh*
> *vegn seeks.*
> "Jews are so busy making children they don't have time
> for sex."

Yiddishkeit is Bill Murray (as Ebenezer Scrooge, after seeing the light, in *Scrooged*) saying, in explanation of his karmic turnaround

> The Jews taught me this great word: *shmuck*. I used to be a
> *shmuck*. But I'm not a *shmuck* any longer.

Yiddishkeit is John Hammond, a Yale Yankee and Columbia talent scout having the "ears" to discover Billie Holiday, Bob Dylan, and Bruce Springsteen. In the old country, similar "ears" were sent through all the Jewish villages in search of potential cantor superstars.

Cantors were the rock stars of the *shtetls* and cities with large

Jewish populations; seats went fast when a special cantor was
traveling through the area for a concert. Like rock stars, the
greatest cantors were pampered, allowed every indulgence, their
eccentricities overlooked. Like rock stars, their handlers treated
them as children—children with magical gifts.

For, as they say in Yiddish,

*Alle chazonim zeinen naronim ober alle naronim kenennen nisht
zingen.*
"All cantors are fools, but not all fools can sing."
Exactly.

FOR TYPE A personalities who overschedule themselves to the
annoyance of loved ones, it is Yiddishkeit to understand that

Nisht ken tanzen tzvai chossene mit ain tuchus.
"You can't dance at two weddings with one ass."

AND, PERHAPS MOST important, Yiddishkeit means:

"Chochme ohn hertz siz poast unal laidick."
"Wisdom without heart is vain and empty."
—Rebbe Aaron of Karlin, famous Chasidic wise man of
the eighteenth century

"WHO WANTS TO know?" as the Yiddish locution has it. Apparently, most everybody in the United States, Jew or Gentile, already knows enough vocabulary.

Performing one's life according to the tenets of Yiddishkeit, with Yiddish itself serving as the backbone, has nothing to do with being Jewish.

And then there is Lenny Bruce's most famous routine, quoted to the point where it's an old saw bordering on cliché. His soul, no doubt, is spinning that the riff has been bowdlerized and stands alone as the epigraph on the first page of the G-rated *Jewish Almanac*.

In the routine, he alters the meanings of Jewish and *goyish*, making "Jewish" signify a warm, loving, soulful *Yiddishe hartz*, not limited to actual Jews. In this paradigm, Mother Teresa, for example, is Jewish. *Goyish* can mean anything from Jewish slumlords to NASCAR auto-racing enthusiasts.

A mentsh with a *Yiddishe hartz* breaks up with girlfriends in person. You open the door for others, and hold the elevator for strangers. You flirt with seventy-five-year-old ladies. You keep secrets, root for your friends, and don't stab people in the back, but call them weasels to their faces. This was *a Yiddishe hartz*, secular version.

"Now I neologize Jewish and Goyish," Bruce begins, banishing for the moment who was actually born as a Jew or Gentile. He uses the word "Jewish" the way many Yiddish speakers call the *mamme-loshn* "Jewish." It is a feeling, not a foreign vocabulary.

"Now I'm Jewish. Count Basie is Jewish. Ray Charles is Jewish. Eddie Cantor is *goyish*. Hadassah, Jewish. Marine Corps, heavy *goyim*, dangerous. Kool-Aid is *goyish*. Black cherry soda is very Jewish. Macaroons are very Jewish. Fruit salad is Jewish. Lime jello is *goyish*. Lime soda is very *goyish*. Trailer parks are so *goyish* that Jews won't go near them. Mouths are Jewish. All Italians are Jewish. Greeks are *goyish*—bad sauce. Eugene O'Neill is Jewish. Dylan Thomas is Jewish. If you're Italian or Puerto Rican and live

in New York City, you're Jewish. If you're Jewish and live in
Butte, Montana, you're *goyish*.

SO WHAT IS a Jew? What constitutes Yiddishkeit?

Maybe there is an intersection of a people who count as its
adherents, everyone from the late Chasidic Rebbe, Menachem
Mendel Schneerson, who decided after a hallowed eighty-plus
years that he was the Messiah, to Sandy Koufax, the youngest
player ever inducted into the Baseball Hall of Fame.

Albert Einstein and the comic movie director and actor Albert Brooks, né Albert Einstein? The *Kohanim*, the priests of Jerusalem's Holy Temple, and the Coen Brothers, of *The Big
Lebowski*?

Katherine Graham, who didn't know she was Jewish until
she was an adult, or Moses Mendelssohn, who converted to
Christianity?

Who's guiltier of what: Meyer Lansky, who arranged for
both the beating of American Nazi Bundists in World War II
and the smuggling of tons of guns to the neonatal state of Israel;
or David Ben-Gurion, who during that same war, ordered his
Jewish troops to sink a boat manned by Jewish gun smugglers
headed his way to help?

Ben-Gurion, Israel's George Washington, who made a point
of dressing down Yiddish anytime he heard it, or Ben "Bugsy"
Siegel, the crazed Jewish gangster who cooked up a plot that
might have actually succeeded in killing Mussolini during World
War II?

What to make of a people who can boast Joey and Tommy
Ramone, Lou Reed (né Rabinowitz), Bob Dylan, as well as the
virulently crazed anti-Semite, former chess champion Bobby
Fischer? Who can explain a tribe that holds to its chest Dr. Albert

B. Sabin, inventor of the polio vaccine, but also has to count as its own Roy Cohn and Judge Irving Kaufman, who illegally conspired in chambers to convict Ethel and Julius Rosenberg, largely so that the case would go down as (good for the Jews)?

Jews fighting Jews?

Yiddish was aware of the dynamic, and sometimes even of its necessity. As long as the Jews were arguing with one another, at least they were still talking among themselves when no one else wanted to get near them.

> *Moyshe rabeynu hot mit di yidn oykh nit gekent oyskumen.*
> "Not even Moses Our Teacher could get along with the
>   Jews."

No one, of course, could, with more affection, needle a Jew than another Jew.

> *Tsu vos darf a yid hoben fis? Az in kheyder muz men im traybn,*
>   *tsu der khupe firt men ihm, in shul arayn geyt er nit, un tsu*
>   *shikeses krikht er, iz tsu vos darf fis?*
> "Why does a Jew need legs? To school he must be forced,
>   to marriage he must be led, to burial he is brought, to
>   synagogue he won't go, and after Gentile girls he
>   crawls. So why does he need legs?"

TWO ILLUSTRATIVE CASES of Yiddishkeit over the last fifty years involve Bob Dylan and Sandy Koufax, each tale mixed amidst the world's last natural Yiddish speakers. Each story shows the power of Yiddish, a lesson especially useful for Jewish baby-boom men, almost all of whom would exchange their souls to the devil to become either Dylan or Koufax for a day.

Stories are still told among eyewitnesses of the Passover night when Dylan showed up at Chasidic rabbi Manis Friedman's door and crashed the seder, immediately downing for hors d'oeuvres a bowl of matzoh ball soup and a plate of gefilte fish.

The Chasidim seemed as interested in Dylan's comings and goings as the general public. Several said they felt the singer's *neshama* (soul) every time he walked into Adath Israel, the mostly Chasidic synagogue a block down from the Friedmans' house, wearing cowboy boots, a leather vest, and a prayer shawl.

"No one knew who he was," one Lubavitcher told me, "but you could tell from the second he walked in, even the way he was dressed, that here was the *neshama* of Yiddishkeit."

In secret, Friedman had blown the mind of Dylan, the mind of his generation. He'd come to Friedman in the late 1980s after spending a decade as a born-again Christian. He left as an Orthodox Jew, warming the innards of every baby-boom Jewish male. "Bob Dylan was Jewish/And then he wasn't/ but now he's back," *Saturday Night Live*'s Adam Sandler sang proudly in his hit Chanukah song. ("'Mary Tyler Moore's husband is Jewish,'" Sandler rhymed the stanza, "Cuz we're pretty good in the sack.")

RABBI FRIEDMAN HAD been the only person in the synagogue who actually knew the J. D. Salinger of popular music. Dylan was usually accompanied to *shul* by his childhood friend Larry Keegan, who'd been paralyzed as a teenager in a diving accident. They'd become friends at Herzl Camp, the same Zionist summer camp in Webster, Wisconsin, that I'd attended. There, he would sit atop the outhouses, a neophyte plunking at his guitar, refusing to come down even when the rabbi who ran the camp would come and order him off.

But it was no camp rabbi yelling at him to come down from an outhouse that apparently turned Dylan into what he was. According to another Lubavitcher, Dylan took his Bar Mitzvah lessons in a room above a motorcycle shop. Embarrassed to be seen going to such a sissy activity on the way up the stairs, he would stop and loiter with the bad boys on the way down.

"That's where he got his rebellious spirit," another young Chasid who prayed in Adath Israel informed me. "It was the combination of Bar Mitzvah lessons and motorcycle shop."

"Dylan is a good family man," Rabbi Friedman let slip one night when he was exhausted and could be briefly induced into talking about his most famous client. "His problem is women."

A few days after Dylan's mother died a few years ago, a fellow Chasidic rabbi visiting the Friedmans asked his host, "Did you just see the poem Bob wrote in yesterday's paper?"

Friedman nodded, saying it was a *mitzvah*, a good deed, for the singer to remember his mother by writing her an ode in the newspaper that she'd read (the *St. Paul Pioneer Press*).

Rabbi Friedman continued silently stroking his beard, waiting, waiting, waiting for a new topic to come up. The reason Dylan talked to him was because he never talked about Dylan.

"How did they get along, Dylan and his mother?" someone then asked.

"His mother," said Manis Friedman, "was his best enemy."

That's Yiddishkeit.

AFTER TIME SPENT studying the holy Hebrew texts of Judaism with Manis Friedman, Dylan could even play guitar again after victimizing himself with gallons upon gallons of *shnapps* he drank during his decade-long stint as a born-again Christian. After seeing Friedman, his voice and sanity also seemed to return.

The rabbi refuses to call himself "Bob Dylan's rabbi"—enough Dylan fans arrive at Friedman's front door unexpectedly as it is, as do reporters from the *New York Times* and assorted rock magazines. Also visiting are spiritual wanderers who've gone off their meds, looking for an audience. Such are the occupational hazards of being a Yiddish-speaking Chasidic wise man.

"Do you know Dylan's songs?" I asked once, and Rabbi Friedman's eyes narrowed. Wrong question. But in Yiddish, the wrong question sometimes leads to the right answer.

Then he spoke. It concerned the Eastern European Jews who made Yiddish a holy language, and their belief in the back-and-forth nonlinear conception of time.

"I don't know his songs," he said. "Didn't he write something about 'The Times Are Changing [*sic*],'" he asked. "What's changing? How do you change *HaShem*'s ["The Name," i.e., God's] time?"

He paused. "And didn't he write, 'The Wind Is Blowing in the Something [*sic*]'? Tell me, where's it blowing?"

So what, in old-world Yiddishkeit terms, could I take from the rabbi's encounters with the voice of a generation?

"Dylan," he said, referring to old-fashioned prayer phylacteries, "wears *tefillin*."

"Yom Kippur is the holiest day of the Jewish religion. The [Dodgers] know that I don't work that day."
   —Sandy Koufax, explaining why he didn't pitch the first game of the 1965 World Series in Minnesota

There is another piece of unknown Yiddishkeit lore involving the Chasids. For forty-two years it has been a mystery, even to Sandy Koufax's biographers, what the Los Angeles Dodgers' Hall of Fame pitcher actually *did* the day he sat out the first game of the World Series in order to set an example for other Jews.

Koufax, as is well known, had become the Nicest Jewish Boy in modern American history by sitting out the opening game of that World Series against the Minnesota Twins because the year's most critical contest fell on Yom Kippur. While his team, stripped of their ace, got whipped in the crucial opening contest, young Sanford was . . . where? Over the years, the story had spread that he'd quietly spent the day at the Conservative Temple of Aaron synagogue in St. Paul in his suit and tie.

Even though Koufax wasn't religious, he'd told contemporary reporters, "I wanted to set a good example" for the rest of Jewish youth—and he promised to somehow make it up to the Dodgers in the best of seven games world championship. Not likely—it would take a miracle for the unhittable pitcher to get into enough games to turn the tide after the Dodgers were walloped so convincingly in game one.

"THAT WAS A great thing Koufax did by not pitching," Chasidic rabbi Moishe Feller says in Rabbi Friedman's living room. "The Rebbe himself mentioned it that week in his talk."

That Yom Kippur, Feller, uninvited, took a new set of *tefillin* and headed down to the stately St. Paul Hotel, the city's finest, where he'd already sniffed out that the Dodgers were staying. "I went up to the desk clerk," Rabbi Feller said, "and asked him if they could ring Sandy Koufax's room. I looked like a rabbi," he said, sweeping his hand four decades later over his long beard and gray suit, "and news of what he'd done had already spread across the world that day. So they figured Sandy himself had sent for me, a rabbi.

"They let me call up to his room," he continued, "and Koufax answers the phone himself and says 'sure, come on up.' When I got to his room he was warming up for the game the next day," Rabbi Feller says, windmilling his left arm in the hallway. "He was alone, and in his *gottkes* [underwear]!"

With that, Rabbi Feller made a laughing aside to Rabbi Friedman: "Which is a lot more than ALLEN GINSBERG was wearing when you had *him* put on *tefillin!*" Feller paused. "The amazing thing is that Koufax *still knew how to put on tefillin.*"

"It was a miracle," Rabbi Feller said about the pitcher, who after almost losing the World Series for his teammates on Yom Kippur, came back to win the second and fifth games, and then, on an unheard-of two days rest and with an aching elbow, the decisive seventh contest. He'd both honored God, and then the National League. Koufax's act was an authentic homage to the past, an exercise in Yiddishkeit.

But honoring Yiddishkeit doesn't have to entail observing Yom Kippur and then winning the World Series. To many Jews, eating the *pupik* (the gizzard) from a home-cooked Sabbath chicken is just as meaningful.

It is a remembrance of the times in the poverty- and hunger-stricken *shtetl* when not an ounce of edible kosher food was thrown away, not even the gizzard or the chicken fat (*shmaltz*) gleaned from the one meal of the week when the peasants ate meat. The phrase "save me the *pupik*" is in itself an act of Yiddishkeit.

And yet, as Abbie Hoffman said, "nostalgia is just another name for depression." (As a defendant in the 1969 Chicago Seven conspiracy trial, Hoffman showed off his Yiddish by yelling at the senescent Jewish judge that he was *a shanda fur di goyim*, "a disgrace in front of the Gentiles.")

Yiddish poet J. Gladstein knew that Yiddishkeit did not live on *pupik* lore alone.

Nostalgia Jewishness is a lullaby for old men /
Gumming soaked white bread.

CHAPTER 9

שׁמײַ׳ר ערשׁ׳ר ויבשׁמײַ׳ר ערשׁ׳ר וי

The Chasidim and Yiddish—Why the Ba'al Shem Tov Was Spanked

The good Orthodox Jews of Slutsk, Russia—coincidentally my direct ancestors, all killed off by the Nazis as they screamed for pity in Yiddish—would have despised Rabbi Manis Friedman.

Today, the Chasidic rabbi is an esteemed Yiddish scholar. Yet if the rabbi had wandered unawares into Slutsk 350 years ago, he would have been led to the town square, forced to drop Chasidic trou, and then literally spanked bare-ass before the entire cheering town.

Not that Slutzniks were philistines toward profound religious thought, which the likes of Friedman thought they'd be offering the citizenry. Slutsk was renowned for its Torah brainiacs. Despite its small size, Slutsk became highly known throughout Eastern Europe over the centuries for its massive output of traditionally trained, genius-level rabbis bearing the intellectually obtuse and conservative judgments that had ruled Jewish life for centuries.

Now Slutsk is remembered, when remembered at all, as the town famous for loathing—more than anywhere else in Jewish

Europe—the revolutionary Chasidim who came knocking on their doors in the eighteenth century.

Before that, the rabbis and populace of Slutsk were also known among other Jews for their arrogance and emotional distance, resulting in the nickname "cold Slutsk." And Friedman, as a Chasid, would have been paid in humiliation if he'd even dared enter the Yiddish-speaking communities that once existed between Minsk, Pinsk, and *Yechupitzville* (any remote, distant, and unimportant small *shtetl* or Jewish City—the American equivalent is Bumfuck, Idaho).

In the eighteenth century, an ignorant Russian-Jewish airhead and ne'er-do-well named the Ba'al Shem Tov ("he of the good name," a.k.a. "the *Besht*") founded the ultra-Orthodox Chasidim. His principles are the ones Friedman lives his life by. The Ba'al Shem Tov, this unremarkable *luftmentsh* went off to the obscure Carpathian Mountains to get away from his temporal failures and to commune with God.

When he returned, the Ba'al Shem Tov had alchemized into a dynamic religious presence and itinerant soul saver bearing news of an exciting and fresh kind of Judaism. Acting as a kind of Jewish Johnny Appleseed, he traveled the land preaching change. There is only one book of his teachings: fifty-two stories and parables collected after his death in *Why the Ba'al Shem Tov Laughed*.

The Ba'al Shem Tov preached to the people that they should live life with joy and pray directly to God. In the past, Eastern European Jews had lived by the pronouncements of the chosen few rabbis who dictatorially insisted on the bleakness of life. Instead, the Chasidim, taught the Besht, would base their existence on ecstasy and joy.

One of the symbols of the aridness of traditional rabbinic-centered Judaism was the *pilpul* (debate over religious and legal minutiae), an old-world staple of maddening, to most, intellectual arguments over points of law or holy texts. Run by the most literate, uncompromising, and dictatorial of rabbis, the *pilpuls* were daily sessions of excruciating intensity for those *yeshiva bochers* under the rabbis' charge.

Over the centuries of the Diaspora, the *pilpul* had evolved into often vociferous and humiliating debate over the old-world Jewish equivalent of how many angels could dance atop the head of a pin. These *pilpuls*, conducted in ramshackle, sunless, and barely ventilated *shtetl shuls* (synagogues) for sometimes eighteen-hour days, ultimately turned the *yeshiva bochers* into the next line of rabbis to rule their domains like feudal fiefdoms.

Yet these new rabbis, the doubtful said, were mere scholars with *kelter neshamas* (cold souls). These *shtetl* rabbis might be adept at dry and sometimes ridiculous debate over every single possible facet, meaning, and pronunciation of one word or sentence of the Torah, other God-given texts, or ancient commentaries written by the likes of Maimonides or Rashi. But they often didn't understand the realities of the Yiddish-speaking citizenry under their old-world control. The rabbis' naïveté over the simple manner in which their poverty-stricken subjects lived with and under was often a topic of ironic *shtetl* humor.

The tale was often told of two poverty-stricken Jews who came to the rabbi with a dispute over whose undernourished cattle belonged to whom. After the matter was adjudicated to everyone's satisfaction, the two men pooled all their resources, and gave the rabbi seven rubles for his help.

The rabbi, whose every need was taken care of by the *shtetl*, looked at the rubles in his hand and was puzzled.

"What are you giving me?" he asked.

"Money," one of them told the rabbi.

"What's money?" the learned man replied.

"It's how people show thankfulness or do business."

"What is this 'business'?" the befuddled rabbi continued. "Why does a rabbi have to know this 'business'?"

"Well," said the second litigant, "you can give it to your family."

"But what can my family do with this money?"

"Rabbi, your wife can use the money to buy fish, meat, potatoes, clothes—everything!"

"Really?" the rabbi said, amazed. "Well, in that case, maybe you should let me have a little more!"

On the other side were joking tales of traditional rabbis' disingenuous greed.

Take the story of a wealthy *apikores* (skeptic and/or learned apostate) who once came to visit a wonder-working old-world rabbi. "Peace be with you, Rabbi," he said, handing the rabbi a five-ruble note.

The rabbi took the money without saying a word. "And peace be with you, my good man," he finally said. "Have you come to see me on a family matter? Does it have to do with having children?"

"No, Rabbi," the man replied, handing him another five-ruble note. "Nothing like that; I'm not married."

"Then perhaps you have come to inquire about some fine point in Jewish law?" the rabbi asked.

"Not at all, Rabbi," the man replied, handing him another five-ruble note. "You see I don't even read Hebrew."

"Then you have come to ask me to bless your business, perhaps?"

"No, Rabbi," the man said, handing over another five rubles. "I'm having a good year, and I only hope that every year will be this good."

"Well, my friend," said the rabbi, "I don't understand. What is it you wish? You must have had a reason for coming to see me."

"Oh yes," the man replied. "I was curious to know how long a man could go on accepting money for nothing."

AND THEN CAME the Ba'al Shem Tov and the Chasidim. In Yiddish, the Ba'al Shem Tov's name means, again, "he of the good name," a highly auspicious moniker: For a Jew, earning a good name for oneself by righteousness and good deeds means possessing a *guten nomen*, an important precept of Yiddishkeit.

And so the Chasidim began striking out at the traditional rabbis more interested in scholarly debate than in teaching the citizens "below" them—citizens they largely considered ignoramuses—how to make a *guten nomen* for themselves, complete with a *varme neshama* (warm soul).

Nachman of Bratslav, one of the original Chasidic *rebbes*, said simply, "It was difficult for Satan alone to mislead the entire world, so he appointed rabbis in various communities."

The Ba'al Shem Tov's fresh kind of Judaism was detested by those satisfied with the old. In his biggest break with traditional rabbinic-based Judaism, the Ba'al Shem Tov preached the notion of God as a Being directly available to even the most ignorant folk, even if those illiterates knew only spoken Yiddish, and had never been deemed smart enough to study holy Hebrew.

"Even a blade of grass," the Besht preached, "carries the Divine spark."

EVERYTHING HAS A spark of life, according to the Chasidim. Even pigs have that ember—a spark of purposeful self-willed evil.

A query posed on a Lubavitch website asks:

Question:
"Why do Jews give the poor old pig such a hard time?
Is the pig more unkosher than other animals?"

Answer:
The pig has copped it pretty badly in the collective Jewish psyche over the years. It has always been the personification of unkosherness. It is not uncommon to find Jews who say "I may not keep kosher, but at least I don't eat pig!"

Although a pig is no more unkosher than a cheeseburger or a lobster, the pig has something to it that is anathema to what Judaism stands for: It is a fraud. There are two signs that identify a kosher species of animal: (1) It has split hooves, and (2) it chews its cud (i.e., it regurgitates its food and chews it over a second time). The first sign is easy to spot— just look at the hooves. But the second is not so apparent. You have to study the animal's digestive system to know if it chews its cud. A cow is an example of an animal that fulfills both requirements, and is thus kosher. A kangaroo is not kosher because it fulfills neither. There is only one animal in existence that seems kosher because it has split hooves, but is really not kosher because it doesn't chew its cud—the pig.

And that's why we denigrate the pig. Every other non-kosher animal is up front about it. The kangaroo says, "I don't have split hooves, so I'm just not kosher." But the pig presents a kosher facade. "Look, I have split hooves, just like a kosher animal should!" But what lies hidden behind that kosher veneer is a nonkosher inside: It doesn't chew its cud. For Judaism, nothing could be worse than making a holy facade when your inside is rotten.

In Chasidism, for good *and* ill, *everything* matters, and has the spark.

In the Chasidic world of the eighteenth century—and now—Yiddish was almost as holy as Hebrew. It was the language of the common man, who, the Chasidim believe, can bypass the traditional rabbinical authorities and go straight to God.

The Chasidim were branded as apostates by the traditional rabbinic authorities who ruled Jewish life in sixteenth-, seventeenth-, and eighteenth-century Eastern Europe. In the *shtetls*, the governing rabbinate deemed the Chasidim heretics and *meshuggeners* of the worst kind.

Their Jewish enemies, of the kind who ruled Slutsk, viewed them as enemy insurgents, challenging the very core of religious rules within the greater *mishpocha* of *yidn*. To the "againster" *mitnaggdim*, the Chasidim were cause for great alarm, what with their peculiar, outrageous, and increasingly popular way of observing Judaism.

In 1772, the Gaon ("genius" or "great one") of Vilna, the most scholarly and revered *mitnaggid* rabbi in Europe, tried to actually excommunicate the Chasidim from Judaism. Among other reasons the "againster" rabbis felt revulsed by the Chasidim was the upstarts' willingness to not only change the unchangeable order of prayers, but to dance in ecstasy to God during their services, allegedly turn somersaults during synagogue prayers.

The Chasidim didn't even want rabbis, or anybody, leading their prayers. And so, the Chasidic prayer services became a leaderless cacophony of braying Jews, their bodies rapidly bowing and twisting, looking for direct, joyful rapture with God. Even the jargon of Yiddish was deemed worthy to pray in.

The Ba'al Shem Tov knew of Slutsk's reputation for hating

Chasidism, Chasids, and especially him. Yet he was, as usual, imperturbable. But when the Ba'al Shem Tov visited Slutsk to proselytize, the town's bare-knuckled *mitnaggdim* gave him the kind of reception reserved for the lowest rank of passing-through scum.

Led to the Slutsk town square, the leader of 1.5 million Jews in Eastern Europe was placed, stomach down, on a rock. His pants pulled down, he was subjected bare-ass to a community-wide spanking machine that seemed highly undignified punishment for a former clay digger turned *meshuggener.*

After Slutsk's *mitnaggid* scholars took a few extra whacks at the Ba'al Shem Tov's *hinten* (a good synonym for ass when you're tired of *tuchus*), the butt-welted Ba'al Shem Tov was driven out of town.

Maybe Rabbi Friedman wouldn't have received the embarrassing corporal punishment visited upon the founder of his way of life in Slutsk in the eighteenth century. Friedman, with his winning ways that have won over everybody from Bob Dylan and Fergie, the Duchess of York, perhaps could have left Slutsk with joyous laughter instead of a sore *tuchus* to remind him of his visit.

Banish the thought, says Friedman: He could never succeed, even 350 years later, where the Besht had been spanked. Still, he reluctantly admits, there is a reason he has been charged in modern times with leading, by himself, the in-country combat mission of guaranteeing a refuge to make kosher meat so kosher that even the Chasidim would be satisfied.

That mission has nothing to do with his status in the pantheon of Yiddish scholars accepted among his demanding Chasidim. It is a tough academic jungle out there among the last group, numbering in the hundreds of thousands, who speak and study Yiddish daily, and who value his kind of scholarship over life itself.

That's swell. But Friedman also owns the quality perhaps least prominent in the world's Chasidic community.

"I guess I'm the Chasid," Friedman says ruefully, yet with a sly smile, "who everybody likes."

Let's hope so.

Tonight, the dangerous crowd he will soon face is in rural twentieth-century Iowa, among the uncircumcised bacon eaters who have sex before marriage, and most of whom have never seen a Jew, let alone a Jew come begging. Compared to this, the eighteenth-century ass-whupping he might have faced in Slutsk would have been as no-stress as a trip to Las Vegas under a phony name.

At least in Slutsk he would have been trying to convince Orthodox Jews who spoke Yiddish, albeit with words meant to shame Rabbi Friedman and send him to hell with the lid off.

TOUGH ROOM TONIGHT, as comedians say about a stone-cold room filled with embalmed patrons.

Yet it's an especially tough room tonight when you're a Chasidic rabbi who needed to slay *Yechupitzville*, i.e., Nowhere, Iowa.

Kein probleme, no problem, thought Manis Friedman as he drove from the metropolitan Twin Cities to the toughest room he'd ever face.

Tonight in Iowa, he was selling an idea, a story, a *megillah*, a *spiel*, not just saying a phrase or two in front of a lost soul who'd come beseeching his attention.

Here in Iowa, he knew he'd need to start with a joke, a *vitz*. And he couldn't bullshit in getting going, à la the manner of emcees or game-show hosts like Georgie Jessel or Wink Martindale. He had the warm, all-inclusive, *haimishe* (homey and warm) style—and with it, Friedman knew he had to immediately, quickly, and humorously explain what Jews were—to a small-town audience in a region where the phrase "Jew me down" was still a common expression. (The sentence was said twice to me by my Catholic ex-wife's farm-town grandfather, ten minutes after we were married.)

Driving South to Iowa from Minnesota, Rabbi Friedman considered his openers, finally settling on the old reliable joke, translated from Yiddish.

"Tsvay yidn, drei meinungern"
"Two Jews, three opinions."

"What is a Jew?" he'd ask the Iowa audience. "Well, if you've got two Jews, you'll have three opinions." It would both be an informative and self-deprecating icebreaker before Friedman had to put *tuchus offen tish,* and get down to business.

If he were far more south, a territory he traveled to frequently, he could always have told the gag about a Chasidic rabbi who, like the Blues Brothers, is on a holy mission from God. In the story, the rabbi's holy mission for some reason meant leaving New York for backwoods Mississippi.

When the bus carrying the rabbi of the joke arrives in Biloxi, the *chochme* (joke) goes, the town's residents are awed by their first sighting of not just an *actual* Jew, but this *kind* of actual Jew, complete with black hat, beard to his knees, sidecurls, and *tzittzit* hanging out of his pants.

Amazed as if Merlin the Magician had just come to town, the villagers follow the Chasidic rabbi in a mass so great that he feels as if he has an unwanted entourage.

The rabbi finally turns to face the befuddled crackers trailing him.

"Vutz the matter?" he asks, "ain'tcha never seen a *yenkee* before?"

FRIEDMAN HAD DELIBERATELY chosen a Yiddish riddle, a riddle so long ago transfused into the American vernacular that unless you were from rural Postville, Iowa, it was probably a cliché. In Postville, most of the population had heard anti-Semitic jokes, but this Chasidic rabbi was the first actual Jew they'd ever seen.

And oh what a Jew he was to see!

Rabbi Friedman looked as if he'd been rented for the evening from Central Casting. As always, the lanky, middle-aged Chasid from the Lubavitch sect of Chasidism was dressed in stark black and white, a graying Smith Brothers beard to his chest, a Sam Spade fedora on his head. He looked as if he had walked out of a painting of an eighteenth-century *shtetl* or a Fred McDarrah photograph of Beat poets in Washington Square Park in the 1950s.

Friedman had fourteen children. Unlike Mel Brooks's two-thousand-year-old man, who had hundreds of children, none of whom ever wrote, Friedman had no complaints about his own brood. All fourteen visited, wrote, had their own families a few minutes away, or still lived at home.

All the men in the Friedman family either have or are in the process of following their father's charismatic-among-the-already-joyful adherents of the Lubavitch sect of Chasidism— the only branch of the movement that encourages its members to reach out to the external temporal world. His sons' ordinations from *yeshivas* around North America makes for easy calling to the Friedman house: One only has to say "Rabbi?" to any male voice, and the answer will almost always be "yes" or "not yet."

But fourteen children? In the third millennium? Isn't that nuts?

It was for just this kind of apparent cuckooness that the Jews of Slutsk so hated Chasids and their *mishegass*.

Hundreds of years later, now, and some Chasidim are still having a dozen children. Many families, even with the rules of Chasidism forbidding birth control, curiously managed to stop at exactly five. Their apparent overbreeding has nothing to do with some twisted religious self-indulgence, as the citizens of Slutsk believed in their campaign to stomp out the Chasidim.

Yiddish *is* the spirit of the Chasidim—like the language, the Lubavitchers were almost completely wiped out in Europe during World War II. The survivors sailed in steerage to New York and their new conclave in Williamsburg, Brooklyn. If they were to survive, the Chasidim would have to regenerate in numbers unheard of to modern American Jews, who with intermarriage and exceedingly low birth rates were barely holding the Jewish population.

Most Jews can't abide them—though Rabbi Friedman is indeed "the Chasid everybody likes."

With their archaic dress and manners, these ultra-Orthodox Jews are derisively called "black hats" by their assimilated coreligionists. Still, the Chasidim were Judaism's leading source of population growth.

Yiddish would never die, says Friedman, because humans, Yiddish, and Yiddishkeit are living in three dimensions at once—past, present, and future. To them, the *mamme-loshn* is simultaneously thriving, surviving, and occasionally having to spend time on life support, as in World War II.

Not even the about-to-be state of Israel wanted these meek ghetto Yiddish speakers, who seemingly hadn't raised a pinkie against the Nazis in self-defense.

Israel wanted—and succeeded—in building a new form of Jew who spoke a secular, modernized Hebrew, symbolic of the strong biblical kings who fought their enemies as hard as the Maccabees, at times before they were even attacked. They would let in young, fit, and strong Zionists, most of whom wanted or were pressured into changing their names from their Eastern European ghetto Yiddish *nomen*, to strong biblical Hebrew monikers.

David Ben-Gurion's original name had been David Gruen, and Golda Meir was Goldie Mabovitch. Yiddish was actively repressed in Israel; in the 1960s, Prime Minister Levi Eshkol was constantly chided by his cabinet whenever he dared use a Yiddish colloquialism in state meetings.

IN HIS NOBEL speech, Isaac Bashevis Singer delineated how Yiddish was indeed diametrically opposed to the relatively fresh concept of tough, Hebrew-talking Israeli men and women who refused to let anyone conquer *their* land, acreage that had put an end to the wandering Jews' Diaspora.

For the Chasidim, Yiddish was not the language of the weak Jew. Beginning in the eighteenth century, Yiddish was a symbol of God's availability to even the most ignorant *shtarker*, a language made holy because He heard the prayers of all.

Today, Yiddish is also spoken as the Chasidic *lingua franca* because it helps keep out, or at least screen, the evil influences of modern society.

But fourteen kids?

To what end this apparently non-eco madness, besides replenishing the Chasidic troops almost completely destroyed sixty years ago? Why did Rabbi Friedman choose to have so many children and constant overnight visitors that he'd numbered the rooms in his home's dormitory-style downstairs to locate who was where when it came time to walk to the synagogue down the road, or sit for dinner at the family's banquet-size table that would comfortably seat an entire Major League Baseball team?

"The Rebbe liked children," Friedman explained, simply, of his procreative predilection. The Rebbe was Menachem Mendel Schneerson, the late holy leader and spiritual-guidance counselor of the ultra-ultra-Orthodox Lubavitchers. Schneerson, as all Chasidic sects' *rebbes*, was viewed as much more than a mere "rabbi," which means just "teacher."

The child-loving, childless Rebbe, unlike mere earthbound rabbis, was considered closer to heaven than plain mortals. And while not having to bear a dozen children may have been a secret *mechaye* (blessing) to the Rebbe's wife, the *rebbe'tzin*, his death without designating an heir left the Lubavitchers leaderless.

In the 1980s, when Schneerson began falling prey to age, one Yiddish magazine in California named Rabbi Friedman to the short list of contenders to be the next Lubavitcher Rebbe. Even now, it is a notion that Friedman is horrified even to hear, as if it were the ravings of a *meshugener apikores*.

To consider oneself worthy of being a *rebbe* was like thinking you were "cool"—the mere fact that you thought you were meant you weren't. Such heretical ideas as succeeding Schneerson weren't even countenanced by the Chasidim after a series of strokes in the 1980s left the heirless Rebbe all but helpless. Schneerson, who'd known fourteen languages and been educated at the Sorbonne, was now unable even to speak Yiddish, let alone name an heir.

Yet while Schneerson was alive and mentally thriving, Rabbi Friedman earned the signal ultra-ultra honor of serving as the

Rebbe's personal translator from Yiddish into English. Friedman had quite a crowd for his simultaneous translation of the often five-hour improvised Yiddish talks beamed by satellite to Lubavitch followers across the world, from Australia to China, every Sunday.

The Chasidim would have been after Friedman's *hinten* if he made one slip-up during those off-the-cuff, Fidel Castro–length sermons of the Rebbe. One mispronounced word, or misunderstood interpretation of a silent hunch of the Rebbe's shoulders, would for Friedman be a signal shame.

Despite the pressure, Friedman was honored to get the prestigious gig. He liked the stress and was good at the job, and had become inadvertently famous among those who watched the Rebbe every Sunday on television. Yet Yiddishkeit, not his genius for Yiddish, still ruled Friedman's world.

He remembered his own roots as the class clown of his Montreal *yeshiva*, a troublemaker for whom "it took years for my Judaism to kick in."

After earning the most prestigious and difficult Yiddish job imaginable, he felt deep remorse over his challengers' losses. "I got the job over four other candidates," Friedman said, "and that was hard. All four had been my teachers."

Rabbi Friedman's power lies not just in the fact that he is a scholar, but that he is a dynamic listener as well as speaker, and one never knows at the time if he's amused, joking, imparting a life lesson, or all three. Traveling the world half the year giving speeches to other Chasidim, Jews of all traditions, Gentiles, and the readership of *Rolling Stone* (which once ran an article about his tutoring Bob Dylan), he no longer even asks what topic he is expected to talk about.

"I'll walk into the hall or synagogue and look at the poster to see what I'm supposed to be talking about," he says. "Sometimes it's Kabbalah. Other times it's 'relationships.' In all cases I say to the audience, 'Just get married!'"

Now that also is Yiddishkeit.

IT WOULD BE a tougher room in rural Iowa that night than on any of the myriad evenings he'd spoken on the Upper West Side of Manhattan, where year after year he'd see the same faces of assimilated Jews wanting to learn how to find a good Jewish mate. Those had been tough crowds; Sarah Ferguson had been more of a breeze to deal with than those love-hungry thirtysomething Jews.

The former Duchess of York sought out Rabbi Friedman and come to his house to discuss the meaning of charity, one of the most vital components of Yiddishkeit. She'd been so eager for an audience with the rabbi that she panicked her handlers by ducking out midway during a book signing at Minnesota's Mall of America.

Friedman was not a rabbi to the stars, but a tool of God. If he'd wanted to be a celebrity rabbi, he'd have long ago moved to Los Angeles, like Shmuley "Kosher Sex" Boteach, his former student (and a now defrocked Chasidic rabbi, punished for giving an interview to *Hustler*).

But Friedman would never move from his tundra outpost to Hollywood; he found Los Angeles merely "an excellent simulation of real life."

And what about Chasidic rabbis holding court in Hollywood? "They're excellent simulations of Chasidic rabbis," he'd said.

So Friedman, instead of spending his time instructing Madonna on how the Kabbalah had nothing to do with wearing red string bracelets, was to appear in rural Iowa that night in the late 1980s. His talk would have nothing to do with his stature as a Torah scholar or brilliant Yiddish linguist.

THAT EVENING IN postville, Iowa, the rabbi stood smiling and alone on the town hall stage. All of Postville seemed to have shown up, and were now shoehorned into an already SRO room filled with several hundred Iowa farmers and their handsome wives. With arms crossed and mouths etched in straight lines, the town stared up at the smiling rabbi, who was wearing a Humphrey Bogart shamus hat as if he were a door-to-door aluminum-siding salesman.

He'd need to read into this audience as well as he'd read into the Rebbe's Yiddish intonations if he were to warm the blocks of granite before him. He did indeed have something to sell these small-town Hawkeyes, but unlike the shyster Harold Hill in *The Music Man*, it wasn't a fictitious boys' band for River City, Iowa. He had no interest in peddling seventy-six nonexistent trombones, a hundred and ten cornets right behind, or as Meredith Wilson's play had it, "here and there a Jew's harp."

Rather, what Friedman—and the world of the Chasidim he was speaking on behalf of that night—wanted was an ultra-ultra-ultra-kosher slaughtering plant. Like Hollywood talent scouts, Chasidim had scoured the country, and come up with Postville as their best bet for the role. The town already had the basic facilities—an abandoned and moldering meat-packing facility on the edge of town. What Friedman could offer the stagnating community were desperately needed jobs.

Before he explained a critical, sticky point to what Postville could expect, Friedman would first have to put the townsfolk at ease about who would be the bosses. For if Postville were to say aye to the rabbi's proposal, the citizens who would work in the revivified slaughterhouse would be under the unyielding direction of demanding Chasidic specialists speaking in rapid-fire, incomprehensible Yiddish.

Their bosses would be men whose lifework was not making *goyim* feel comfortable, but overseeing the proper and amazingly unappetizing way to make cattle kosher by first slashing their throats and then letting them bleed out. That specially prepared meat would be shipped to carnivorous Chasidim across the country, and the workers' overseers would not have Friedman's patience or tact.

Their bosses would brook no shortcuts among the laborers doing the heavy *shlepping* involved in turning cows into kosher carcasses. Yet the people of Postville didn't know *that* yet.

So before he could get down to David Mamet's *Glengarry Glen Ross* business maxim of ABC—Always Be Closing—he would have to explain what exactly Jews were.

Personally, it didn't really matter to Friedman if a particular Jew were ultra-Orthodox, atheist, or a culinary Jew who showed his ethnic pride by savoring a lean corned beef sandwich, whether it was kosher or not.

"It's not relevant whether you're a good Jew or a bad Jew," he told me with a laugh one more time, after I asked him if I was one of the bad. "You're a Jew, and we're stuck with you."

In Postville, he began by asking the crowd, "What are Jews?"

"*Tzvay yidn,*" he thought in Yiddish, "*drei meinungen.*"

"If you have two Jews," he continued, translating his thoughts to the audience, "you'll have three opinions."

The crowd erupted.

Friedman then got down to business, finally putting *tuchus offen tish*. And the Chasidim won their packing plant.

(Years later, the Chasidim running the Postville slaughterhouse were excoriated from sources ranging from the *Forward*,

in a searing front-page investigation, to People for the Ethical
Treatment of Animals. The charges included overly dangerous
working conditions for the mostly Mexican workers and cruelty
to cattle in the process of koshering. Friedman was not involved.)

Long after, I asked the rabbi if he thought the joke he told the
good people of Postville was true. Could two Jews really dis-
agree with three opinions?

"The single most important issue is whether Jews can get
along with each other," Friedman said, pausing for effect.

"And the answer is no."

There is, for example, the story, updated for every adminis-
tration, of what happened when the late Prime Minister Yitzhak
Rabin, the leader of Israel, visited Bill Clinton at Camp David.

"It's very difficult to be president of three hundred million
people," Clinton said with a sigh.

"I know *exactly* what you mean," Rabin said with an even
heavier sigh.

"How can you possibly know what I mean?" Clinton re-
torted. "I'm president of three hundred million people. Your
population is only several million."

"Yes, but while you are president of three hundred million
people," Rabin said, "I am president of several million presidents."

And remember the thoughts of the great German poet Heinrich Heine, who converted from Judaism to Christianity in order to have entrée to the strictly Christian aristocratic salons of
Deutschland. According to Heine, no such conversion to Christ
could be genuine and heartfelt, because no Jew could ever believe in the divinity of another.

In his autobiography, screenwriter and Zionist *agent provocateur* Ben Hecht recalled the opinion Peter Bergson offered on

the topic of Jew-versus-Jew. Bergson was a militant Zionist trying to arm, often illegally, the barely armed Jews of the new Israel. He'd come to America to fund-raise for the cause, and was not surprised that none of the assorted Jewish committees and official delegations he pitched proposals to would do anything but argue against him.

"It is the same old story," Bergson said. "Jews must always battle Jews. It's the only politics open to a stateless people. The only victories they can hope to enjoy are victories over each other."

A very Yiddish point of view.

CHAPTER 10

שׁעַפּׁעָ֥גׁ זׁ֥֥ועֶ֣עֶ זׁ֥֥יׁ שׁ֥ע֣עעֶ

Yiddish: Or, Envy in America

Geshmak iz der fish oyf yenems tish.
"Tasty is fish on someone else's dish."

I t is said that the number of poetry *readers* in the United States is exactly the same as the number of poetry *writers*.

Experts in the *mamme-loshn* perhaps outmultiply people who can actually speak the language by about 50:1. Curiously, virtually the last speakers of this language meant since its birth to be spoken aren't the professional Yiddishists, the Ph.D.s who've imposed Yiddish grammar on the untamable language. Granted, these experts have also given Yiddish a legitimacy it never before enjoyed in its one-thousand-year history of being treated by Jews as a *momzer*, a bastard stepchild whom no one wants to claim. (*Momzer* is also an oft-used and excellent word to use against a stone-asshole.)

Yiddish's legitimacy was brought about in large part by scholars such as New York University's Uriel Weinreich, who in his brief thirty-nine years compiled the first authoriatative college Yiddish textbook, as well as the first comprehensive (according to most) English-Yiddish/Yiddish-English dictionary.

Uriel's widow, Beatrice, has meantime become the world's

leading chronicler of Yiddish folktales, as well as the unfortunate butt of jokes for her and Uriel's *Say It in Yiddish* travel book that gives instructions on such things as "Where is the casino?"

Michael Chabon, Pulitzer Prize–winning novelist, the best writer of his generation, and the author who writes better than anybody on matters of Yiddishkeit, wrote a touching and humorous essay in 1997 about why this useless book is the saddest volume in his personal library, kicking off a firestorm of controversy and defenses of Beatrice in every Yiddish online publication in the land.

Then there was Uriel's father, Max, who headed the Yiddish Research Institute, known as YIVO, a virtual Library of Congress for the *mamme-loshn*. He also wrote a multivolume history of Yiddish, only two out of four volumes of which have been translated from Yiddish into English.

Michael Wex was dead wrong in saying the essence of Yiddish is *kvetching*. As Lou Reed, ne' Louis Rabinowitz, titled one of his best albums, the heart of Yiddish is magic and loss. Yet when Jews bitch, they are mostly likely to complain about each other. The Jews' own history taught them the efficacy of keeping their *kvetching*, like Sister Sledge, in the family—it's safer that way. And perhaps nowhere is this intramural bickering more evident than in most matters Yiddish.

Take the late, poor Leo Rosten, author of the enormous bestseller *The Joys of Yiddish*, a lexicon of the *mamme-loshn* which was first published in 1968, and most recently revised with the aid of Lawrence Bush. *The Joys of Yiddish*, along with *Fiddler on the Roof* (despite the play's frequent lapses into sentimental treacle), were probably the two productions most responsible for reigniting in assimilated Jews a search for the meaning of Yiddishkeit during the 1960s.

And if any one volume can be said to have sparked renewed mass interest in Yiddish itself, it is Rosten's informal, often comic dictionary. Even if that interest among readers was only in deciphering the difference between a *shlemiel* and a *shlimazel* or a *shmuck* and a *putz*—well, it's important to know the difference between a *shmuck* and a *putz*.

Irving Howe, however, was not such a fan. The late Howe was no mere *kvetcher*. Howe was a literary heavyweight: a probing intellectual, critic, bon vivant, founder of the intellectual journal *Dissent* and author of *World of Our Fathers*, the definitive study of the tide of immigration of the 2.5 million Yiddish-speaking Jews from Eastern Europe to America between 1880 and 1920, and their struggle of acculturation in the *Goldene Medina*.

Howe brutalized the just-published *Joys of Yiddish* in his review of the book in the *New York Times*. He'd long been bothered by how succeeding generations of American Jews had lost complete touch for the feel and meaning of the Yiddish of their immigrant forebears. In Rosten's work, he declaimed, "Yiddish is torn out of its cultural context, its integral world of meaning and reference."

Rosten's book, wrote Howe, was a compendium of trivia without any deeper meaning, a work that carried the kind of nonexistent intellectual arc of a game of *Jeopardy!*. Behind the tinsel of Rosten's good-natured humor, Howe charged, was just more tinsel.

Rosten was pummeled as a faux philosopher, linguist, and philistine. (He actually held a doctorate from the University of Chicago, taught at Yale and the University of California at Berkeley, and first made a name for himself by publishing his short stories frequently in the *New Yorker*.)

Not that Howe was any sort of fuddy-duddy when it came

to the *mamme-loshn*. Howe also wrote in the *Times* that "no, not everything written about Yiddish need be dry, solemn, or scholarly," and "there should be room for tasteful popularization," he continued, "but something about the Broadway-cum-TV tone of Mr. Rosten's book—the tone of elbowing, backslapping 'local color'—gives me the chills."

Nor was Howe, who'd grown up speaking Yiddish, trying to shoo away anybody who dared wander onto his turf. In the 1950s, he convinced Saul Bellow to translate Isaac Bashevis Singer's *Gimpel the Fool* into English, then ran portions in his magazine. As a happy result, he proudly saw his literary find become famous and published in the *New Yorker*.

Rosten took vigorous hits from a variety of sources. Professor Ilan Stavans of Amherst College wrote an insightful appreciation in 2006 of *The Joys of Yiddish* in *Pakn Treger*, the magazine published by the Yiddish Book Center. In his article, Stavans praised Rosten and his efforts with *The Joys of Yiddish* against the backdrop of Howe's—and other highbrows'—disgust with the book (or perhaps its massive popularity).

"Accusations of inaccuracy [against Rosten] were published in periodicals such as the most important Yiddish paper in the country, the *Forverts* [a.k.a. the *Forward*]," Stavans wrote.

"One periodical even nominated Rosten for a 'shanda award,'" he noted, a term of high disparagement usually saved for Jewish swindlers, adulterers, or *luftmentshen* who managed to live in the clouds with the grudging financial support of their fathers-in-law.

And Howe?

"We are what we speak," Stavans continued, "kitsch and all. In [Howe's] *kvetching*, he failed to see the superb qualities of *The Joys of Yiddish*."

Stavans's critique was both understanding and respectful to

all concerned. "The Broadway-cum-TV tone of Mr. Rosten's book," Professor Stavans continued, "the tone of Howe's allergy to *schmaltz* culture kept him from realizing [*The Joys of Yiddish*] is an homage to American individualism and creativity. If the lexicon might be said to have an overall message, it is not about selfishness but about human flexibility."

The *kvetching* came from all directions. Yiddishists and Yiddish writers with public personas of critical generosity took their swings at Rosten as if his head were atop a children's tee-ball post. Professor Stavans took note that "even Isaac Bashevis Singer, who himself was often accused of misrepresenting Yiddish . . . in private conversations derided *The Joys of Yiddish* as impure, just as he derided mainstream phenomena like the Broadway musical *Fiddler on the Roof.*"

The chain of *kvetching* about everyone and everything Yiddish went on and on and on. . . .

Isaac Singer was spat upon with equal enthusiasm as Rosten. Even Professor Stavans, editor of the Library of America's three-volume edition of Singer's writing, admitted after the books came out that "my grandmother thought he was trash."

Singer was also the object of special enmity and profound disgust from his fellow Yiddish writers who did not share his luck, pretty women translators, and gift for self-promotion. Cynthia Ozick, in her classic, perfect short story "Envy: Or, Yiddish in America," brilliantly teased out the horrific jealousy, well founded or not, of Singer's contemporaries in Yiddish fiction and poetry.

Thinly veiled by Ozick as Yankel Ostrover, Singer is pilloried in the short story by other Yiddish writers, especially Avram Edelshtein. His fellow Yiddish writers, Ozick wrote, perhaps recalled the Yiddish idiom

*Dem yidn shat nit azoy zany eygener dales vi dem anderns
ashires.*
"A Jew isn't bothered so much by his own poverty as by
another's wealth."

And she wrote:

> They hated [Ostrover] for the amazing thing that had hap-
> pened to him—his fame—but this they never referred to.
> Instead they discussed his style: his Yiddish was impure,
> his sentences lacked grace and sweep, his paragraph transi-
> tions were amateur, vile. Or else they raged against his
> subject matter, which was insanely sexual, pornographic,
> paranoid, freakish—men who embraced men, women
> who caressed women, sodomists of every variety, boys
> copulating with hens, butchers who drank blood for
> strength.
>   And why Ostrover? Why not somebody else? Was Ostro-
> ver more gifted than Komorsky? Did he think up better sto-
> ries than Horowitz? Why does the world outside pick on an
> Ostrover instead of an Edelshtein or even a Baumsweig?

In 2004, on the one hundredth anniversary of Singer's birth
(he died in 1991 at age eighty-seven), the Library of America and
the National Endowment for the Humanities sponsored a
several-month series of lectures, readings, panel discussions, ex-
hibits of the lost world of Yiddish, and idolatrous memories of
Singer. Elsewhere there was rage.

Not all Yiddish experts or writers were pleased that Singer
had focused his career scribbling about old-world prostitutes,
dybbuks, otherworldly spirits, and mysticism instead of concentrating

on the destruction of that world, and the people he'd known who'd disappeared into the ash of the Holocaust.

"I profoundly despise [Singer]," Inna Grade, the seventy-five-year-old widow of Chaim Grade, told the *New York Times* in an article about the Nobel prize-winner's centennial celebrations. Grade, high in the pantheon of Yiddish writers, was barely known to American audiences during his lifetime due to a dearth of translations of his work into English—the most common plaint of Yiddish masters, real or would-be, and the focus of much of Ozick's "Envy: Or, Yiddish in America."

"I profoundly despise all those who eat the bread into which the blasphemous buffoon has urinated," Grade's widow ranted on in the piece written for the *New York Times* by Alana Newhouse, arts and culture editor of the English-language version of the *Forward*.

In 2001, Rabbi Emanuel Rackman, chancellor of Israel's Bar-Ilan University, wrote in collaboration with Stephen Wagner that "the issue is not that Chaim Grade does not have the Nobel Prize, but that, from the Jewish perspective, the least suitable, the worst possible writer has it."

Even Elie Wiesel, who is almost never anything but utterly charitable toward fellow writers, hinted at his qualms about Singer via his praise of Grade.

"The work of Chaim Grade, by its vision and its scope," he wrote, "establishes him . . . as one of the great—if not the greatest—of Yiddish novelists. Surely he is the most authentic." Itche Goldberg, the always good-natured Yiddish writer, and editor of the Yiddish literary journal *Yidishe kultur* for forty years, also had his qualms about Singer. His 2007 obituary in the *New York Times*, written after Goldberg died at 102, mentioned that Itche "published an essay criticizing Singer as failing to reflect the humanist and social ideals that Mr. Goldberg felt were the central themes of Yiddish culture."

Relative to Singer, Grade got crumbs. When New York's Yeshiva University awarded him an honorary degree in 1980, college president Norman Lamm seemed less to be honoring Grade as dropping a safe on Singer's head when he said, "Yiddish literature often wallows in the mud of cynicism and frivolity, in the scatological swap of amorality when it heralds the fascination with the demonic and with sexual weirdness."

Could anything else but the ways and means of Yiddish politics inspire the head of an Orthodox Jewish university to say "scatological swap of amorality" and "sexual weirdness"?

Grade *was* a finalist for a Pulitzer Prize in fiction in 1983—a year after he died—for *Rabbis and Wives*. Later, his heirs were awarded $500 for Hadassah's first Harold U. Ribalow prize for fiction. When he died, the *New York Times* gave Grade 575 words for his obituary; Singer received 2,424 words and a picture on the front page of the newspaper.

Alana Newhouse's *New York Times* article, where Mrs. Grade compared Singer's writing to urine, continued with condemnations of Singer from the likes of Allan Nadler, the head of Drew University's Jewish studies department, and the former research director at the YIVO (Institute for Jewish Research).

"When Abraham Sutzkever was starving," Nadler said, "fighting Nazis with the partisans in Lithuanian woods and writing great Yiddish poetry about the tragic fate of the Jews on fragments of bark, Singer was eating cheese blintzes . . . on 72nd Street and thinking about Polish whores and Yiddish devils."

It is easy to find, if one is looking for proof, that Singer was a self-absorbed narcissist who cared little for Yiddishkeit.

In a short story entitled "The Third One," Singer writes:

It was sweltering outside, but the cafeteria was cool. During the day, between three and five, it was almost empty. I took a table near the wall, drank coffee, nibbled a piece of apple cake, and looked into an occult magazine. In the letters to the editor, a woman wrote that her cat had been run over by a car and she had buried it but still it came to visit her every night. . . . But does the astral body really exist? I wondered. And do animals possess it, too? If so, my whole philosophy must be revised.

Before I could undertake so large an order, I went to the counter and got another cup of coffee. "One reality has nothing to do with the other," I said to myself.

Singer, rather than taking the insults to heart, almost seemed to revel in them. He enjoyed telling a story of an encounter he had with a Brooklyn Yiddish *vinkl* (literally "circle," meaning a club) in the mid-1970s, when he was already famous.

"By us, you can read your story in Yiddish—to *lantzmen* [fellow Jews, especially from the same town, village, or country] who understand," the president of the group had said on the phone as he wheedled a personal appearance from Singer. He promised Singer that the club's members "were not like those university types who laugh at the wrong places and make fun of your accent behind your back."

"What could I do?" Singer would ask in retelling the story. Himself in his seventies, Singer offered *rachmones* (empathy, sympathy, or even pity) because, he said, "These are old people."

Unfortunately, since the club had no money to pay even his transportation, Singer said he took a $30 cab ride from his Upper West Side home to Brooklyn, where the club's president began by flattering him to the extreme when he showed.

He'd arrived at the president's house to find only eight people in attendance. Singer read a story, whereupon the president declaimed, "This is not a good story. This is a *shmutz adikeh* [dirty] story. I spit on your story."

He then hocked a loogy on the rug underneath Singer's chair—and there is no phlegm like that spat by an embittered old Jewish man. In Yiddish there is the phrase

Ikh her vie er khraket in gass!
"I hear him hawking up an oyster [way *treyf!*] outside in the street!"

Then, everyone else in the Yiddish club took their turn literally spitting at and on Singer. One member bitched loudly because Singer's yarn wasn't a properly Zionist tale.

Another complained because his creation wasn't about keeping kosher. One more spat on his shoes because the story wasn't good history. The next one took phlegmy aim at the Nobelist's shoes because Singer's Yiddish was allegedly a bastardized form of the *mamme-loshn*.

Another Yiddish club member spat twice at the writer. The first goober came because the story was not Orthodox enough, and the second because the tale was a *shanda fur di goyim*.

"Imagine," Singer said, "eight people and nine spits!" Before he left for another self-paid $30 cab ride home on his own dime, he gave the group a handful of money, and told them to buy pencils and notebooks and "go home and write a story. Then at your next meeting you'll hear exactly the stories you want. Don't call me."

Still, there were broad hints of self-loathing. In *Gimpel the Fool*, the book that got Singer noticed in non-Yiddish circles, he wrote, "I had seven names in all: imbecile, donkey, flax-head, dope, glump, ninny, and fool."

Or perhaps that's just Yiddish being Yiddish. By using only seven terms of self-deprecation, perhaps Singer was being an egoist. After all, there are almost a dozen thick columns under the heading *narishkayt* (foolishness) in Nahum Stutchkoff's Yiddish thesaurus.

It was because of the plethora of available and varied Yiddish put-downs that the *New Yorker's* S. J. Perelman sprinkled them liberally throughout his work. Perelman had a classically Yiddish split persona; he was simultaneously the last century's funniest satirist and the most personally bitter humorist this side of James Thurber.

Post–Nobel Prize, Singer became an Upper West Side cynosure, often seen feeding the pigeons of Broadway, an always besuited elf in a William Burroughs–style hat. The world—not just America but Europe too—responded to Singer's *shtick*.

Rumor even had it that Singer kept his name listed in the phone book so young women could ring him up. Then, in 1985, the son he'd abandoned (along with his wife) when he came to America before World War II appeared. With a properly Hebrew moniker of Israel Zamir, he published an oddly fond memoir of the father he never knew growing up: *Journey to My Father, Isaac Bashevis Singer.*

Singer was never truly comfortable with his person, persona, and eminence as the figurehead of worldwide Yiddish. Beneath his charm he was bitter, manipulative with women, someone scratching away inside his own skin. As his biographer Florence Noiville points out, sometimes he even referred to himself as "the pig."

It was a name that other Yiddish writers specially reserved for him, at least according to Cynthia Ozick's "Envy: Or, Yiddish in America," the fictionalized account of Singer and his best enemies.

"Why did Singer still seem agitated in spite of his success, torn between pride and self-hatred?" Noiville asked in her estimable biography. "Apparently he was repelled by something within himself. But what?"

In the end, to the delight of the jealous and hurt Yiddish writers who'd outlived him, Singer did indeed get his. After he was buried, Singer's name was spelled wrong on his tombstone, which also honored him in etched granite for winning the "Noble Prize."

The monument's errata remained unfixed for almost six years. Finally, the misspellings were corrected with a pathetic little plaque glued over the errors. The grave looked worse than ever, as if it had been touched up by a Little League–trophy repairman—it would have also been more respectful, it seemed, if he'd been buried in a potter's field accompanied by the anonymous ghosts Singer so loved writing about.

Old World Shtetls and Ghettos: Yiddish Weaklings, Yiddish Beliefs, the Yiddish God, and Yiddish Revenge

Nekome iz a guter bisn.
"Revenge is a tasty morsel."

"I wouldn't say it's acting. I don't think I'm a good actor. But there's a dybbuk *inside, you know, greased with chicken soup, that says, 'Survive! Survive!' "*
—Abbie Hoffman

oes Yiddish culture make Jews cowards?
No.
Yiddish knew the truth:

Der yid iz fun keseyder on an ish milkhome—shtendik shlogt er zikh mit der deye.
"A Jew is forever warlike—always fighting with his conscience."

Still, there is that . . . stereotype. And is history, or that myth, telling us something?

There were mighty exceptions of course. Isaac Babel wrote of the gangster "Benya Krik," whose real name was Michael Yaponchik, the Jewish organized-crime boss in Odessa, Babel admired Yaponchik not just because he was a true Jewish fighting force, a Yiddish Robin Hood who would spread the wealth among his poverty-stricken *lantzmen* in the *yidns'* Moldavanka ghetto. At night, he and his gang would also patrol the Jewish streets and protect its citizens from harassment by race-baiting Gentiles.

Babel loathed his childhood Jewish education and teachers— pale, bespectacled weenies who were pessimistic, frightened of the world and any human excess, and who, in his indelible phrase, carried "autumn in [their] hearts."

In Lionel Trilling's famous essay on Babel, the brilliant late Columbia professor wrote:

> It is in writing about Benya that Babel uses the phrase that sets so far apart the intellectual and the man of action. The exploration of Benya's pre-eminence among gangsters does indeed take into account his personal endowment—Benya was a "lion," a "tiger," a "cat"; he "could spend the night with a Russian woman and satisfy her."

Disparaging his own simple father—a drayman and religious Jew, Babel asks, "What would you have done in Benya Krik's place? You would have done nothing. But *he* did something."

Yet in the early twentieth century, the Socialist Yiddish writer Israel Efroikin, staffer on the *Yiddishe Velt,* the "Jewish World," in Vilna, Lithuania, pondered the Jews' purported unwillingness to veer from an almost self-nihilistic pacifism, even when at least a motley response of self-defense was called for:

Everybody knows the legend that Jews are cowards. Lots of Jews today repeat it. How much sneering there is in our modern Yiddish literature, at the Jewish innkeeper and Jewish tenant farmer whom the local landowner, the uncontrolled lord of his life and possessions, forced to dance before him and his friends and sing. The singing Jew became with us a synonym for cowardice and lack of human dignity and self-respect. It was meant to foster contempt for the ghetto Jew, for the Jew of the Dispersion.

Why didn't these Jews of the Dispersion, almost all Yiddish speakers, fight back?

Ever?

They did. Not very often, however. And with certain exceptions, usually not very well. And even then, almost always they fought against their will.

There were the massively outnumbered Maccabees, the heavy underdogs who beat an insurmountable point spread and conquered the Greeks circa 170 B.C.E. And the Arabs' unsuccessful 1948 war launched against Israel just as the Jewish state's independence was declared.

And the Yiddish-loathing, Hebrew-loving country's halfdozen Middle East conflicts since. They were wars that, contrary to Yiddishkeit tradition, not only had to be fought but won. Between 170 B.C.E. and 1948 there were few battles or wars for Jews to celebrate victory.

Then again, what could be expected from a people who, by choice, belonged nowhere, sought almost no allies, and spoke a language nobody else understood? As Yiddish spread across invisible borders in a world virtually always unfriendly, it became a tongue that united the humbled Jews, while enraging their uncomprehending enemies.

Yet what *could* they really do to survive as Jews? As part of their Yiddishkeit tradition, they'd made themselves purposefully defenseless, without anything on their side but a most peculiar God indeed. A God certainly not living up to a Divinity's putative potential or ancient biblical reputation for sending, just in time, thunderbolts, plagues, and locusts at His Chosen people's enemies.

So why wasn't God parting any seas as the Jews of the Diaspora were chased from one land that didn't want them to another? A God who'd stopped the miracles thousands of years before the Jews could have really used some grand magic to help salve their torments, which they wailed in Yiddish to an unanswering heaven?

All this, at a time when Yiddish taught:

On nisim ken a yid nit lebn.
"A Jew can't live without miracles."

In the meantime, the Jews chided their God:

Ata bekhartanu mikol ha'amin—unfarn sheygets hostu moyre?
"Thou didst choose us from among the nations—and
    You're afraid of the Gentile boys?"

And yet, even as the Jews *kvetched* about their Lord's seemingly lackluster performance, they held on to their beliefs in God, even as they teased Him in the most damning, loving language on earth.

"For it was the word that counted most," Irving Howe wrote, continuing:

Yiddish culture was oriented toward speech: its God was a
God who spoke. And He was a plebeian—or, if you wish, a

folk—God, perhaps immanent but hardly transcendant. Toward Him the Jews could feel a peculiar sense of intimacy; and indeed, they had suffered enough in His behalf.

In prayer His name could not be spoken; yet in or out of prayer He could always be spoken to. Because the East European Jew felt so close to God he could complain to Him freely, and complain about Him too. Thus Rabbi Levi-Yitzchok of Berditchev, a leader of the Chasidic movement, wrote a chant [in Yiddish] that is an indictment, though a loving indictment, of God.

The rabbi bitches to God in a manner reminiscent of the Yiddishkeit reality that Jews often can't stand one another. Yet he also stresses that Jews must never stop loving one another, and always stay as close as possible in proximity and thought while they waited for their omnipotent God.

No, it isn't apostasy according to Yiddishkeit to speak about and to God this way. "Always live life with joy," says Yiddish scholar and Chasidic wise man Rabbi Manis Friedman. "Forget intermediaries, go straight to God. Make fun of yourself, make fun of other Jews, make fun of the world, make fun of God. But go straight to Him, not because you need Him, but because He needs you. Why? No one knows, and to ask—now *that* is blasphemy!"

Wrote fellow holy man and chasid Levi-Yitzchok of Berditchev centuries ago:

Good morning to You, Lord of the Universe! I, Levi-Yitzchok, son of Sarah of Berditchev, Have come with a claim against You On behalf of Your people Israel. What do You have against Your people Israel? Why do you afflict Your people Israel?

And I, Levi-Yitzchok, son of Sarah of Berditchev, say, I shall not stir from here. From this spot I shall not stir, There must be an end to this, The exile must come to an end! Magnified and sanctified be His Name!"

LIFE IN THE *shtetl* was almost unrelievedly bleak, and rules were not meant to be broken, but to keep everybody huddled closely together. If a son married a *shiksa*, he was declared legally dead and his parents went into mourning.

Daughters were alternately warned from the *shagetz*, a non-Jewish man. True, according to the rules of the Jewish matriarchy, at least the grandchildren would be Jewish. But there would still have to be a hell of a lot of explaining to the neighbors.

And worse. The tribe would seem no less in danger.

In a Dovid Bergelson Yiddish short story, the daughter of *shtetl* inhabitant Moyshe-Leyb Yanashov falls in love with a non-Jew, a justice of the peace who lived nearby. Once, several Jews ran into her and "her wee four-year-old, whose eyes were even bigger and blacker than her mother's."

He would give the Jews such a curious look of surprise, as if they, the whole community, all Jews from near and far, were related to him on his mother's side. One of the Jews even began teasing him with his finger, motioned to him with his wrinkled forehead, his nose, and his entire smiling face, and he mumbled to him in Yiddish:

"Come here, you little bugger, come here. . . ."

But the little creature was frightened by these motions. He heard his mother's voice, and hurried back with a thumping heart, pounding his feet loudly and running quickly, as if terror-stricken.

IN THE EUROPEAN rural *shtetl* and urban ghetto, fear of Gentiles seemed to course in the blood as a genetic trait. But you could only run so far, isolate so long.

Perhaps Avrom Reyzen's short story, "Acquiring a Graveyard," provides the best, most moving look into the zeitgeist of the *shtetl*. It was written right after the great Kishniev pogrom of 1903, sanctioned by the czar, that sent thousands of Yiddish-speaking Jewish atheist radicals, as well as God-fearing, God-insulting peasants, scurrying for safer shores.

Reyzen begins by describing a mythical *shtetl* completely isolated from the world. So remote was the village that its inhabitants never even heard the faintest echoes from Russian cities or towns. No one but the *shtetl's* own residents needed or were interested in it, and the *shtetl* didn't need anybody.

The Jews there grew their own potatoes, made flour from a village windmill, and found meat in sheep they'd herded themselves. The *shtetl* didn't even need a graveyard; its population was so tiny that the mortality rate was near zero; "the few old people there were diehards; they kept on living."

The only person from the village who anyone could remember passing away was ancient Hendel the bagel maker, who, "after thinking it over, slipped off to Palestine" to die. Describing this *shtetl* of such splendid isolation that it didn't require a cemetery, Reyzen wrote:

> Leybe the Tailor was a genius at his trade, and he sewed for both men and women. True, the material was brought in from the city, but this was done by Yankel, who was practi-

cally the only storekeeper in town; once a year, he would travel to the state capital to buy various goods. . . . And he was so quiet about his trip that it almost seemed like a secret. Every year, he would vanish for two days with no sign of life, and when he came back, only a few people, not all, would find out where he'd been.

And then, "the war broke out" and soldiers came. Yonkel the storekeeper was positive he'd do good business, for he'd heard that soldiers did a lot of buying—and these were soldiers from the Jews' own Russia.

"But these soldiers were of a different kidney," Reyzen wrote. They plundered Yonkel's store and stuck a rifle to his chest.

And Yonkel's face lit up with a good-natured smile, as if to say, "C'mon now! Would you shoot one of your own countrymen? Wait till the enemy comes! You'll have enough work on your hands then!"

The Russian soldiers, however, took Yonkel's smile as an insult and shot him dead. And the town now realized "that a graveyard is an important matter, and that there is indeed such a thing as death."

A few days later, Mottl the butcher was publicly hung for allegedly being an enemy spy. And then, "The enemy army arrived. The battle took place behind the *shtetl*. The shrapnel and the bullets flew over the *shtetl* like hail. The Jews' . . . hiding places were of little use."

After three days of fighting, 12 Jews lay dead in the street. The survivors could never have imagined so many corpses. Being new to such matters, they tried to awaken the bodies as though they were asleep. But none of them got up—they were dead.

Old Hendel [the *shtetl* wise man] freely admitted, "Yes, now we've got to have a graveyard! This is just the right time!"

But one of the younger men waved him off: "The whole town's become a gravcyard!"

"*a goy blaybt a goy*," as they say in Yiddish: "A Gentile remains a Gentile," i.e., scratch below the surface of any non-Jew and you'll find an anti-Semite; they can't help it.

And yet, as is also said: "Better in Gentile hands than in Jewish mouths." "*Beser in goyishe hent eyder in yidishe mayler.*"

PERHAPS THE WORST punishments doled out to the Jews came in 1827, when Czar Nicholas I enacted the "Cantonist Decrees," ordering that young, reasonably fit Jewish males were to be pressed into his army for twenty-five-year hitches. Especially targeted were Jewish boys between the ages of five and eighteen.

Alexander Herzen (1812–1870), the famous Russian journalist, was allowed to watch a group of Jewish boys-cum-soldiers beginning their training, and interviewed the officer in charge of keeping the lines moving.

"Whom do you carry?" Herzen asked.

"Well sir, you see, they got together a bunch of the accursed Jewish youngsters," the commander complained. "The officer that turned them over to me told me they were an awful nuisance. A third of them remained on the road (at this the officer pointed with his finger to the ground). Half of them will not get to their destination."

"Epidemics, I suppose?" I inquired, stirred to the very core.

"No, not exactly epidemics, but they just fall like flies. These Jewish boys are so tiny and delicate. They can't stand mixing dirt for ten hours, with dry biscuits to live on. . . . Pale, worn out, with scared looks, this is the way they stood in their uncomfortable, rough soldier uniforms. Everywhere strange folks. No father, no mother, no caresses. You just hear a cough and the youngster is dead. . . . Children, without care, exposed to the wind which blows unhindered from the Arctic ocean were marching to their death."

The point was not only to torture the Jews and their children by ripping the youngsters away from their parents' arms. The heinous draft—enforced by government agents traveling from *shtetl* to *shtetl*—was also the czar's way of beginning the final, forced assimilation of the *yidn* into Russian society, complete with the utter abandonment of children's Jewishness.

These newly refashioned Jews were to speak in Russian, and fight in a most un-Yiddishkeit battle of other people's wars. (The Jews, used to a life lived underground, kept the Yiddish academies open in basements and barns, and a few publications continued publishing. But the draft, *oy*, the draft—each *shtetl* was given a minimum quota of children to be given up.)

The kidnapped children, sentenced to terms in the army three times as long as they'd been alive, had few memories of their years as Jews. The boys were snatched dressed in typical young-boy short pants, and were quickly forced to eat swine, abandon all other semblances of keeping kosher, and learn how to kill. They would cease to be Jews.

At first, the only exemptions were granted to married men. So, *shtetl* children began being married off to *shtetl* girls at the ages of six and seven. The story was told of an old Jew who saw a tiny young boy on the streets during the day. The old man asked the boy why he wasn't in school.

"I don't go to school anymore," the tyke replied. "I was married yesterday."

The old Jew continued pressing. "If you got married yesterday and are now head of a family," he asked, "why aren't you wearing long pants?"

The child replied, "Yesterday I got married, so I wore the pants; today my little brother is getting married, so he's wearing the pants."

Grown-up bachelors, meantime, hoped to gain the rare beneficence of the czar's agents by pretending to be children: They could be seen playing marbles in the town square wearing short pants.

Not long after the czar's decree, exemptions for married men were eliminated. The only way to get out of the Russian army was to be declared physically unfit. So, Jewish men began volunteering to be hideously maimed, "fixed," by the *shtetl* smithy, utilizing his searing, volcanically white-hot poker.

The infamous title character in Bernard Malamud's *shtetl* novel *The Fixer* was no joke. Hoping to avoid fleeing Russia and his family, my then-eighteen-year-old grandfather, set to be drafted during the next agent's visit, had gone to see the local "fixer" at the edge of town.

There, he paid the *shtetl* blacksmith to shove a molten rod through his groin. The wound, hopefully, would make the young man deemed unfit for military service. Unfortunately, the *shtetl* fixer botched the job, my father detailed to me, leaving my grandfather with a massive hernia that would plague him his entire life—yet at the time still a bull-strong fellow fit for active military service in the Russian army.

And so, my father went on, repeating the story I'd heard so many decades before, my grandfather had to flee one night, leaving behind my grandmother and his two young daughters— my aunts. He had barely enough kopecks to get himself across the ocean; he would send for them as soon as he'd raised enough money if he somehow escaped and made it to the new world.

The only things he brought would not have to pay steerage. Besides his *tefillin* (prayer phylacteries) and *tallis* (prayer shawl), he carried only one other reminder of home.

It probably would have been wiser for him to choose something light and easy to conceal for his third keepsake. Instead, he took his bulky winepress, which he carried on his back as he fled across most of Europe, then transported over the Atlantic to America.

That winepress could travel free; his wife and children would have had to pay. His plan to quickly earn a grubstake and send for my grandmother and two aunts was *kiboshe*d by World War I's arrival and, in its wake, America's new and particularly anti-Jewish restrictive immigration laws.

So it was seven years before he could send for them, to come to someplace called Minnesota. His older brother with the Yiddish name Markle had been unable to avoid the czar's army, and had been shot in a German prisoner of war camp.

When my grandmother and aunts finally made it to America and joined him, the family soon grew by one with the birth of my father. As per Yiddishkeit tradition, he was named after a dead relative. Hence he became "Markle Karlen"—a first name no one I've ever met anywhere has heard before.

In the meantime, my grandfather began using his winepress

in his new world, which was overflowing with Scandinavians; for the uneducated country boy who refused to learn English, the winepress was home.

My grandfather made sweet peasant wine. In the old country, his homemade wine was so righteously tasty, he had won the honor of making it for religious sacraments in the village. His wine came from a secret recipe, with all that entails.

It was never written down, of course. Only one family member in each generation was taught the precise combination of ingredients that yielded the wine, which was sacramental enough to please the village's religious leaders, yet carried the wallop of a Joe Louis uppercut.

My grandfather, an Orthodox Jew, arrived in a land populated by Norwegians and Swedes and kept making the wine that had made him famous back home. He had a small but appreciative audience among his *lantzmen*, who, like the grandfathers of Bob Dylan and Joel and Ethan Coen, had emigrated from czarist Russia to the banks of the upper Mississippi. Because of his wine, my grandfather was a celebrity.

Prohibition? Not for him. He received a religious exemption for his sacramental wine. And if the leftovers went to the neighbors, so what? He never charged anybody.

By the 1930s, his Mason jars of wine were going out as Christmas Eve presents to neighbors named Olson, Swenson, and Andersen. Always willing to provide a free ecumenical snort to the good Lutherans, my grandfather died in 1974, as Willie Loman would have had it, "well liked."

BACK HOME IN Yiddish-speaking Russia, Poland, Lithuania, and Romania, the peasants continued their love-hate-but-really-love relationship with God.

A got hobn mir—aza you oyf undz un a folk hot er—aza your
oyf im!
"A God we have—woe to us; and a people He has—woe to
Him!"

The humor that is so essentially Yiddish, it is no secret, was
largely born of pure and earned fear and paranoia. As William
Novak wrote in *The Big Book of Jewish Humor,* the language is
"optimistic in the long run, but pessimistic about the present
and the immediate future," with "twin currents of anxiety and
skepticism that can become so strong that even the ancient
sources of Jewish optimism are swept up in them."

So, when possible, when faced with their own destruction, it
meant simply trying to flee, in order to flee alive again another
day, with another handy quip, hopefully.

Even then, however, the joking often belied more than a not-
so-subtle put-down of the *goyim*—in a language, of course, no
Gentile could understand. Also evident was the special kind of
historic, Yiddish-based, argumentative, Jew-versus-Jew antipa-
thy, bathed in the love and specialness of a people so isolated and
oppressed by the non-Jews they made fun of.

There is the old-country folktale that says:

If you tell a joke to a [Gentile] peasant he will laugh three
times—when you tell it, when you explain it, and when he
understands it.

A [non-Jewish] landowner [there could be no Jewish
landowners] laughs only twice—when he hears the joke and
when you explain it. Of course he never understands it.

An army officer laughs once—when you tell the joke.
He never lets you explain it, and it goes without saying that
he is unable to understand it.

But when you start telling a joke to another Jew, he interrupts you. "Go on! That's an old one!" And he proceeds to show you how much better he can tell it himself.

Yet as Yiddishkeit demands:

Oyf a shlektn goy tor men keyn nekome nit betn.
"Don't pray for revenge, even on a wicked Gentile."

And yet Yiddish never has minded contradicting itself:

Got shtroft, der mentsh iz zikh noykem.
"God punishes, man takes revenge."

No matter how often their heads were sliced off and their Torahs burned—atrocities that spurred the birth, growth, and protective shield of Yiddish—Jews refused to suspend their disbelief that the Jews were Chosen, the one people out of all the Lord's tribes picked to receive God's gift of the Torah.

God would show up, that's what all the *tsoris* in their lives were all about: He would come and save the Jews, just as soon as the Jews made themselves and the outside world worthy of His and Her presence (the Chasidim believe God has equal male and female forms). That outside world, different civilizations that had so strafed the running Jews for millennia, translated to *"goyim"*—simply this planet that wasn't Jewish.

Forget the saving grace of Jesus, for whom Yiddish had a devilish saying—a metaphor degrees of separation away from any Gentile knowing he was being mocked by these lowly cowards.

Nisht geshtoygn, nisht gefloygn.

Literally, this meant in Yiddish something that "didn't climb, didn't fly"—that is, anything that just plain didn't work, from a *shtetl* stove to a rusted ghetto gate.

In reality, the something that didn't climb and didn't fly was Jesus himself, who like so many other self-declared Jewish messiahs duped the masses, and neither climbed nor flew to heaven for our sins.

While they waited for their own Messiah, Jews could read from the Torah what would happen once their Old Testament God announced Himself as the new Sheriff in town.

God would be their stone, the anti-Semites a fragile water pitcher. And as Sancho Panza, Don Quixote's squire, said, "whether the stone hits the pitcher, or the pitcher hits the stone, it's going to be bad for the pitcher."

Samuel L. Jackson, playing a hit man in Quentin Tarantino's *Pulp Fiction*, liked to quote the Old Testament's Book of Ezekiel, chapter 25, verse 17, to his victims' faces immediately before killing them. In truth, the passage was a *mish-mosh* of Ezekiel 25:17, the Twenty-third Psalm, and a declaration from one of Tarantino's favorite chop-socky films.

But it sounded real, and the point was made: When the Jews' God came, there would be hell, literally, to pay in revenge.

"Ezekiel 25:17," Jackson said, pointing his gun between the eyes of whomever had sinned against his underworld boss.

The path of the righteous man is beset on all sides by the iniquities of the selfish and the tyranny of evil men. Blessed is he who, in the name of charity and good will, shepherds the weak through the valley of the darkness. For he is truly his brother's keeper and the finder of lost children. And I will strike down upon thee with great vengeance and furious anger those who attempt to poison and destroy my brothers. And you will KNOW I am the Lord, WHEN I LAY MY VENGEANCE UPON YOU!!!

BLAM BLAM BLAM BLAM

But until the Jewish God arrived, the Jews would have no BLAM BLAM BLAM BLAM against their enemies. They would be on their own, helpless on purpose, with nothing to protect them but their shared faith and language to redeem them from their wanderings.

But again, and again, why?

As usual, Yiddish has at least two contradictory ideas: one involving a "whaddya gonna do?" hunch of the shoulders, the other expressing the irony of the Jews' virtually unyielding slaughter.

Fun nakhes lebt men nit, fun tsores shtarbt men nit.
"From joy you can't live, from troubles you can't die."

Yet, on the other hand:

Zint es iz oyfgekumen dos shtarbn iz men nit zikher mitn lebn.
"Since dying became fashionable, living isn't safe."

THE ANSWERS ARE not easy in uncovering the meaning and purpose of revenge. Or why a people chooses to suffer for no known reason, except so at least a sliver of its small population can hang on to life and suffer some more. The reasons are no simpler to deduce than knowing what was really in Shylock's heart when he demanded his pound of flesh for a lifetime of debasement.

It was appropriate that the play Shakespeare originally titled *The Jew of Venice* was translated into Yiddish and performed on Second Avenue's "Knish Alley." After all, Shylock would have spoken Yiddish behind the unscalable gates of Venice's ghetto, that prison which Jews were locked into every night.

YET UNTIL REVENGE was turned against the Jews' tormentors— and God's revenge seemed the only way *that* could happen— there would be mostly suffering.

"Pain thresholds vary among peoples as among people; the threshold of East European Jews was exceedingly high, perhaps even excessively high, if pain is to serve as a warning of moral danger," wrote Harvard professor of Yiddish Ruth R. Wisse in *The Shlemiel as Modern Hero.*

And yet, Wisse continued, perhaps what bonded the Jews *was* that life was so precious, even if expendable, for the right idea. So, the Jews of Eastern Europe were so willing to get knocked down, struggle back to their feet, dust themselves off, and go back to living a life of Yiddishkeit.

Professor Wisse wrote, "The community learned to absorb severe shock without abandoning the image of man to which it had pledged itself, and without losing its love or desire for life."

And why didn't the Jews, entrapped by the moods of the people whose countries they'd wandered into, abandon that Pollyannaish, too-forgiving image of man? What was more important—to just stay Jews, without help from somebody's cavalry that would never come charging to their rescue?

Israel Efroikin, the Yiddish writer, pitched in on that one too. "Jews were taught to have a horror of shedding blood," he wrote. And of all the cultures on earth, he said, Jews were the only ones not to indulge or define themselves with tales of mythic or real heroic strongmen, à la the Vikings or Alexander the Great.

"What is a hero according to the Jewish conception?" Efroikin went on. "Not he who kills another, but lets himself be killed rather than do wrong, rather than break his covenant with God.

"The true Jewish coward," he said, was one "who was ashamed to speak in the presence of non-Jews—his language, not theirs!"

These Jews who refused to even speak Yiddish in front of Gentiles, or who tried to fit in by appeasing their enemies, were the real cowards, Efroiken continued.

"They were deserters, near-renegades, practically apostates. Their numbers grew and but for a remnant of the old-type Jews we might have perished as a people."

So perhaps that was indeed the point. To be left with enough *lantzmen* after any unprovoked outrage against them—be it a spontaneous pogrom or a scientifically planned Holocaust—to just stumble on as a people.

In ways, it worked. Again, where are all the tribes of the Bible who'd walked alongside the Jews now?

THE WISDOM OF Jews accepting without complaint their own weakness tweaked nostalgic thoughts in even macho, unsentimental Ben Hecht, the screenwriter, novelist, Zionist *agent provocateur*, and leading fund-raiser for buying and boating illegal guns to Israel during its War of Independence. In his 1950 memoirs, Hecht wrote:

I have believed in a nation of Jews and worked for that belief. But there are moments when I think wistfully of the
lost innocence of the Jews, when the only politics they had
was the management of heaven. Nations rose and fell, blood
baths drowned the earth; jackal heroes screamed its peoples on to carnage; unsated neurotics in togas, gold braid
and high hats slashed at the veins of life, crying, "Glory!
Glory!"

And with this evil the Jews had nothing to do. They
were the birds that got tumbled out of their nests when the
winds blew hard. They had no more to do with the historical winds of the world than to die in them.

Again, why?
Because, Yiddish explained:
A Jew is like any other person: only more so.
Another key precept of Yiddishkeit:

Ver es hot nit keyn bushe in ponim un keyn rakhmones in horts
    der kumt nit aroys fun yidn.
"Whoever has not tasted humiliation and feels no pity
    doesn't descend from Jews."

Treating someone as a human, and not a Darwinian survivor, lies at the heart of Yiddishkeit. Take John Turturro, playing
a Jewish character nicknamed "the Shmatte" in the Coen Brothers film *Miller's Crossing*. Taken deep into the woods to be shot,
Turturro seems less concerned that he is about to die than the
manner in which he'll be left.

"You're going to let me die out here like a *wild animal?*" he
asks. "Don't let me die out here like a *wild animal!*"

Unlike the modern state of Israel, the Yiddish nation could

only fight one-front battles. Waging war against their own consciences, as the Yiddish idiom went, Jews were left with few resources to fight enemies either far away or nose-to-nose. From outside looking in, it was a worldview that seemed to embrace masochism as a lifestyle.

And so, this most tortured people who proudly didn't know how or refused to battle with sticks, fought back with words. Specifically, Yiddish words. More precisely, the jokes and ironic twists soldered into the soul and sinews of this humble day-to-day language.

"In foreign surroundings," Frank Kafka wrote, "the native and the familiar becomes clearer and more distinct to us. That—I think—is the source of Jewish jokes about Jews."

Still, it seems a lot for a language to serve in place of cannons. How could this self-loathing language of a universally loathed tribe evolve so as to be able to put an end to this orphan tribe's wanderings?

The measly words of Yiddish, it turned out, were armed—and especially directed at oneself or fellow Jews. In time, that vocabulary formed a line of defense, both psychic and real. Yiddish's words weren't a defense *mechanism*, but an actual way to defend one's self and soul.

So, in resonances still heard today, Jews knew to throw a self-deprecating joke when in doubt about the hostility that surrounded them. "Aggression turned against the self seems to be an essential feature of the truly Jewish joke," wrote Martin Grotjahn, a psychoanalyst. "It's as if the Jew tells his enemies: 'You do not need to attack us. We can do that ourselves—and even better.'"

Mel Brooks's comeback to his *lantzman* came decades later, when Brooks was once again playing the two-thousand-year-old man, ad-libbing answers to Carl Reiner's questions.

Q. I gather, sir, that you are a famous psychoanalyst?
A. That is correct.

Q. Who analyzed you?
A. I was analyzed by No. 1 himself.

Q. You mean the great Sigmund Freud?
A. In person. Took me during lunchtime, charged me a nickel.

Q. What kind of man was he?
A. Lovely little fellow. I shall never forget the hours we spent together, me lying on the couch, him right there beside me, wearing a nice off-the-shoulder dress.

Q. [Did] he have an Oedipus complex?
A. What is that?

Q. You're an analyst, sir, and you never heard of an Oedipus complex?
A. Never in my life.

Q. Well, sir, it's when a man has a passionate desire to make love to his own mother.
A. (after a pause) That's the dirtiest thing I ever heard. Where do you get that filth?

Q. It comes from a famous play by Sophocles.
A. Was he Jewish?

Q. No sir, he was Greek.

A. With a Greek, who knows? But with a Jew, you don't do a thing like that even to your wife, let alone your mother.

FOR REVENGE AND protection, Jews had the mythical Golem, lodged in Yiddish superstition and the mysticism of the Kaballah. The Golem was the Jews' avenging monster, a tragic creature given a body and strength, but no soul or feelings.

Tales involving the Golem involved the monster eventually destroying its maker, usually a rabbi. Mary Shelley swiped her notion of Dr. Frankenstein and his monster from tales of the Golem dating to the Middle Ages; an episode of the *X-Files* even featured a Golem in a guest-starring role.

Only learned priests with secret Kabbalistic incantations could call forth the Golem, who was supposed to do only good with his strength, then be made to disappear until he was needed again. If his maker made a misstep and the Golem slipped out of control, the Jewish monster could become, well, a *monster*.

I'D LEARNED OF the Golem when I was twelve. I'd been sent to the library one afternoon in Hebrew school after I'd been banished from class for getting busted renting out, by fifteen-minute increments, a copy I'd shoplifted of *Everything You Always Wanted to Know About Sex*.

My business destroyed, stuck for two hours with nothing to do, I craned my neck to see the top of the shelf behind the librarian's desk, in search of books about Nazis, especially ones that showed them being hung.

Instead, I spied two matched green volumes, one with the

enticing title *Jewish Magic and Superstition*. Its companion was something called *On the Kabbalah and Its Symbolism*, by Gershom Scholem.

They were kept out of normal sight lines; the Kabbalah was restricted to "mature" scholars over forty who had already been through all the holy (and linear) texts. When the librarian went out of the room, I ran the book ladder behind his desk, shimmied to the top of the shelf, and leaped a few times until I could get the books to fall from their perch and onto the floor.

After quickly replacing the ladder, I took out the first green book, with the sexy title about magic, copyrighted in 1939 by one Joshua Trachtenberg. I opened it up and was introduced into the confusing, exciting Jewish world of devilish *dybbuks*, monstrous Golems, and Kabbalistic incantations encompassing magic, both black and white.

Led by a reference to another book, I then read of one Rabbi Judah Loew of sixteenth-century Prague, who activated a Golem against the city's anti-Semites by taking a lump of clay and invoking seventy-two specific letters of the Hebrew alphabet that spelled out a special word for "God."

Those letters, put together in secret combinations, and pronounced in specific breathing patterns, could animate a lump of clay into the monster. Warnings about not playing with Golems came in the other green book, the one by the late Gershom Scholem—one of the top few scholars of Jewish mysticism over the last hundred years.

"Mistakes in carrying out the directions [for making the monster] do not impair the Golem," he wrote, "they destroy its creator."

According to the Kabbalah's "Sefer Yetzirah," quoted Scholem, a Golem maker must:

Take a bowl full of pure water and a small spoon, fill it with earth—but he must know the exact weight of the earth before he stirs it and also the exact measurement of the spoon with which he is to measure [adds Scholem: "But this information is not imparted in writing"]. When he has filled it, he should scatter it and slowly blow it over the water. While beginning to blow the first spoonful of earth, he should utter a consonant of the Name in a loud voice and pronounce it in a single breath, until he can blow it no longer. While he is doing this, his face should be turned downward. And so, beginning with the combinations that constitute the parts of the head, he should form all the members in a definite order, until a figure emerges.

Unfortunately, to animate the monster one needed to know that special seventy-two-letter name for God. It was a name spoken in ancient times only once a year, by a priest in the holy of holies, the Temple in Jerusalem. The word was handed down orally through the generations to a special few holy men and mystics who could be trusted with the Divine power of the seventy-two-letter Divine Name.

Before Rabbi Loew in Prague rediscovered it, that name had been lost to the ages. After he'd made his Golem, Rabbi Loew wrote the Hebrew and the Yiddish word for truth on its forehead: Though they are spelled the same, in Hebrew the word for truth is *eh-met*; in Yiddish, *em'mes*.

When the being's job was done and the anti-Semites slapped back in their place, the rabbi erased the first letter on the monster's head, making the word *em'mes*—"truth"—into the word *mate*, which means "dead."

With that fancy doodle-work, the Golem returned to clay. Less successful than Rabbi Loew and his Golem-work, I read on, was another Prague rabbi whose Golem grew so tall and huge that the holy man could no longer reach the monster's forehead to erase the key letter that would return his monster to dust.

Out of reach, the rabbi thought fast, and ordered his creature to tie his master's shoelaces. The Golem bent down, the rabbi erased a letter of the word "truth" to make the word "dead," and the creature immediately disintegrated. Unfortunately, he collapsed on the rabbi, who was pulverized.

Yet I. L. (Isaac Leib) Peretz (1851–1915) had a different take on the Golem. Peretz, along with Sholem Aleichem and Mendele Mocher Seforim, was considered the third star in the trinity of great Yiddish writers. And the brief short story in which Peretz rewrote the parable about the monster, said Irving Howe, was not about the power and possibilities of revenge, but "the decline of faith, the loss of ancient wisdom, the dust of skepticism."

In "The Golem," Peretz wrote:

Great men were once capable of great miracles. When the ghetto of Prague was being attacked, and they were about to rape the women, roast the children, and slaughter the rest; when it seemed that the end had finally come, the great Rabbi Loe[w] put aside his Gemarah, went into the street, stopped before a heap of clay in front of the teacher's house, and molded a clay image. He blew into the nose of the golem—and it began to stir; then he whispered the Name into its ear, and our golem left the ghetto. The rabbi returned to the House of Prayer, and the golem fell upon our enemies, threshing them as with flails. Men fell on all sides.

Prague was filled with corpses.

It lasted, so they say, through Wednesday and Thursday. Now it is already Friday, the clock strikes twelve, and the golem is still busy at its work.

"Rabbi," cries the head of the ghetto, "the golem is slaughtering all of Prague! There will not be a gentile left to light the Sabbath fires or take down the Sabbath lamps."

Once again the rabbi left his study. He went to the altar and began singing the psalm "A Song of the Sabbath."

The golem ceased its slaughter. It returned to the ghetto, entered the House of Prayer, and waited before the rabbi. And again the rabbi whispered into its ear. The eyes of the golem closed, the soul that had dwelt in it flew out, and it was once more a golem of clay.

To this day the golem lies hidden in the attic of the Prague synagogue, covered with cobwebs that extend from wall to wall. No living creature may look at it, particularly women in pregnancy. No one may touch the cobwebs, for whoever touches them dies. Even the oldest people no longer remember the golem, the wise man Zvi, the grandson of the great Rabbi Loe[w], ponders the problem: may such a golem be included in a congregation of worshippers or not?

The golem, you see, had not been forgotten. It is still here! But the Name by which it could be called to life in a day of need, the Name has disappeared. And the cobwebs grow and grow, and no one may touch them.

What are we to do?

THE GOLEM'S METAPHYSICAL cousin in the Kabbalah was the usually less frightening *dybbuk*. Diabolically mischievous instead of overtly murderous, the *dybbuk*, the opposite of the Golem, had a spirit and feelings but no physical form. He could enter someone's body and haunt their soul, as powerfully and perversely as the *dybbuk* deemed necessary. *Dybbuks* could also help the needy if they chose.

The best modern portrait of a *dybbuk* at work comes in *The Dance of Genghis Cohn* by Romain Gary. Gary, a Jew, wrote a masterwork of black comedy in his tale of a lousy ventriloquist, stage name "Genghis" Cohn, shot at Auschwitz in 1944. Twenty-four years later, Cohn, reborn as a *dybbuk,* makes his haunting presence known to Schatz, the S.S. officer who killed him, now a good citizen and the police chief of a small German town. The *dybbuk* relates:

> We became inseparable, Schatzchi and I, on a certain beautiful, cold day of April 1944. Schatz has sheltered me since: for almost 24 years he's been hiding a Jew. I try not to take advantage of his hospitality, not to take up too much room. People often say that we [Jews] were pushing, give us a finger and we'll grab the whole hand, and I try to show them how discreet and tactful we can be. I always leave [Schatz] alone in the bathroom, and when he has a romance underway I'm very careful not to show up at an awkward moment. When two people have to live so close together [like the *dybbuk* and Schatz], discretion and restraint are essential.

Cohn *does* gain some fun shocking Schatz. "I'm pleased to note that it shakes him a bit," says Cohen.

> Let me tell you that I make quite a sight. I'm wearing a long black coat over my Auschwitz-style striped pajamas and, right over the heart, the infamous yellow Star of David. My face is very pale, ghastly white, in fact: no matter how courageous you are, when the machine gun's aimed at you and the order *Feur!* is already on the officer's lips, it does something to you, no use denying that . . . we were made to dig our own graves

[and] it was there that Schatz, who was the young officer in charge of the execution, picked me up, without realizing it.

YET THERE WERE times when even imagined Yiddish demons could wreak havoc on the superstitious Jews of Eastern Europe.

Isaac Singer addressed this issue in typically heartbreaking terms in his short story "Taibele and Her Demon." In the town of Lashnik, not far from Lublin, he wrote, was a couple named Chaim Nossen and Taibele. They had three children, but all died in infancy, "and after that, Taibele's womb closed up."

Distraught, Chaim Nossen takes off, just like the husbands in America who in real-life abandoned their wives when they hit Ellis Island.

Chaim had fled Taibele without granting a *get*, meaning she was unable to marry again. Without a spouse, or hope for one, or children, she was doomed, she knew, to spend her life alone.

Every day, Taibele would gather with her friends and gossip. Shortly before, she'd bought a book from a peddler "about a young Jewish woman, and a demon who had ravished her and lived with as man and woman." "The women," wrote Singer, "huddled closer together, joined hands, spat to ward off evil, and laughed the kind of laughter that came from fear."

"Why didn't she make a journey to a holy rabbi?"

"The demon warned her that he would choke if she revealed the secret," Taibele answered.

Alchonen, "a dissipated fellow full of cunning goatish tricks," . . . walked past and heard the tale. That night, and for each night following, he would sneak into Taibele's room, make love to her, and tell her he was the demon in the story. "As the saying goes," Singer beautifully wrote, "may God protect and preserve us from all that we can get accustomed to."

And even if she was holding the devil, she became accustomed to holding on to him to make her feel less alone. In time, the town gossips noticed that Alchonen was not going to *shul* much anymore. He now escorted only the children of the poor and rarely ate and was always thirsty. And then he died.

Whereupon Taibele no longer was visited by her loving demon, and she "remained alone, doubly deserted. . . . She aged quickly. Nothing was left to her of the past except a secret that could never be told and would be believed by no one. There are secrets that the heart cannot reveal to the lips. They are carried to the grave. The willows murmur of them, the rooks caw about them, the gravestones converse about them silently, in the language of stone. The dead will awaken one day, but their secrets will abide with the Almighty and His judgment until the end of all generations."

FINALLY, BY THE last half of the nineteenth century, some European Jews began to learn to fight for themselves. In the past, Russian-Jewish writer Israel Efroikin wrote that the Jews had been saved by refusing to fight, or in any way giving in to the outside world.

But these were different times. "And the God of Israel," Efroikin wrote, "helped by sending us new Jewish heroes, the Jewish revolutionaries in the countries of the Diaspora."

These Russian-based revolutionaries and labor organizers were almost uniformly Jewish, speaking in Yiddish, the language of the people. So, in 1881, a Jew was among the cabal of plotters who threw a bomb into Czar Alexander II's carriage, killing him.

And before he was nine, Meier Suchowljansky, so little he would never grow taller than five feet two inches, had witnessed the terrible pogrom in his beloved town of Grodno, in Russian Poland.

Not long after, a Jewish revolutionary came to Grodno and addressed a meeting of survivors of the pogrom. The conclave was held in the *shtetl* home of Meier Suchowljansky's grandfather.

"Jews! [the speaker said in Yiddish.] Why do you just sit around like stupid sheep and allow them to come and kill you, steal your money, kill your sons, and rape your daughters? Aren't you ashamed?"

"*Yidn! Fahr vos zittzen ihr vi narishke shepslach un der loiben zei tsu kumen und Hargener eich, galvenen eir gelt, Hargenen eire zene, fargvaldicken dei eier Techter? Shemt zicht ihr!*"

"You must stand up and fight, [the revolutionary continued].

"You are men like others. I have been a soldier in the Turkish army. I was taught to fight. A Jew can fight. I will teach you how. We have no arms, but it doesn't matter. We can use sticks and stones. Even if you're going to die, at least do it with honor! Fight back! Stop being cowards! Stop lying down like stupid sheep! Don't be frightened. Hit them and they'll run. If you are going to die, then die fighting. Protect your beloved ones. Your womenfolk should be able to rely on you."

Meier Suchowljansky listened intently.

A year later, he emigrated to New York, where his name was changed at Ellis Island to Meyer Lansky. He soon met Benjamin "Bugsy" Siegel.

Eventually, with other Jewish gangsters like Mickey Cohen, Lansky and Siegel did more to fight fascism during World War II and save their people overseas than all the official Jewish committees in the United States combined. Virtually all of those organizations were composed of genteel American-Jewish leaders who were afraid to make the fight resonate as a "Jewish war."

To Lansky et al., a Jewish war was what was, finally, called for.

By the 1930s, anti-Semitism was flourishing as never before in the United States. In Des Moines, Iowa, Charles Lindbergh, head of the America First committee, pointed to the Jews in particular as those who would be singled out for punishment if their "propagandizers" for getting the United States involved in entering World War II were successful.

His speech, entitled "Who Are the War Agitators?" specifically named the Jews (as well as the British and Franklin Roosevelt) for leading the United States into a war unwanted by "us"—true Americans. (Two months later, after Pearl Harbor, Lindbergh shut his mouth. The journals of his wife, Anne Morrow Lindbergh, expurgated upon first publication, were finally reprinted in whole and revealed her brutal anti-Semitism.)

In Des Moines that 1941 night, Lucky Lindy warned "us" Americans that Jews were "not Americans." He continued:

> Instead of agitating for war, the Jewish groups in this country should be opposing it in every possible way, for they will be the first to feel its consequences. A few farsighted Jewish people realize this and stand opposed to intervention. But the majority still do not. Their greatest danger to this country lies in their large ownership and influence in our motion pictures, our press, and our government . . . the entire future of America rests upon our shoulders.

In Detroit, Father Charles Coughlin was preaching over the national airwaves for Jews to be excluded from all positions of power, while brigades of pro-Nazi "Silver Shirts" were massing in Minneapolis and beginning to terrorize the local Jews. In New York, the "Brown Shirts" of the German-American Bund were holding huge rallies in support of the Germans.

Jewish leaders in New York had no idea how to strike back; they had no legal recourse. So New York State Judge Nathan Perlman personally got in touch with Meyer Lansky and asked for help. He didn't want the American Nazis killed, Perlman told Lansky, just their rallies broken up. Perlman offered Lansky payment, but it was the only part of his proposal that the Jewish gangster refused.

"I was a Jew," Lansky later said, "and felt those Jews in Europe who were suffering. They were my brothers."

Historian Robert Rockaway chronicled in *But He Was Good to His Mother: The Lives and Crimes of Jewish Gangsters* how for months on end, dozens of Bund rallies were broken up by Jewish gangs. "Nazi arms, legs and ribs were broken and skulls were cracked," he wrote, "but no one died."

Lansky himself remembered one rally in particular held by the Brown Shirts in the German Yorkville section of New York. "The stage was decorated with a swastika and a picture of Hitler. The speakers started ranting. There were only fifteen of us, but we went into action. We threw some of them out the windows. Most of the Nazis panicked and ran out. We chased them and beat them up. We wanted to show them Jews would not always sit back and accept insults."

The horrors of the old world would be recalled . . . and its lessons remembered.

CHAPTER 12

שׁמַאסַֿ‏ן‏יַ‏שׁ‏עַ‏שׁ‏יַ‏ן‏סַֿמַאשׁ

Coming to America I:
Yiddish and German-Jewish Self-Loathing

Oh, the Protestants hate the Catholics
And the Catholics hate the Protestants
And the Hindus hate the Muslims
And everybody hates the Jews.
—*Tom Lehrer, "National Brotherhood Week"*

Estimates have it that from two million to around two and a half million Yiddish-speaking peasants arrived in America from Russia, Poland, Romania, and points east between 1880 and 1920. About 70 percent of them stayed in New York after reaching Ellis Island, utterly remaking the urban landscape.

New York became a new city. In 1870, only eighty thousand Jews lived in the nascent metropolis, comprising less than 9 percent of the city's population. By 1907, New York's Jewish population numbered almost a million, with ninety thousand new immigrants arriving every year. Less than a decade later, nearly 1.5 million *yidn* had squeezed in, representing 28 percent of the entire city.

The mass of German Jews had arrived first, somewhere around the corners of the Civil War. The Sephardim, the true royalty of Judaism, naturally beat them here. Judah P. Benjamin, a Sephardic Jew, served as attorney general, secretary of war, and secretary of state of the Confederacy, and appears on most Confederate two-dollar bills. During the war, he was called "the brains of the Confederacy."

A political progressive, Benjamin was deeply involved in drawing up a Confederate Emancipation Proclamation. After Lincoln's assassination, wrote biographer Eli Evans, Benjamin was blamed by "a nation of Christ-haunted people [who] searched instinctively for the Jewish scapegoat." After the Civil War, he had to flee to England.

While the Sephardim had little use for the German Jews, the latter did not exactly roll out the welcome wagon for their Yiddish-speaking brethren from Eastern Europe. Most of them had arrived from Germany decades before the tsunami of Jewish peasants arrived. Few of the German Jews had memories or even handed down stories of their ancestors' *Judenstrasse*, the streets of Deutschland's Jewish ghetto.

True, those German alleys had once been home to as much poverty and oppression as the Russian and Polish *shtetls*. But Jews from Germany had gotten to America first, and many were already flourishing when they landed. And when the German Jews emigrated, they *strode*. Decades later, the newly arriving Jewish immigrants from Eastern Europe had *fled*.

And by the time most of the peasantry arrived, the Jews who'd emigrated from Germany had more or less successfully melted into American society. Though they were still considered by the Gentile citizenry as what literary theorist Edward Said termed "other," at least the generally well-off German Jews were able to make reasonable facsimiles of the venues from which they were shut out.

Still banned from the WASP white-shoe financial houses, many German Jews earned their fortunes by simply setting up their own shops and investment firms. Prime among them was Jacob Schiff, who arrived at age eighteen from Germany in 1865 already well off.

Twenty years later he was in charge of the investment banking group of Kuhn, Loeb, and Company—the second richest and most influential institution in the country after J. P. Morgan's bank. By 1891, he was on the committee of German Jews who lobbied President Benjamin Harrison to completely stem further immigration of peasant Jews from Eastern Europe.

They wanted Harrison to twist the Russian government's arm not to "force groups of its people . . . to seek refuge in another country, and that country would be our own."

Of course, it was still unthinkable to allow any kind of Jew, no matter how wealthy or cultured, into the steadfastly Christian *fin de siècle* social register representing the four hundred leading New York aristocrats who it was said could fit into John Jacob Astor's private ballroom.

Yet the German Jews made do with their own high society, dubbed "Our Crowd" by author Stephen Birmingham in his admirable chronicle of the same name. And even if those German Jews could not step foot near the haughty salons of the Gentiles, they could at least find ironic comfort in the fact that the Astors themselves were frequently slurred as Jews-in-hiding by the Christians who would eat their caviar and drink their champagne.

The Rest of Us is what Birmingham aptly named his later chronicle of the rise of the teeming Eastern European Jewish immigrants shoehorned into Lower East Side tenements. Un-like the Germans, *those* immigrants did not arrive in America with *gelt,* walking sticks, cravats, or the ability to hum along with the libretto at the opera.

Instead, *der greeners* (greenhorns) streamed through Ellis Is-land speaking Yiddish and, if they were lucky, carrying more than just the clothes on their backs. Some had accumulated enough money in the old world to bring their families along with them in steerage. If not, it could be years before a sum could be sent back home for passage across the ocean for the rest of the *mishpocha.*

Many were illiterate, or wore side locks and beards they would never cut or shave off. They arrived in sack dresses and pants made at home in the *shtetl* with gnarled working-class hands that had clutched religious prayer shawls and phylacteries on the boat over.

These simple, uneducated masses, arriving in the new world with their old-world ways, immediately encountered an espe-cially virulent form of Jewish self-loathing that had first begun emerging in Germany in the 1700s. The hatred now came from New York's Upper West Side, and was symbolized by the Ger-man Jews' loathing of the mere sound of Yiddish.

"Few kinds of hate are as potent as self-hate," wrote Dovid Katz, author, educator, and a resident in the pantheon of great Yiddishists. And few brands of *yidn* hated the dictates and tradi-tions of their people more than "Our Crowd." When those Jews looked downtown at their newly arrived co-religionists, they reacted with shock, embarrassment, and a knee-jerk need to distance themselves not only geographically but genetically.

That those *other* Jews spoke Yiddish was proof enough, opined the uptown English-language *Hebrew Standard,* that their Eastern European brethren were more from the world of "Ori-entalism than Americanism."

Further, the paper warned, "assimilation for these wretched souls will perhaps never take place."

The *Hebrew Standard* went so far as to claim approvingly that their well-to-do German readership had closer spiritual and intellectual ties to Christians than to these "Orientals."

The *Hebrew Standard* reassured its subscribers that they were "thoroughly acclimated American Jews [who have] no religious, social or intellectual superstitions. [They are] closer to the Christian sentiment around him than to the Judaism of these miserable darkened [Jews downtown]."

Yiddish, the English-language *American Hebrew* proclaimed, was a "piggish jargon" while the Yiddish theater was "barbarous." And the dozen Yiddish daily newspapers that had sprouted downtown espoused dastardly "socialism."

Those shrill Yiddish periodicals, declared the *American Hebrew*, catered perfectly in style to their readership of monolingual Eastern European Jewish immigrants who were horrifyingly "pushy."

The *American Hebrew* saved special vituperation for Abraham Cahan's Socialist *Forverts* (*Forward*), the most popular and influential Yiddish newspaper. The daily *Forward* was nothing more, declared the German Jews' house organ, than a "revolutionary rag."

Yiddish had long been purged not only from these German-American Jews' vocabularies, but from their collective unconscious as well. In the world of *their* fathers, and their fathers' fathers, the *mamme-loshn* was nothing more than improvised old-world barnyard babble. And anyone who spoke or even knew the language in America was considered tenement rabble.

Meantime, Yiddishkeit, the intrinsically *Jewish* way of living and behaving, had also long ago been thrown out with the filthy ghetto bathwater filled with old-world superstition that had been replaced by the eighteenth-century Enlightenment. In the new world, the Yiddish language was barely fit even for the downtown Jews' anarchic streets—never mind the uptown Jews' sparkling new apartment buildings shooting impossibly sky high on Central Park West and Riverside Drive.

Up there, the Germans yearned not for the tang and folk wisdom of the mother tongue, but instead the culture, reason, and good taste of the Fatherland's most select salons. Not that many Gentiles cared. For the century before the 1980s, as Steven Gaines wrote, the Upper West Side of New York was "denigrated as the bourgeois, Jewish aunt of the WASPy, blond, patrician [East Side] Fifth Avenue."

The German Jews may have wanted to expunge Yiddish as an alarming back step in the march toward assimilation. But the public anti-Semitism of Gentiles toward the Germans more than matched the German Jews' own anti-Semitism toward the *yidn* downtown.

As late as 1939, *Fortune* magazine—Henry Luce's Torah of the Christian Establishment—declared that the Upper West Side was "inhabited chiefly, though by no means exclusively, by New York–born Jews who have standards of their own but whose interest in social prestige is practically nil . . . but they know how to get the most out of it for their money . . . [their] maid (probably a Negro) gets $60 a month wages and has no style."

Then there were the rich uptown-born Jews who didn't understand the meaning of the few commonplace and simple Yiddish words they apparently thought they knew. Even A. J. Liebling, the great *New Yorker* writer whose beat included "low life" profiles was befuddled when he tried to work the *mammeloshn* into his otherwise exemplary work concerning the charming side of Times Square hustlers, con men, and special peculiar folks to whom he lovingly gave his attention.

"Times Square's language was a Yiddish, showbiz, midway

patois," James Traub aptly described in his definitive 2004 history of the neighborhood, *The Devil's Playground: A Century of Pleasure and Profit in Times Square.*

Unfortunately, the "Broadway folklorist," as Traub described Liebling, apparently knew *gornisht* (less than nothing) about the special language of his people.

In the story "Tummler," Liebling began by grossly misinterpreting the standard Yiddish word *tummler.* In the 1930s, Liebling liked to write about a Broadway cigar shop owned and presided over by Izzy Yereshevsky, and largely populated by Jewish Damon Runyon characters not too far removed from disembarking from Ellis Island's docks.

"To the boys of the I. & Y. [Izzy's store], Hymie Katz is a hero," Liebling begins his nonfiction report. " 'Hymie is a *tummler,*' " the boys as the I. & Y. say. " 'Hymie is a man what knows to get a dollar.' "

Yiddish sentence construction for sure. Unfortunately, *tummler* has nothing to do with being "a man what knows to get a dollar." According to Rosten and Bush in the updated *New Joys of Yiddish,* a *tummler* is "one who creates a lot of noise but accomplishes little."

Other definitions, delineate the duo, are "the 'life of the party,' " and of course there is the *tummler* at old-time Catskill Borsht Belt resorts—a " 'hilarity organizer,' " whose "guiding principle is 'Have Fun!' " (*Tummlers* who served their time as young entertainers in the Jewish resorts include Danny Kaye, Jackie Mason, Sid Caesar, Shelly Winters, Buddy Hackett, and Tony Curtis.)

Poor Liebling, to the Jewish manner born, with no Jewish learning. Poor ignorant Liebling, such a brilliant writer, proved ignorant of Yiddish again in his classic work, *The Jollity Building,* in which he defined *bupkes* as "a Yiddish word which means 'large beans.' "

According to Rosten and Bush:

"'Bubkes!' is not used to designate beans (belblakh does that) but to describe [something] with considerable scorn. Bubkes must be uttered with sarcasm, indignation, or contempt. The expletive takes over where 'Nonsense!' 'Baloney,' or 'Bushwa!' stops for a rest."

Liebling, a gourmand, didn't know that belbakh would give him gas; while bubkes is what your lying, no-goodnik of a brother-in-law paid back after you lent him one hundred dollars.

Gentile snobbery, if not the anti-Semitism, remains. Gay Talese, speaking to the New York Times, declared, "On the West Side . . . the men, though carrying books you may want to read, are all in need of dental work. . . . [the doormen are] wearing Yankee jackets and listening to the baseball game while double-parking cars in front of lobbies where the paint is flaking and there is a playpen full of kids running wild."

The West Side German Jews may have been vexed by their inability to crack the true power elite, but they busied themselves setting up their own social hierarchy. "Our Crowd" may have been exclusively Jewish, but they were not shy about enforcing their own gentleman's agreement about not mixing with anyone bearing a hint of a Yiddish accent.

Take Mrs. Phillip J. Goodhart, née Lehman, a doyenne of German-Jewish society in the 1930s. She was a doyenne not just because her brother Herbert was New York's chief executive and a "pally," as per Dean Martin, of President Roosevelt. When Governor Lehman was still in diapers, the family already bore one of the most prestigious names among the prestige-mad community of German Jews.

"Goodhart" was a "good" name, though it had nothing to do with the Yiddish notion of earning a *guten nomen* by humbly performing good deeds. Rather, "Goodhart" was an Upper West

Side Jewish badge that allowed its holder to join the Schiffs, Kahns, Warburgs, Goldmans, Loebs, and even Lehmans.

Ward McAllister, who helped concoct Mrs. Astor's infamous all-Christian list of four hundred people "who mattered," had the notion that "our good Jews" come up with a list for themselves. The "good Jews" didn't need a list: They knew who they were, and none of them bore an Eastern European accent, or surname ending in "sky."

Mrs. Goodhart tried to soft-pedal her disdain for mixing with the déclassé Jews who spoke Yiddish. She divided her world into "people we wouldn't visit" and "people we visit."

If a Jew she didn't know was mentioned, she would ask, "Is it someone we would visit?" And if one of her kin was courting or being courted, Mrs. Goodhart would query, for an example, that "there are some Cohens in Baltimore. We visit them. Are you one of them?"

Of course, even though they were all allegedly from the same tribe, Yiddish speakers were *not* people Mrs. Goodhart would ever even dream to visit.

THE WHOLE *MISHEGASS* of Jews pretending they were aristocrats began in earnest in eighteenth-century Germany. With the Enlightenment providing the cover of social and intellectual modernity, even the most obvious Jews began to take vicious aim at their own people's manners, habits, and traditions.

Theirs was the apostasy of such urbane German sophisticates as the poet Heinrich Heine, who converted to Christianity because he didn't feel his Judaism was a religion, people, or culture—but an "accursed affliction."

Even more troubling, however, was the fact that the German Jews who struck most maliciously at the heart of their religious community were those who ostensibly spoke on its *behalf.* Berlin's official rabbinate damned Yiddish as the malignant *Judendialekt*—the "Jews' dialect." In 1778, they called for the outright suppression of the *mamme-loshn.*

"This was not a campaign against singing, writing, or reading in Yiddish but against what the [Jewish] Berliners considered a subhuman, degrading jargon," wrote Dovid Katz. Yiddish, "a language that had been around for many centuries, in which hundreds of books were published, was suddenly being recast as a non-language."

The German rabbis were not alone in their attempts to stamp out the language that had been one of the most critical components of Jewish survival during the Diaspora. The German-Jewish philosopher Moses Mendelssohn (1729–1786) believed that "Yiddish was an archenemy of the people, period. He had to debunk and humiliate the language and those who spoke it."

Mendelssohn converted to Christianity, less as an act of faith than as a social lubricant into German high society. Strict and didactic, he believed belittling Yiddish speakers was one tool to help Jews "overcome their handicap."

In a sentence that would forever overshadow Mendelssohn's greatest works, he wrote, "This jargon has contributed much to the immorality of common Jews."

One of Mendelssohn's most zealous protégés was David Friedlander (1750–1834), best known for his *Epistle to the German Jews.* That 1788 screed clanked linguistically as Friedlander attempted to show his fellow Jews the correct path by writing to them in German, using Yiddish script.

Calling the *mamme-loshn* "Judeo-German," Friedlander declared:

Once the child is stuck into the so-called Judeo-German language he cannot have any correct conception of a single thing in this world. How can he be expected to act later on in accordance with any proper principles of behavior?

DURING THE GENERATIONS on either side of 1900, American Jews of German extraction did more than belittle Yiddish and their ignorant, unwashed brethren from Eastern Europe who spoke it. They also promoted the newfangled "Reform" branch of Judaism that had been hatched in their ancestral country with the goal of emancipating Jews from the ancient rites and superstitions that had historically brought the wrath down of both polite and/or uncivilized Christian society.

These were among the first Jews who unabashedly ate nice hams and erected Christmas trees in their living rooms. In America, on occasions when Reform Jews prayed, it was in English, with men *sans* skullcaps sitting next to women (blasphemy to Orthodox Jews). Synagogues were to be called "temples," and were constructed to resemble the most lavishly ornate churches.

Reform Jewish Germans in New York purposely made themselves a lighthouse in 1870 when they built the munificent Temple Emanu-El, perhaps the largest synagogue in the world. The *New York Times*, owned by German Jews, immediately praised it as one of the grandest wonders of modern religion.

The temple, said the *Times*, was "the first to stand forward before the world and proclaim the dominion of reason over blind and bigoted faith."

They were words that would have sent spasms of horror through the overwhelmingly religious and Yiddish-speaking

Lower East Side—if only many in that Jewish community had then been able to read English. It got worse.

The temple, the *Times* wrote, would unite via reason the "universal communion" of mankind by honoring "the Judaism of the heart, the Judaism which proclaims the spirit of religion as being of more importance than the letter."

Then, in 1873, Temple Emanu-El invited Gustav Gottheil from Manchester, England, to guest-speak about this new kind of Judaism. He also received a rave review, especially since he spoke "in impeccable English accents, comprehensible to all New Yorkers."

Who, and what language, were they *not* referring to?

ALMOST A CENTURY later, professional Jewish comics who'd grown up in more traditional settings than a Reform temple were still being greeted with howls of approval from audiences for their pokes at the new form of Judaism.

Not even Lenny Bruce, the high priest of apostasism, could resist. In one of his routines, he declared:

Come Saturday, they would make every kind of *shul* a drive-in Frank Lloyd Wright [temple.] They would put statues in:
"Are you putting a *madonna* in the *shul?*"
"Yes, it's contemporary, that's all."

Bruce continued:

Reform rabbi[s.] So reformed they're ashamed that they're Jewish. Rabbis that had this kind of sound: "*Heyyy, mein Liebe, heyyyyy. . . .*"

And now these rabbis have turned into doctors of law and all have this sound:

REFORM RABBI [clipped, hearty, good-fellow British articulation]: Ha ha! This Sabbath we discuss Is-roy-el. Where is Is-roy-el? Quench yon flaming *yortsite* candle! Alas, poor Yossel . . . Deah deah deah! Today, on Chin-ukka, with Rose-o-shonah approaching, do you know, some had the chutz-pah to ask me, "Tell me something, doctor of law, is there a God, or not?" What cheek! To ask this in a temple! We're not here to talk of God—we're here to sell bonds for Israel! Remember that! A pox upon you, Christ and Moses! Go among them and kiss their empty *mezuzahs.*

JEW: Rabbi, that was a beautiful speech!

RABBI [Jewish accent]: Danksalot! Ya like dot? Vat de hell, tosset oof de top mine head, dot's all. *Und tsi gurnisht.* ("And it wasn't anything.")

So Moses is depressed. The *shuls* are gone. No more *shuls.* He breaks open a *mezuzah*—nothing inside!

"*GEVALT!*"

But a piece of paper that says:

"Made in Japan."

EVEN THE PROUD atheist Woody Allen included a bit about the German-Jewish religious movement in his 1960s stage act, de-claring that his rabbi was so Reform he was a Nazi.

Over the last couple of decades, the Reform movement has

become more and more traditional. A truly progressive strain of social action has entered the movement, along with its new emphasis on ritual. Today a Reform rabbi may be man or woman, gay or straight. Now, children learning their Bar or Bat Mitzvahs at most Reform synagogues must be able to read Hebrew, and chant Torah and Haftorah portions longer than those sometimes demanded by Conservative synagogues.

Both men and women in the congregation may choose whether or not to wear *yarmulkes*: In the newer Reform synagogues about 50 percent do. And the symbolic ritual of the Bar or Bat Mitzvah child reaching adulthood? In a move that would make the founders of Temple Emanu-El gag—a *tallis*, a prayer shawl, that most unthinkable of old-world garments, is draped over a child's shoulders, to be kept for a lifetime of observing ritual and progressive thinking.

THE MOST EXTREME form of self-hatred—pretending one wasn't even Jewish—became in itself a piece of farcical American Yiddishkeit. In the United States, attempts to completely plow over one's Jewish roots weren't akin to the faux self-abnegation of the medieval Jewish *marranos* of Spain and Portugal.

They'd kept their fingers and toes crossed as they pretended to convert to Catholicism, in often vain attempts to avoid the Inquisitors' torch. *That* kind of covering up of *who* you were at least was in the service of keeping *what* you were—alive, as an underground Jew.

But in modern America, simulating a Gentile provided the kind of cognitive dissonance and self-delusion of Joshua Abraham Norton, an English-born Jew who proclaimed himself Norton I, Emperor of the United States, in 1859. For twenty years, the

San Francisco eccentric was granted an official uniform, title, and observation post and chair at the California State Senate. Norton's delusions were harmless psychopathology.

In Yiddishkeit lore, tales are often told in amusingly bitter-sweet fashion of noninsane Jews who think they can hide their Jewishness in plain sight. They are the kind of stories of self-denial that went on so spectacularly in families like that of Katherine Graham, née Meyer.

The parents of the late publisher of the *Washington Post* never explained why she wasn't ever invited to Gentile friends' homes. And long before Mrs. Graham became the crusading Jewish queen mother of the Watergate scandal, she was married off, in a church, as an Episcopalian.

To her credit, she looked back at her peculiar upbringing with a grace and humor made all the more charming by her George Plimpton-esque enunciation of the English language. There were tragedies in other familes, to be sure: John Kerry knew his father's father, Fritz, had committed suicide in 1921. His paternal grandmother was also Jewish. But the senator wasn't aware until told by a *Boston Globe* reporter that Grandfather Kerry was, in fact, his *Zeyde* Kohn, and that he'd changed the family name and religion before shooting himself in a Boston hotel. (Kerry's paternal grandmother was also Jewish.)

Almost as tragic a tale of Yiddishkeit self-denial is that of "Duke" Wolff. In the 1970s, his son Geoffrey published *The Duke of Deception*, a magical and tragic memoir of his deeply flawed, yet loving father—a professional con man so on the run from reality that not only did he never admit he was Jewish, he espoused a brutal form of anti-Semitism.

Though the Meyers, Kohns, and Wolffs were all Jews descended from Germans, more recently arrived Eastern Europeans also got into the act.

Literally.

Well before Emma Lazarus wrote her poem on the Statue of Liberty about the wretched immigrant refuse yearning to breathe free, there have been a bevy of jokes among American Jews about fellow *yidn* who got off the boat at Ellis Island—and then tried to pass themselves off as highbrows whose ancestors were on the *Mayflower*.

The joke made it all the way into the movies. In the Marx Brothers film *Animal Crackers*, Chico *shnorrs* his way into the mansion of grande dame Margaret Dumont, where he recognizes one of the invited high society guests. The visitor Chico identifies *isn't* who he claims to be: Roscoe W. Chandler, a highbrow international art expert who speaks with a baronial European accent.

In truth, he is Abe Kabibble, not long before a Yiddish-speaking Lower East Side fish peddler who'd emigrated from Czechoslovakia. Kabibble refuses to acknowledge that he isn't Roscoe W. Chandler until Chico, as usual playing an Italian ne'er-do-well, begins loudly singing, "Abie, the fishman! Abie, the fishman!"

Exposed, Kabibble shushes Chico before any of the other guests hear:

ROSCOE W. CHANDLER [sotto voce]: I confess, I *was* Abie the fishman from Czechoslovakia.

CHICO [as Ravelli]: How did you get to be Roscoe W. Chandler?

ROSCOE W. CHANDLER: Say, how did you get to be an Italian?

CHICO: Never mind that, whose confession is this?

Perhaps the most popular such joke among Jews involves an aristocratic man wearing pince-nez glasses, a custom-made suit from London, a walrus mustache, and a diamond stickpin. He gets out of the backseat of a limousine on the Lower East Side and starts looking at the sights as if he's a curious slummer. Suddenly, he is accosted by a butcher wearing a blood-splattered apron.

"Hey, I know you!" the butcher exclaims loudly in a deep, Yiddish-inflected accent. "You're Moishe the pickle vendor!"

"My good man," the baron says, looking around to see if anybody is watching, "I am C. D. Rivington, the great industrialist!"

"Hey, Moish," says the butcher, "whatcha doing in the old neighborhood? We haven't seen you in a few years."

"Sir, I am no such person. I am C. D. Rivington."

"Moish," the butcher goes on, undeterred, "I understand how you picked your last name: You grew up right here on Rivington Street. But what's 'C. D.' stand for?"

The faux aristocrat once again warily looks around for witnesses, then whispers the name of the cross street of his childhood in a deep Yiddish accent of his own.

"Corner Delancy."

THE JOKES CONTINUE into more modern times. Lenny Bruce showed the dichotomy between the old-world generation longing for a better life for their children, and their new-world children wishing their parents would just go away.

"Now we take you a young boy who's returning home from Fort Loeb. But first we dissolve to the interior of the home, on Second Avenue."

JEWISH MOTHER: Vell, jus' tink. Soon, he'll be home. Our boy's comink home from military school. I

saved every penny vot ve had to bring him der
success dot der outside vorld vud neffer gif him.
Ah, soon our boy vill be home, from overseas in
Delaware.

"Now dissolve to the kid, on the steps, going through the
trauma of going home."

> KID [Ivy League voice]: I don't wanna be there with
> those [kikes]. I don't wanna look at them any-
> more, with their onion-roll breaths. I found some-
> thing new at Fort Loeb, and a girl who doesn't
> know anything about the Lower East Side.

> KID: Hello, Mom.
> MOM [OVERPOWERINGLY]: *Hello, dolling!*
> KID: Aaagghhh!
> MOM: What's da matta vit chew?
> KID: Nothing, Mother. I'm just so excited about see-
> ing Bellevue [*sic: Bubbe*] and Zeder [*sic: Zeyde*], I
> just don't know how to say . . .
> MOM: Awright, you'll siddown, you'll have some
> soup get into.
> KID: Bronx [sheenie]! Aaggghh! [briskly]. Well,
> Taddy, I have to run back now to school and I
> hope that you and your people . . .

Or:

It's weird. I met a guy the other night. I want to relax him.
He was very La Boheme, he had the [beatnik] beard, you

know. So I used talk in a hip idiom, so I started talking. I said, "What's shaking, man?" And he started talking Jewish [Yiddish]! He was a rabbi! Said, *"gurnisht* (nothing) health!" and he gave me a couple [illegal] pills.

Yet even Bruce copped to the fact that he had suffered from the mere self-loathing he'd internalized in order to gain the acceptance of the *goyim*, just as much as C. D. Rivington, Abe Kabbible, and Duke Wolff. What had changed his mind to be able to 'fess up to mixed audiences and announce his Jewish self-loathing say his real last name, a respectable name, a last name given tailors in the old country.

"Louis. That's my name. In Yiddish [it's] Lepke."
    "Why haven't you got 'Louis Schneider' [people ask] up on the marquee?"
    "Well, 'cause it's not show business. It doesn't fit."
    "No, no, I don't wanna hear that. You Jewish?"
    "Yeah."
    "You ashamed of it?"
    "Yeah."
    "Why are you ashamed you're Jewish?"
    "I'm not married anymore! But it used to be a problem. Until *Playboy* magazine came out with their [IN-OUT] list."
    "Yeah. That's right. IN-OUT. You just can't be that urbane bachelor [*Playboy* caters to] and drive down the street driving a Jag or a Lotus yelling 'nigger' and 'kike.' It don't fit. That's what really happened."

CHAPTER 13

שׁאבּאדיקﬠﬥﬨﬧﬠﬥﬠﬢﬡ

Coming to America II:
The Rest of Us

L ife was anything but *shtick* for most of the impoverished Yiddish-speaking Jews, mostly stuffed into downtown New York's thirty thousand "dumbbell" tenements. There, almost a million people were squished into a square acre of blocks on the Lower East Side.

The hovels, thrown up beginning in 1879 by real estate speculators, "were six or seven-story structures pinched in the middle to create airshafts. Four apartments occupied each floor of the building, light and air entering directly into only one room of each flat."

Elevators were unheard of; mothers dropped lunches and schoolbooks via a long rope to their kids in the street. Sanitation was a horror; privacy didn't exist, long lines gathering outside of the one bathroom per floor—"or in the worst of the tenements, in the lot behind the building. Baths didn't exist at all."

It was a density higher than Bombay or Hong Kong. The *New York Times* called the tenements, "the filthiest places in the western continent."

In 1908, George Price investigated the Lower East Side. His account was especially appalling because it was true:

"These buildings in which the Jews live were crowded, damp, without elementary sanitary facilities, half in ruins. The flats were dark, dank, emitting an unbearable stench, particularly those flats which also served as shops. The inhabitants were in a poor state of health. Children died like flies during frequent epidemics. Parents were forced to have their children help in tobacco or tailoring work or else send them—at the age of six or seven—to work in a shop, which meant physical, psychological, and moral deterioration. . . . Not infrequently, we came across buildings housing one hundred families with eight persons (800 people)."

"You couldn't get to love a tenement flat," wrote Maurice Hindus. "It was not a home." Perhaps the only positive to emerge from these horror chambers was a new infusion of Yiddish words borrowed directly from English: "next doorke," "downstairske," "oppstairske," and "lendler," the man who came in person to collect his rents of nine or ten dollars a month.

Despair was a common denominator. And the most extreme reactions to this new-world kind of suffering was not unusual, all the way up to suicide.

In the mid-1970s, the late Kenneth Tynan was researching his classic profile of Mel Brooks for the *New Yorker*. Considering his subject's upbringing, he wrote about Brooks—inventor and player of the Yiddish-speaking Indian chief in *Blazing Saddles*—that "to be Jewish, Brooklyn-born, fatherless, impoverished, and below average stature—no more classic recipe could be imagined for an American comedian. Or, one might suppose, for an American suicide."

Brooks concurred. Memories of those tenements he'd grown

up in had never stopped haunting. Even when he was a highly paid comedy writer in the 1950s on Sid Caesar's *Your Show of Shows*, Brooks said, "There were fourteen or fifteen occasions when I seriously thought of killing myself. I even had the pills."

Colleagues on the show recall when he snapped out of a suicidal depression in the writers' room by grabbing a straw hat and cane and manically ad-libbing an upbeat song-and-dance number that concluded with:

> *Life may be rotten today, folks,*
> *But I take it all in stride.*
> *'Cause tomorrow I'm on my way, folks—*
> *I'm committing suicide!*

Tynan later recalled Brooks's suicidal ideation to a wealthy Jewish movie producer who pooh-poohed the notion. "Nonsense, that's self-dramatization," remarked the producer. "Jews don't kill themselves. Look at their history. They're too busy fighting to survive."

Brooks was appalled when Tynan told him of the conversation.

"You were talking to a rich Jew. Poor people kill themselves, and a lot of poor people are Jews. One evening, when I was a kid, a woman jumped off the top of a building next door to where I lived. She was Jewish. And there were plenty of other Jewish suicides during the Depression."

Another image melted into his consciousness came from when he was playing in the street a few blocks from home. Brooks heard ambulance and police sirens wailing, and Edvard Munch–style screams amplified to life. Running to see what the commotion was, he saw a corpse being loaded into an ambulance, and was told that a Jewish mother had killed herself by taking the gas pipe.

Only the decedent's shoes were visible poking out from under the sheet, and Brooks swore he knew them as his mother's. He ran home to an empty apartment, not knowing that she'd taken an extra shift at her job in Manhattan. He waited alone for hours until she returned home, and he at last knew she wasn't dead. They were the most scarring hours, he said, of a life born of the Jewish ghetto.

SIMILAR JEWISH GHETTOS, of course, weren't *sui generis* to New York. There was Chicago's Jewish main drag, which Ira Berkow captured perfectly in just the title of his grandly evocative 1977 book, *Maxwell Street: Survival in a Bazaar.*

Jewish immigrants were the primary tenants of Maxwell Street between 1880 and 1920. By 1900, Jews comprised 90 percent of Maxwell Street's population. As Irving Cutler wrote in *The Jews of Chicago: From Shtetl to Suburb* (1996)

> [Maxwell Street] housed kosher meat markets and chicken stores, matzo bakeries, tailor and seamstress shops, bathhouse and peddlers' stables. Its rich and varied religious and cultural life included synagogues, Hebrew schools, literary organizations, Yiddish newspapers, and Yiddish theaters.

Ira Berkow includes a list of Jews who rose to prominence from Maxwell Street, many of whom got their first job on its avenues. Off those Jewish street corners came a panoply of personalities ranging from Admiral Hyman Rickover to Jack Ruby (né Jacob Rubinstein); CBS founder William Paley to heavyweight boxing chump Kingfish Levinsky; Supreme Court Justice Arthur Goldberg to Jake "Greasy Thumb" Guzik, Al Capone's money man; Benny Goodman to Paramount Pictures president Barney Balaban; and boxing champions Jackie Fields, né Jacob Finkelstein, and Barney Ross, né Beryl Rosofsky.

The Maxwell Street Jews were a tightly knit group: Barney Ross's mentor was Jackie Fields, and Ross stayed close friends with Jack Ruby his entire life, talking with Jack on the phone until virtually the day Ruby killed Lee Harvey Oswald. Ross was happy to oblige the Warren Commission, and serve, virtually alone, as a witness testifying to Ruby's positive character.

Montreal, meantime, became one of the leading Jewish centers in North America; it is recalled with black, loving humor in the late, great Mordecai Richler's novels (among the most memorable are *The Apprenticeship of Duddy Kravitz, St. Urbain's Horseman,* and *Solomon Gursky Was Here*). Most of the novels were set in or near St. Urbain, the avenue that served as Montreal's equivalent to New York's Delancey or Chicago's Maxwell streets.

Montreal also had one of the great Yiddish newspapers, the *Keneder Odler,* Canada's *Forum.* In Washington, the Seattle Hebrew Free Loan Society was concurrently faux-"lending" money to both middle-class and poverty-stricken Jews unable to gain loans from the anti-Semitic banking industry. The Seattle group was founded by a women's sewing circle; their society was called a *landsmanshaft,* and provided mutual support for *lantzmen.*

In 1948, sociologist Carey McWilliams, also the editor of *The Nation,* wrote that Minneapolis was "the capital of anti-Semitism in the United States." With nowhere else to turn for help but themselves, the Jewish community there stuck together to create one of the most successful *landsmanshaftn* and burial societies in

America. Meantime, in Philadelphia, the Shefa Fund still oper-
ates as an umbrella organization serving to gather together family foundations, synagogues, and Jewish federations.

Landsmanshaftn were a staple of almost all cities with more
than a dollop of Jews. From 1877 to 1879, the Union of American
Hebrew Congregations held the first census of American Jews;
they discovered that every state and new territory but Okla-
homa could claim Jewish residents.

Yet no matter where these mostly Eastern European Jews
eventually ended up, a huge proportion began their American
lives near New York's Statue of Liberty. Moses Rischin provided
a dazzling description of what those Jews had gone through to
get here. Wrote Rischin:

> These immigrants packed their few household belongings,
> pots and pans, samovars, pillows and bedding, much of
> which would be lost or pilfered on the way, and forsook
> their native towns and villages to embark on the greatest
> journey of their lives. They parted with loved ones, seem-
> ing forever, and made their way by foot, coach, and train to
> the bewildering port cities of Western Europe.
>
> There they sailed direct from Hamburg or Bremen at a
> cost of thirty-four dollars, some for a saving of nine dollars
> traveling by way of Liverpool. Crammed into steerage for
> as long as three weeks, Jewish immigrants were confined
> to herring, black bread, and tea by their loyalty to dietary
> laws, until the water journey's end.
>
> It was "a kind of hell that cleanses a man of his sins
> before coming to Columbus' island," insisted a popular
> immigrant guidebook that attempted to minimize the tor-
> ments of the voyage. Whatever the spiritually therapeutic

values of that epic crossing, few immigrants would ever
forget its terrors.

THE MOST CRUSADING non-Jew who poked his nose into the
horror was Jacob Riis (1849–1914), the famous muckraking journalist and crusader supreme.

Riis's *How the Other Half Lives* was a major *mechaye*, a blessing, for the Jews, as well as a critical, popular, and society-
shaking success. In the wake of his investigations, there came
actual change within the hideous housing where almost all of
the impoverished Jews who emigrated from Eastern Europe
between 1880 and 1920 lived. To call Riis's work a tour de force
is to minimize its ultimate effect.

In his book, Riis wrote:

THE HOME—A WORKSHOP

The homes of the Hebrew quarter are its workshops
also. . . . You are made fully aware of it before you have
traveled the length of a single block in any of these Eastside
streets, by the whir of a thousand sewing machines, worked
at high pressure from earliest dawn till mind and muscle
give out together. Every member of the family, from the
youngest to the oldest, bears a hand, shut in the qualmy
rooms, where meals are cooked and clothing washed and
dried beside, the livelong day. It is not unusual to find a
dozen persons—men, women, and children—at work in a
single small room.

When in the midnight hour, the noise of the sewing-
machine was stilled at last, I have gone the rounds of Ludlow and Hester and Essex Streets among the poorest of the

Russian Jews, with the sanitary police, and counted four, five, and even six of the little ones in a single bed, sometimes a shake-down on the hard floor, often a pile of half-finished clothing brought home from the sweaters [sweatshops] in the stuffy rooms of their tenements.

In one I visited very lately, the only bed was occupied by the entire family lying lengthwise and crosswise, literally in layers, three children at the feet, all except a boy of ten or twelve, for whom there was no room. He slept with clothes on to keep him warm, in a pile of rags just inside the door. It seemed too impossible that families of children could be raised at all in such dens as I had my daily and nightly walks in. . . . And yet the vital statistics and all close observation agree in allotting to these Jews even an unusual degree of good health. The records of the Sanitary Bureau show that while the Italians have the highest death rate, the mortality in the lower part of the Tenth Ward of which Ludlow Street is the heart [where the Jews live] is the lowest in the city. Even the baby death rate is very low.

But for the fact that the ravages of diphtheria, croup, and measles run up the record in the house occupied entirely by tailors—in other words, in sweater district, where contagion always runs riot—the Tenth Ward would seem to be the healthiest spot in the city, as well as the dirtiest and the most crowded.

The temperate habits of the Jew and his freedom from enfeebling vices generally must account for this, along with his marvelous vitality. I cannot now recall ever having known a Jewish drunkard. On the other hand, I have never come across a Prohibitionist among them. The absence of the one renders the other superfluous.

MORALS AND FAMILY LIFE

Whatever the effect upon the physical health of the children, it cannot be otherwise, of course, than that such conditions should corrupt their morals. I have the authority of a distinguished rabbi, whose field and daily walk are among the poorest of his people, to support me in the statement that the moral tone of the young girls is distinctly lower than it was.

The entire absence of privacy in their homes and the foul contact of the sweaters shops, where men and women work side by side from morning till night, scarcely half-clad in the hot summer weather, does for the girls what the street completes in the boy.

But for the patriarchal family life of the Jew that is his strongest virtue, their ruin would have long since been complete . . . and on the Sabbath eve when he gathers his household about his board, scant though the fare be, dignifies the darkest slum of Jewtown.

In America, the new *Goldene Medina*, the golden land, Yiddish once again became the street and marketplace patois. Even the scores of Jewish prostitutes lounging on the steps of Hester Street walk-ups would entice customers by offering, in Yiddish, wares to be dispensed in alleys and tenement rooftops.

The watchful pimps spoke Yiddish, as did the *balebostes*, (housewives), trying to get to the kosher butcher hours before Friday dusk, so as to have enough time to cook a spindly chicken for *Shabbos* dinner that night. Religious Jews had a *Shabbos goy* come over to light the stove because they refused to turn on a light or rip a piece of grass on the Jewish Sabbath.

These observant Jews were *shomer Shabbos*, literally "guardians" of the Sabbath. A guardian's dictates are outlined in the Coen brothers' film, *The Big Lebowski*. In *Lebowski*, John Goodman plays Walter Sobchack, a profane Orthodox Jew with a profound case of post-tramautic stress syndrome from his years spent fighting the Viet Cong under canopy jungle.

Trying to describe to his kegling buddies, Jeff Bridges and Steve Buscemi, why he can't bowl on the Sabbath, he explains, "I'm *shomer Shabbos*. That means I can't drive, ride in a car, turn on the stove, talk on the telephone, handle money—and I sure as SHIT don't roll! *Shomer* fucking *Shabbos!*"

Wedged into their own well-defined and defended neighborhoods, both observant and apostate Jews bonded tighter together in kinship and friendship circles than any other immigrant minorities. In America, the old country *shtetl* had morphed into the corner of Delancey and Rivington.

The crushing poverty, anonymous existences, and almost pathetic devotion to culture endemic in the Jewish ghetto were movingly presented in "Wedding Presents," by B. Kovner, a short story reminiscent of a Yiddish O. Henry tale. It was originally published in the *Forverts,* where at the time of publication he'd already ground out ten thousand daily columns.

"Wedding Presents" was translated into English and gathered in a compendium of his work, the oddly named *Laugh, Jew, Laugh* (1936). Kovner's tale is of a spiritually broken, nameless young man and woman, both destitute *greeners* with tuberculosis and no English, who save their pennies to sate their hungers for all the political and cultural news presented in American Yiddish newspapers.

The story starts:

Both he and she were working [making] ladies' waists [coats] for the same boss and in the same [sweat] shop.

One day he said to her: "Since we are both sick, poor, and lonely we ought to get married."

"Then what?" she asked.

"Then it will be better for the both of us," he replied. "You'll go to work and I'll go to work and we will manage somehow to make a living."

"But we are sick," she said coughing the while.

"For this very reason we should be married. Even to be sick it is better when two are together. When you'll be confined to bed I'll tend to you, and when I'll be too sick to go to work, you'll be my nurse."

To marry and rent a tenement apartment bearing only a bedroom and kitchen, he hocked his watch and chain and borrowed "a five spot" from his cousin Benny for a marriage license and a one-dollar wedding ring. They planned a three-dollar wedding. There would be no money left over for furniture.

He said, coughing with a squeak, "We'll get that in presents. We will invite the people of our shop to the wedding. One will send us a table, another one chairs, a third one a bed, a fourth one a rug."

Meanwhile they slept on the bare floor upon Yiddish newspapers . . . [and] covered themselves, she with a native shawl that her mother had sent her from the other side with a landsman, and he with his old [world] overcoat.

Instead of furnishings, they received for wedding presents from their equally poor co-workers an ancient, used pair of opera glasses; a two-volume set of Karl Marx's *Das Kapital*; photographs of Eddie Cantor and Charlie Chaplin; and a small plaster figurine of Venus de Milo, the goddess of Love. The new husband said Venus had no hands because she had lived in a world "without bosses and factories, therefore 'hands' are not necessary."

The newlyweds remained without furniture, and the story ends with them still sleeping on a bare floor covered with downtown ghetto Yiddish newspapers instead of rugs. At night in the unheated tenement, "she [still slept] with her native shawl and he with the old overcoat having thrust his feet in the sleeves to keep him warm."

FOR THOSE MORE adaptable to the United States, Yiddish provided an answer to explain the pitched battles between street-corner hustlers vying for a better sidewalk to park their sidecars or peddle newspapers.

Handlschaft iz nit keyn brudershaft.
"Livelihood isn't brotherhood."

And scholarship often had to take a second place to the hunger pangs accompanying trying to *macht a leben.*

Mit khokhme aleyn geyt men nit in mark.
"With wisdom alone you don't go to market."

AMONG THE MOST humiliated in the American Jewish ghetto were the *melamdim* (elementary-school teachers) of the *cheders* (Hebrew schools). The *melamdim* were most often old men who hated everything about the new world, and started teaching American ghetto kids, whom they also usually despised, as a means to make a bare living.

"Thousands of pupils," wrote Irving Howe, "would remember the *melamed* with a cordial hatred."

★ ★ ★

IRONICALLY, OR PERHAPS not, were what both Jewish gangsters and their civilian brethren long meant when later in life they referred to prison as *cheder*, as in "he's away at *cheder*."

There is an interesting parallel here in Jewish education among youngsters between (1) early-twentieth-century *melamdim* terrorizing their American charges with rulers banged against the children's wrists during their hideously boring Bar Mitzvah lessons, and (2) modern Jewish children's acting like juvenile delinquents toward teachers at Talmud Torah, which has long been dubbed "Talmud Torture" by kids who are so often A students in their secular, "regular" schools.

In the old days, many *melamdim* were

> earnest, medieval men, zealously trying to impart unwished-for-knowledge to unwilling youngsters. . . . [Others] are ignorant men who spend their morning in peddling wares and evenings . . . selling the little Jewish knowledge they have to American children. . . . The usual procedure is for a group of boys to gather in the home of the self-appointed "Rabbi," and to wait their turn or "next." While one pupil drawls meaninglessly the Hebrew words of the prayer book, the rest play or fight.

Menachem Dolitsky, the Hebrew poet, once looked back with irreverence at his own time as a *melamed*:

> A Jew rents a room, hangs up a sign reading, "Expert Teacher, Alphabet, Bar Mitzvah"—and he's in business as teacher. He doesn't make enough out of just teaching, so he takes on a few sidelines . . . and he puts on his sign: "Expert Mohel [ritual circumciser], Expert Marriage Performer, Ex-

pert Matchmaker, Expert Evil-Eye Exorciser, Expert Hem-
orrhoid Remover," etc.

ONE OF THE more unusual oral chroniclers of what life in the
Jewish ghetto felt and smelled like was Maxie Shapiro, a light-
weight professional boxing contender whose father had come to
the United States from Poland in 1910. Even in Shapiro's unstudied
ways of describing horror and happiness, he sensed the spirit and
reality of the street better than most of the muckraking reporters.

"I was born on the Lower East Side," he remembered at age
seventy, during an interview in 1977:

> That's lower Manhattan, We used to call it "the ghetto" at
> that time. A ghetto is a gathering of, well, not the wealthy
> people. The more financially well-to-do went to Browns-
> ville, a pretty classy section in East New York. By Sutter
> Avenue. Had an aunt that lived there. Went to visit her and
> we thought she was wealthy because she had a downstairs
> bell and a backyard. And in buildings [where we lived], the
> housing there was not what it is today. You know it had
> bathrooms in the hallways, no showers, no steam heat and
> we used a coal stove to keep warm. And there was gaslight
> and stuff like that.
>
> I never went to Hebrew school, but we had a rabbi who
> lived in the tenement right in the neighborhood. After our
> Bar Mitzvah you quit going to synagogue, har har. My fa-
> ther wasn't too pious. Mother would go to represent the
> family in the synagogue. My father and me only [went] to
> synagogue on the High Holidays, [but] she kept a kosher
> house. That was a must at that time.

And of course there was no eating on Yom Kippur. I used to run to the Automat with some of the guys, on Fourteenth Street on Yom Kippur and eat. I wasn't too good at following the rules.

Shapiro went on to describe the children of his neighborhood:

There was a junior high school a block away from where we lived on the Lower East Side. It was called Seward, and it was on Hester and Ludlow streets.

All my friends were Jewish. At that time *everybody* was Jewish. Even my teachers were Jewish—I had David Cohen, Irving Cohen. It was strange to see the one Italian kid in the class. All these years later I can still remember his name, "Calvado."

Every neighborhood was a section. The Lower East Side where I lived was Jewish people, and a few blocks away there was a boundary line, the Bowery. The Italian neighborhood, Mulberry Street. So we never went there and they never came over to us. Everybody stayed in his own backyard.

The Chinese were right where they are today. In Chinatown. Didn't see any Irish. They were right down by the East River. They had a section there, McAllen Park. The Polish were also in a different section, about a mile away. Avenue A and Tenth Street.

You could sleep in the park, you could sleep on the roof. There was no fear like today that you had to worry about anybody grabbing your pocketbook or people being mugged. No one had nothing. But that was nothing. They had their safety and their peace of mind. In that way it was easy living at that time.

★ ★ ★

IRVING BERLIN, né Israel Isidor Baline, the immigrant son of a Belarussian rabbi, remembered differently. Berlin, the composer of "White Christmas" who later tried to cover his tracks as a young writer of published Yiddish songs, recalled that any Jew who mistakenly ventured into Irish territory on All Saints Day was, if caught, dragged to the East Side docks, then tossed into the East River.

In *The Time That Was Then*, Harry Roskolenko's autobiography, he described another such foray onto the wrong blocks, as well as the clash of Jewish generations, with the elders appalled at sons who would even dare fight back against their enemies. Once, while walking quickly through the Irish neighborhood trying to get back to his own turf, he'd been trapped while taking a round-about route beneath one of New York's mighty bridges, which unfortunately still lay behind enemy lines. On the way, Roskolenko recalled:

"I'd been roughly [told] I'd killed Christ seventeen different times by [Irish roughnecks], and [I always] found myself about to be bloodied, under the Manhattan Bridge."

"When I came back [home], bloodied, my father, who had no sympathy for my non-newspaper-selling wanderings, would ask, before I got the thunder of his Orthodox dissent:

" 'Was it an Irisher?'

" 'No! I was washing my bloody nose at the sink.'

" 'Ah Poll-yack?'

" 'Maybe . . . I did not have time to ask. They hit, I hit—and then I ran home.'

" 'Did you hit well? With blood, too?'

" 'With blood, too—and teeth.'

" 'Teeth? Another boy's teeth? A *shanda!* [disgrace!]'

"And my father, opening my mouth, still full of teeth, slapped my face, shouting, 'Never the teeth and never the eyes—*smarkatsh* [snotnose].'

"'And a hole in the head?' I asked, having given up crying at his rigid ways. 'Is a hole in the head all right?'

"'Not in your head! Read—don't walk under bridges!'"

YET BOXING BECAME the Jewish sport of choice for "second-generation young men from Eastern European immigrant working-class families." Between 1910 and and 1939, there was only one year in which at least two Jews didn't hold a boxing championship.

One day, a tenement dweller named Ahuva Leiner read right past a Yiddish *Forward* story extolling a Jewish boxer named "Benny Leonard," soon to be the greatest Jewish boxer ever.

Later that day, a large bus pulled up a few feet from the Leiner family's tenement, and she saw it filled with fight fans and banners extolling said Benny Leonard.

"Who's that?" she inquired of a neighbor, in a story recounted later in the *Forward*.

"Your *son!*" said a neighbor proudly.

Before Mrs. Leiner fainted, she asked only, *"Vos tet such du?"* ("What's happening here?") She soon came to, and began yelling a *shanda!* "He's going to disgrace us in front of the neighbors! A prize fighteh! A Jewish boy, a prize fighteh who's ashamed of his own name!" (Leonard had changed his ring name to avoid such a scene.)

When Leonard came home, he was confronted by his father, a tailor who made $10 a week working sixteen-hour days. His father also was yelling what a disgrace his son had become. Leonard then took the $35 he got for the match and gave it to his father.

"Vos is dos?" ("What is this?"), a story in the *Forward* recalled years later. Leonard told his father the money was his payday for this one fight. His father immediately calmed down. "This is what you got for one fight, on one night?" he asked.

He then looked at his son, and said only, "Benny, when are you going to fight again?"

Increasingly, boxing was capturing the attention of an ever-growing trickle, then flood, of first- and second-generation assimilating American Jews. In 2005, David Margolick published an expansively researched, exactingly reported, and trenchantly written book called *Beyond Glory: Joe Louis vs. Max Schmeling and a World on the Brink.* In it, Margolick writes the heretofore unsayable:

> In America, Jews were all over boxing, not just as fighters and fans but as everything in between: promoters, trainers, managers, referees, propagandists, suppliers, chroniclers. No major ethnic group in American history ever so dominated an important sport. The phenomenon is largely forgotten, in part because it was scantily scrutinized at the time. For Gentile writers, the topic may have been too embarrassing. The various strains of Jewish culture at the time—elite German Jewry; secular, socialist eastern European Yiddishists, the religiously observant—all disdained the sport as *"goyishe naches,"* the kind of foolishness Christians enjoyed.

Danks Gott zeinen a goyishe nachas (thank God there is *goyishe nachas*), especially June 22, 1938, when Joe Louis fought Germany's Max Schmeling, the Fuhrer's favorite specimen of Aryan superiority.

"It was Joe versus Hitler Day," wrote communist Michael

Gold, author of one of the true classics of twentieth-century proletarian literature: *Jews Without Money.*

For one night, Louis, an African-American, became much more than an honorary Jew: he was black Moses with a deadly uppercut.

Press credentials were issued to three daily Yiddish papers— the *Forverts, Morn-zhurnal,* and *Der Tog.* At ringside a Brooklyn rabbi sat together with a Baptist minister.

IN ABRAHAM CAHAN'S 1896 collection, *Yekl the Imported Bridegroom and Other Tales of Yiddish New York,* Yekl, der *greener* (greenhorn) finds relief from his sweatshop job—and proof of his Jewish-Americanism—by becoming a boxing fan.

Asked by his friend Jake, the pants presser, if John L. Sullivan "is still heavyweight champion of the world," Yekl shouted:

"'Oh no!'"

Jake responded with what he considered a Yankee jerk of the head.

Yekl responded:

"Why don't you know? Jimmie Corbett *leak*ed him, and Jimmy *leak*ed Chollie Meetchel, too. You can *betch you 'bootsh'!* Johnnie could *leak* Chollie *because* is a big *bluffer,* Chollie is," he pursued, his clean-shaven, florid face beaming with enthusiasm for his subject, and with pride, in the diminutive proper nouns he flaunted.

"But Jimmie punished him, *Oh, didn't he knock him out of shight!* He came near making a meatball of him"—with a chuckle. "He *tzettled* him in three *roynds.*"

Ironically, a slew of eventual Jewish boxing champions learned the Sweet Science at the Educational Alliance, founded by German Jews Isidor Straus and Judge Samuel Greenbaum to bring culture, class, and proper American habits and, hopefully, employment to their Yiddish-speaking brethren. (Jacob Schiff, who'd apparently learned the error of his anti-Semitic ways toward his Eastern European brethren, was also one of the Alliance's founders.)

The official purpose of the Alliance on East Broadway was "Americanization" in this new "Palace of Immigrants." And among the Alliance's offerings, utilized by upward of 37,000 immigrants a week, were classes in etiquette, American history—and physical education, including, unknown to its founders, boxing.

Learning English was the primary educational goal, and at first Yiddish was forbidden (a rule later rescinded).

The patriotic song "America" would be first rendered in Yiddish:

AMERIKA

Mein land, mit guts gekroint,
Vuzieseh freiheit voint,
Fun dir ich zing;
Land fun die Pilgrims' tzeit,
Mein folk hot dort geleit,
Berger af yeder zeit,
Mit freiheit kling.

And then in English:

AMERICA

My country 'tis of thee,
Sweet land of liberty,

Of thee I sing;
Land where my father died,
Land of the Pilgrims' pride,
From every mountain side,
Let Freedom Ring.

LEO ROSTEN, A generation before he wrote *The Joys of Yiddish*, began publishing short stories in the *New Yorker* under the name "Leonard Q. Ross." The cumulative results were gathered together in a best-selling 1937 novel.

The book was entitled *The Education of H★Y★M★A★N K★A★P★L★A★N*, and told the story of a Yiddish-speaking greenhorn so eager to show his allegiance to his adopted country that he put stars between the letters of his name. By day, Hyman slaved in a dressmaking sweatshop, but he lived for the nights and his English classes at an Alliance-like school for new Americans.

For one of his first English assignments, he wrote a missive to his brother in Warsaw. Though the words may clang, his joyful enthusiasm bursts through the malapropisms:

> "Do you feeling fine? I suppose. Is all ok? You should begin right now learning about ok. Here you gotto say ok. All the time, ok the wether, ok the potatos, ok the prazident Roosevelt."

Hyman also wrote admiringly of a trio of American heroes:

> "Judge Vashington, Abram Lincohen, an' Jake Popper."
> "Vashington," Kaplan wrote on, "vas fightink for Friddom, against de Kink Ingland, Kink Jawdge Number Tree,

dat terrible autocarp who vas puddink stemps on tea even, so it tasted bad."

"Lincohen made American slaves free, like Moses liberated the Jews ind Egypt. Meantime, Jake Popper was a beloved deli owner 'mit a hot like gold.' Struck ill, Popper, who insulted odder doctors [and received] blood confusions . . . efter a vhile, Honest Jake Popper pest away."

UNTOLD HUNDREDS OF thousands of other immigrants proudly never gave up their Yiddish. They had no use, ever, for the English that was their children's first language, the tongue they spoke in school and in the street. My grandfather was one such Yiddish refusenik. The women, meantime, were often like Eddie Cantor's mother, who kept a strictly kosher home, and whose ultimate declaration of hopelessness came when her son ran out of their tenement to play.

"You, you, baseball player, you!" Cantor's mother yelled, the worst English epithet she could think of.

(Abraham Cahan, when editor of the Yiddish *Forverts*, lectured in a column to a worried mother that baseball was a healthy and productive way for Jewish children to build muscles and get fresh air. He also included a sketch of the New York Giants' Polo Grounds to educate the masses about baseball's intricacies. But he turned up his nose at football, then mostly played in WASPy colleges where Jews weren't admitted.)

AND THEN THERE were the immigrants who, with their deep Yiddish accents intact, were able to claw, with grit and seemingly no shame, their way from being a *greener* right off the boat to the top of American society, if not quite polite American society.

Some of these were *allrightniks,* who had done "all right" in America but, like vulgar *bulvons,* couldn't stop boasting about their success.

And then there were the *Amerikane gonifs,* who were the one kind of *gonifs* who had nothing, or not much, to do with thievery. Rather, they were first-generation immigrant men and women who had gained grand success in America in ways their simple *shtetl-*mates in the old world considered a most peculiar and *meshugga* way.

"Only in America" was the head-shaking thesis when letters came back to Eastern Europe from former *shtetl-*mates who'd gone to the United States—and who now told of riches they'd made selling tons of scrap iron; becoming the plumbing king of Cincinnati; inventing the tea bag; or patenting the little iron twist tie at the top of salamis. In the old world, they were all "*Amerikane gonifs,*" able to make fortunes by seemingly ridiculous if legal means.

In Eastern Europe, *Amerikane gonif* was often a term of envy *and* disgust, for people still bound by strict religious and superstitious codes who'd never dreamed or wanted a chance for worldly and secular riches. Especially in an unknown country where straight off the boat, formerly righteous men supposedly shaved off their beards, while their wives stopped bothering to keep kosher.

To them, to be an *Amerikane gonif* was another way that the United States was deemed a nightmarish place. There, said *lantzmen* who'd fled back to Eastern Europe after trying America, even well-intentioned *mishpocha* had to dangerously mix with Gentiles only blocks away, as well as the loathed German Jewish *apikoreses* (nonbelievers and apostates).

Worst of all, went the reports, brethren were shedding centuries of old traditions the second they hit Ellis Island. Even beloved Yiddish was being infused with base English street terms, and was being increasingly dropped because it was viewed as a profound business liability by *goyim* every bit as anti-Semitic as the Cossacks.

There was little mention that, astonishingly, sometimes Yiddish was actually a plus in nascent industries like Hollywood showbiz. True, it was a new business with the rules of the fourteenth-century high seas. Yet the Jews had to invent Hollywood and other unheard-of industries because they were shut out of virtually every preexisting profession where a Yiddish accent, never mind being Jewish, was fatal.

The cliché "think Yiddish, cast British" has been a truism in the entertainment business for generations. That's how Jimmy Cagney, who learned his fluent Yiddish as a boy serving as a *Shabbos goy*, was always able to negotiate from a position of power from what the studio bosses and their immediate underlings had planned for him.

(The moguls often talked to each other in the *mamme-loshn* to strategize salary offers while *hondling* [hard-core bargaining] in front of their uncomprehending Gentile stars.)

In America, meantime, the term *Amerikane gonif* was usually said with pride, especially by the *gonifs* themselves who'd made it big. For their first-generation immigrant brethren who hadn't struck the mother lode, the term denoted that here in the United States, a man or woman with pluck, luck, and a willingness to play hardball and an asshole could overcome the humiliations dumped on them by Gentiles.

For these new Jews waiting for their piece of the American pie, the United States was indeed a *Goldene Medina*, a potential land of gold. *Amerikane gonifs* were proof that even peasant

Jews—from Helena Rubinstein to Samuel Bronfman—with the
right attitude could succeed beyond anybody's wildest dreams,
except their own.

Meantime, the American Jews knew, their *lantzmen* in Eastern Europe were still looking over their shoulders. When would
the next pogrom come, or the latest in the Yiddishkeit tradition
of facing Final Solutions that dated all the way back to Haman
and Queen Esther?

PERHAPS THE MOST memorable *Amerikane gonif* was Samuel
Goldwyn, who changed his name twice from Shmuel Gelbfisch,
after running away from his family in the Warsaw ghetto and
immigrating alone to America in 1896 at age fourteen. Gelbfisch
left without a passport, documents, or any desire to follow in his
father's footsteps as a "Man of the Book [who] spent most hours
endlessly studying the Talmud."

Sometimes Gelbfisch was just a regular *gonif.* Before walking
toward the German border in pursuit of a place in steerage in
the port of Bremen, Gelbfisch had stolen some rubles from his
mother's cash box, as well as one of his father's suits, which a
tailor friend altered to his size.

Then, after forcing his way to the top of the neonatal film
business, he still didn't mind playing a real, old-fashioned thief.
He offered Anita Loos $5,000 a week on a year's contract that
called for her to write one screenplay he wanted.

The deal horrified Goldwyn's colleagues, who toted up
her coming salary to be $260,000 a year. "Don't worry, I can
get out of the contract when I'm through with her," Goldwyn said—and did.

The Warsaw *gonif* noticed that early filmgoers laughed whenever his adopted American name—Samuel Goldfish—came on the screen. And so, Samuel Goldwyn was born.

In Hollywood he was forever considered an hellacious *shtunk*—"a stinker, a nasty person . . . ungrateful [and] mean."

And yet even in his famous "Goldwynisms"—considered proof of his woeful ignorance—one can hear loud echoes of the bent Yiddish wisdom that never escaped him or his accent.

"Include me out," he said, so similar to the lauded Groucho Marx's declaration "that whatever it is, I'm against it."

"A verbal contract isn't worth the paper it's written on," Goldwyn argued. One needn't be a member of the Sanhedrin, the old-world Jewish courts that adjudicated *shtetl* disputes, to find the truth in that.

"Bon voyage! Bon voyage! Bon voyage to you all!" he called out to several employees as he took off for a cruise to Hawaii. Yet when he returned, he fired many of those who'd come to wave good-bye.

Lifting his glass to toast the visiting British World War II hero Field Marshal Montgomery, he said, "A long life to Marshal Field Montgomery Ward," properly puncturing the balloon of the monomaniacal Monty.

And who could argue with his observation that it seemed, "every Tom, Dick, and Harry is named John"?

There is the phrase of Yiddish wisdom:

Beser a guter soyne eyder a shlekhter fraynd.
"Better a good enemy than a bad friend."

That *Yiddish* idiom has always been judged a true *chochme* (wise statement, or a smart joke). Yet Goldwyn was considered *cockamamie* (ridiculous) when he denied he was even feuding

with his longtime enemy, fellow Eastern European Jewish immigrant Louis B. Mayer. "What?" Goldwyn declared when asked
about his good enemy, "we're like friends, we're like brothers.
We love each other. We'd do anything for each other. We'd even
cut each other's throats for each other!"

True, some Goldwynisms seemed plain idiotic: Yet "I took
the whole thing with a dose of salts," echoes with Yiddish
irony.

When told by Edna Ferber that she was working on her autobiography, he asked, "What's it about?" In the age of James Frey
and his faux memoir *A Million Little Pieces*, perhaps the virtually
illiterate Goldwyn was somehow being prescient about the future of literature.

And why he is considered a *nar*, Yiddish for a fool and a buffoon, by responding to a question with "Let me sum it up for you
in two words—im possible!" when there is a phrase in the mother
tongue that "a wise man hears one question and thinks of two."

Goldwyn's favorite gesture was poking his index finger painfully into another man's chest—a classic old country Yiddish *zetz*
(a punch or verbal needle)—practiced upon anyone who questions a *ganze macher's* (big shot's) way of conducting business.

"I make a rule for you," he said, "a happy company makes a
bad picture."

Why is that considered tyrannical and petty when the macho ex–*Washington Post* editor Ben Bradlee, considered one of
the great journalists of the twentieth century, said he liked to
create an atmosphere of "creative tension" in the workplace,
because few scoops come out of a happy newsroom?

And who can't laugh at the kind of classic Yiddish character
Goldwyn often played—a *Moishe Kapoyr*—*mamme-loshn* for a
type of *nudnik* who always gets things upside down? (*Kapoyr* is
Yiddish for "backward," "the other way around," or "reverse.")

"Let me pinpoint for you the approximate date," he also said *Kapoyr*-ishly.

Or, similarly, there was the time he called theater mogul Marcus Loew's son from Los Angeles at two o'clock in the morning New York time. "My God, Sam, do you know what time it is?" Arthur Loew railed.

To which Goldwyn turned to his wife, Frances, and asked, "Frances, Arthur wants to know what time it is."

So what was Goldwyn, really? A *shmuck* savant, a *Moishe Kapoyr*, or perhaps a "wise man [*sic*] of Chelm" (a mythical Jewish town in Eastern Europe composed entirely of the forever befuddled)? On paper, he was a less-than-ordinary, larcenous *shmeckel* who'd escaped the tyranny that beset his Eastern European ghetto, as well as the glovemaking sweatshop where he briefly worked upon arriving from Warsaw, with the money and a cut-up suit he'd stolen from his parents.

A *gonif*, and an *Amerikane gonif*, he was also the rare *luftmentsh* who made his quixotic daydreams come true by helping invent the ultimate Dream Factory.

That's Yiddishkeit.

CHAPTER 14

שׁרײַבן אָדער בײַבן שׁרײַבן אָדער בײַבן

The Yiddish Daily Newspaper

Stop the presses! It's the scoop of the century! Hold the back page!

Every [Jewish immigrant] read a Yiddish paper, even those who knew little more than the alef-bet (alphabet). There were seldom many books in the average immigrant's home, but the Yiddish paper came in every day. After dinner, our family would leaf through it page by page and sometimes father would read some items aloud. Not to take a paper was to confess you were a barbarian. For ordinary Jews who worked in the shops or ran little stores, the Yiddish paper was their main tie, perhaps their only tie, with the outside world.

Such was the import in America of devouring a daily Yiddish newspaper, recaptured above from Ronald Sander's *The Downtown Jews: Portraits of an Immigrant Generation.* Reading news and views of the day's world was a habit virtually none of the Jewish immigrants brought with them from the old world. (Though Yiddish publications had existed for several years in

Eastern Europe, they were by and large for the intelligentsia, Bundists, and Socialists.)

When the Eastern European Jews reached America, Yiddish was the only language most could speak. Written in the Hebrew script of their *shtetl* prayer books, the Yiddish words that they'd lived by but before had only heard spoken could now be sounded out.

Now, in America, those words of their beloved *mamme-loshn* arrived daily, in ink, with a precious kind of regularity unknown for anything in their precarious lives in the *shtetls*. The Yiddish newspapers, bitterly fighting each other for the minds of the masses, first won their hearts.

In the printed Yiddish words, each paper's readership could find their lost-forever worlds. And in their paper's pages, they could find the reasons behind why they'd had to flee so far and leave so much behind.

Wherever these *greeners* had landed in the Americas, and whatever their persuasion or interests, the mystifying and unexplainable of their new existences could now be explained. The Yiddish newspapers helped give life to the lost, whether providing them with the finer points of boxing or detailing how to overthrow the bourgeoisie.

By the 1920s, Irving Howe recounted in *World of Our Fathers*, "anyone who took a subway from Brooklyn or the Bronx on a weekday morning would see garment workers poring over copies of the *Forward* (*der Forverts*), or *The Day* (*der Tog*) both substantial [Yiddish] dailies, and this was a cultural fact of some importance, signifying a step toward modern consciousness."

The newspaper, Howe continued, "is, after all, a habit fairly recent in the history of mankind, announcing a relation with the external world and a sense of time as economic commodity which few old country Jews either knew to exist or would have cared to acquire."

Soon, with their own theaters, literature, and printed weather reports, Yiddish speakers no longer had to put down their own language as *Jhargon*.

"Yiddish we all called 'Jargon,' and we never thought about it," wrote Simon Dubnow, a Jewish historian murdered in the Soviet Union by the Germans in 1941. In an essay titled "From Jargon to Yiddish," he continued, "the whole situation changed at the turn of the [twentieth] century."

"Several good Yiddish periodicals began to appear, like the *Freind* in St. Petersburg in 1903. I came to see Mendele Mocher Seforim, the grandfather of modern Yiddish literature," Dubnow recalled. "I asked him how he liked the new [*Freind*]. 'I like it very much,' he said, 'but why must they slap themselves in the face?' And he pointed out the subtitle: 'The First Jargon Daily in Russia.'"

"'Why must they call it Jargon?' [Seforim] asked, 'Why not *Yiddish*?'"

"And this was the turning point," wrote Dubnow.

As late as the 1890s, Yiddish culture was still a nascent phenomenon in America. "There was only the beginning of a modern Yiddish literature at that time and a fledgling Yiddish theater. The Yiddishist movement had not yet crystallized." This made left-wing workers' unions, almost universally supported by the neonatal American Yiddish press, as the main conduits of Jewish news, emerging ideologies, and opinion.

In America, all the greatest men and women of Yiddish letters first printed their work in several different Yiddish newspapers. As a form of acculturation, reading those papers in America was arguably the most important first step from the old world to the new. One of the most popular mediums for personal tale-telling and words of woe or joy came in the back pages of the *Forverts*.

Laid out there was the paper's most popular feature, "A Bintel Brief" ("a Bundle of Letters"). Through those often pleading missives, the new immigrants could learn, day by day, in a "Dear Abby"–style format, what it meant to be an American, and how to act like one.

The questions, written and mailed in to the editors, dealt with every topic from how to use a handkerchief to what should be done if a Jewish daughter wants to marry an Italian.

"I am a Socialist and my boss is a fine man. I know he's a Capitalist but I like him. Am I doing something wrong?"

Or, "My son is already twenty-six years old and doesn't want to get married. He says he is a freethinker and he is too busy. Socialism is Socialism is Socialism, but getting married is important too."

Or, "My husband reads the *Forward*, but where does he read it? In the barbershop, where he goes all the time with those other card players. Let him see this letter in the barbershop instead of at home."

Or, "Is it a sin to use face powder? Shouldn't a girl look beautiful? My father does not want me to use face powder. Is it a sin?"

Yet was Irving Howe being hyperbolic in asserting that Yiddish newspapers—with features like "A Bintel Brief" the pleas for help or advice from frightened immigrants—were a "cultural fact of some importance"?

Not at all, wrote Hutchins Hapgood contemporaneously in the *New York Sun*, the American newspaper that was the most literate agent of social change in journalism at the turn of the twentieth century.

"The Yiddish press," wrote Hapgood, "particularly the social branch of it, is an educational element in the Ghetto. It has largely replaced the rabbi in a position of teacher of the people."

In the *Forverts's* "Bintel Brief," battles were openly waged between American-born grown-up children and their Eastern European immigrant parents. Usually, the elders who wrote in were befuddled by their offspring, and saw no reason for a changing of the guard in the new world of Jewish family tradition.

Often, the debates centered on Yiddish as the symbol of the war between new and old. Those interfamily crises over the *mamme-loshn* provided perhaps the most fevered questions the *Forverts* editors had to field and try to solve. The disputes were aired in the pages of a people's Yiddish paper, in numbers seemingly equal to those of Lower East Side Jewish families struggling to make sense of the new world.

From "A Bintel Brief":

Worthy Editor,

I am sure that the problem I'm writing about affects many Jewish homes. It deals with immigrant parents and their American-born children. My parents, who have been readers of your paper for years, came from Europe. They have been here in this country over thirty years and were married twenty-eight years ago. They have five sons, and I am one of them. The oldest of us is twenty-seven and the youngest twenty-one.

We are all making a decent living. One of us works for the State Department. A second is a manager in a large store, two are in business and the youngest is studying law. Our parents do not need our help because our father has a good job.

We, the five brothers, always speak English to each other. Our parents know English too, but they speak Yiddish, not just among themselves but to us too, and to our American friends who come to visit us.

We beg them not to speak Yiddish in the presence of our friends, since they can speak English, but they don't want to. It's a sort of stubbornness on their part, and a great deal of quarreling goes on between our parents and ourselves because of it.

Their answer [to us]: "Children, we ask you not to try to teach us how to talk to people. We are older than you."

Imagine, even when we go with our father to buy something on Fifth Avenue, New York, he insists on speaking Yiddish. We are not ashamed of our parents, God forbid, but they ought to know where it's proper and where it is not. If they talk Yiddish at home amongst themselves or to us, it's bad enough, but among strangers and Christians? Is that nice? It looks as if they're doing it to spite us. Petty spats grow out of it. They want to keep only to their old ways and don't want to take up our new ways.

We, beg you, friend Editor, to express your opinion on this question, and if possible send us your answer in English, because we can't read Yiddish.

Accept our thanks for your answer, which we expect soon,

Respectively,

I and the Four Brothers.

"A Bintel Brief's" answer:

We see absolutely no crime in the parents' speaking Yiddish to their sons. The language is dear to them and they want to speak in that language to their children and all who understand it. It may also be that they are ashamed to speak their imperfect English among strangers so they prefer to use their mother tongue.

From the letter we get the impression that the parents are not fanatics, and with their speaking Yiddish they are not out to spite the children but it would certainly not be wrong if the parents were to speak English too, to the children. People should and must learn the language of their country.

THE ABRASIVE ABRAHAM Cahan helped found the *Forverts* in 1897, but soon quit after a spat with his colleagues. (In 1886, he'd launched with a friend in New York *Di Naye Tsayt* [*The New Era*], a Socialist newspaper he wanted "written in the simplest Yiddish so that even the most uneducated worker could understand it.")

After storming out of the *Forverts*, Cahan joined the English-language *New York Sun*, then the *Commercial Advertiser*, where Lincoln Steffens was city editor and which boasted a young staff of crusading muckrakers including Hutchins Hapgood and Jacob Riis.

While working at the English-language newspapers, Cahan learned the essentials of proper reporting. He also perfected a highly personal writing style while pursuing investigative journalism in the slums.

Cahan's stories were composed in prose that predated by half a century the "New Journalism" of the 1960s. Those tales have resulted in at least one modern book-length academic analysis of his style, titled *Grandma Never Lived in America: The New Journalism of Abraham Cahan.*

As Cahan perfected his English writing style, he continued

raking muck in his first-person accounts of the horrors of the downtown Jewish ghetto. There, the *Commercial Advertiser* estimated, over 50 percent of all prostitutes were Jewish, even in neighborhoods that were largely composed of Italians and Irish.

By the time Cahan returned to the Yiddish press and the *Forverts* a few years later, the forum he rejoined was singled out for praise by the *Sun*'s own Robert Ezra Park.

"No other foreign language press has succeeded in reflecting so much of the intimate life of the people it represents," Park wrote, "or reacted so powerfully upon their opinion, thoughts, and inspiration for which it exists. This is particularly true of the Yiddish daily newspapers in New York City."

A significant number of new-world husbands seemingly vaporized by the time the women they'd married in the old country finally found the means to make it over to putatively join them. Yet many husbands took a powder before their wives arrived, often with a new-world vixen as a fresh spouse. The *Forverts* became swamped with pleas for help from abandoned wives describing what their husbands looked like and their own dire straits.

So, the *Forverts* began frequently running a rogues's row titled "The Gallery of Missing Husbands," where they printed pictures of the missing men, a great number of whom were located in this early forerunner of *America's Most Wanted*. The trend eventually became the stuff of art for those who read Isaac Bashevis Singer's *Enemies: A Love Story*, or saw Paul Mazursky's 1989 film version of Singer's tale of romance, adultery, and ghosts, starring Ron Silver and Anjelica Huston.

In real life, assimilating Jewish husbands on the run from old-world spouses now also had to deal with the National Desertion Bureau, created in 1911 by New York's Jewish Social Service. The bureau's purpose was more than just to reestablish chivalry in the hearts of wayward husbands: Religious Jewish women couldn't obtain a divorce unless their husbands agreed, a sexist religious process known as getting a *get*.

There was no *get* to be gotten, however, if the ne'er-do-well *shmuck* of a husband couldn't be found, leaving his wife stranded, often with a family, in a kind of limbo. Without their husbands' granting a *get* that would allow the abandoned wives to be awarded a religious divorce, the women could neither be single and available in the city, nor enjoy the security of having a decent man to head the household, and lead the family to whatever destiny the new world had in store.

During the two decades on either side of 1900, hundreds of notices were printed in the largest Yiddish newspapers. By far the majority of husbands stuck around: Quite often it was the Yiddish-speaking *mamme* in charge anyway.

The classic joke, told for over a century, concerns a young Jewish boy who comes home from school one day and tells his mother he's been cast in the sixth-grade play as "the Jewish husband."

The mother is outraged: "You go back to that school," she says, "and demand a *speaking* part!"

Though the *Forverts's* readers were largely the transplanted peasants of downtown New York, it was mailed across the world. And the unlikable Abraham Cahan, who ran the *Forverts* for fifty years until the day he died in 1951, became the most famous and influential Yiddish editor ever.

Besides Yiddish journalism, Cahan also wrote novels in English (many of his detractors claimed his fiction also showed up in the *Forward's* news stories). His first book, *Yekl the Imported Bridegroom and Other Stories of Yiddish New York* (1896), received rave reviews from the unlikely likes of William Dean Howells, who hailed Cahan "as a new star of realism" and compared him to Stephen Crane. And *Yekl*, the centerpiece story of the book, even served a quarter-century after Cahan's death as the basis for the 1975 Hollywood film *Hester Street*, directed by Joan Micklin Silver and starring Carol Kane as Gitl.

Not all of the American intelligentsia were impressed by Cahan's style of literary realism, or the teeming avenues of the Jewish ghetto filled with Eastern Europeans speaking Yiddish. Henry James had a Dickensian view of the vast immigration of illiterate Jews, seeing them as "shabby, swarming, immigrants without a visible church, a visible society, a visible past."

IN THE RISE *of David Levinsky*, Cahan's second work of English fiction, he told of the immigrant audiences that flocked to the Yiddish theaters featuring plays of a special oeuvre critics officially called *shund* (trash).

In *Levinsky*, Cahan made the masses of *shund* lovers look laughably philistine. Never mind that these theatergoers were largely transplanted peasants seeking a short respite from the sweatshop via *shmaltzy* melodramas often set in the old country, or on the grotesque ghetto streets they now knew only too well. Strangely, the Jews he put down in his novels were the same audience Cahan spent half a century defending in the pages of the *Forverts*.

Yet while the often bombastic Cahan lectured his readership for the need of a serious theater, he also engaged in a bizarre, one-way public feud with Jacob Gordin, one of the top playwrights ever to scribble for the Yiddish stage. Gordin's most famous work was an adaptation of Shakespeare titled *The Jewish King Lear*, starring Jacob Adler.

The proletarian audience was so stunned after the premiere of *The Jewish King Lear* that they called out, "Author, author,"

wanting a peek at this unknown "Velvele Shakespeare." Adler
had to retake the stage to announce that the playwright was in
England and would not be able to make an appearance.

Eventually, almost two dozen Yiddish theaters lined the
Lower East Side's Second Avenue, a.k.a. "Knish Alley," the
mamme-loshn's Broadway. There, theatergoers were presented
with the most famous works of Shakespeare, Ibsen, and Arthur
Schnitzler translated into Yiddish. From August 1918 to May
1919, Maurice Schwartz began his first year at the helm of the
Yiddish Art Theater, a brand-new, nine-hundred-seat drama emporium in the Irving Place Theatre.

That first year, Schwartz opened thirty-five different plays,
some new work, others translations from *goyishe* classics, with a
healthy sprinkling of productions that were famous Yiddish sta-
ples. For his theater's debut season, Schwartz offered Yiddish
translations of *Mrs. Warren's Profession* by George Bernard Shaw;
Ghosts, Hedda Gabler, and *A Doll's House* by Henrik Ibsen; *The
Jewish King Lear* by Jacob Gordin; *The Father* by August Strind-
berg; *An Ideal Husband* by Oscar Wilde; and *People* by Sholom
Aleichem.

People failed at the box office and with the critics, as did most
of Aleichem's plays produced in America. Yet successful productions were also staged that inaugural season by such Yiddish
heavyweight writers, now mostly forgotten, as David Pinski
and Peretz Hirschbein.

Playwright Jacob Gordin, also one of the two most famous
Yiddish actors of his time, was able to open his own theater on
Second Avenue on the strength of his crowd-pleasing *The Jewish
King Lear.* Meantime, Schwartz moved his repertory company
in 1922 to a specially built, two-thousand-seat theater on
Twelfth Street and Second Avenue, where a multiplex movie
theater now sits.

During the thirty years Schwartz was able to keep his Yiddish Art Theater alive, his actors included Leonard Nimoy; Stella Adler (Jacob Adler's daughter, as well as the only American actor or actress ever to study with Konstantin Stanislavski, and Marlon Brando's first serious acting teacher); and Muni Weisenfreund (who went to Hollywood as Paul Muni, where he impersonated Al Capone in *Scarface*, and starred in *I Am a Fugitive from a Chain Gang*, *The Life of Emile Zola*, and *The Louis Pasteur Story*, for which he won the 1936 Academy Award for best actor).

Though Yiddish was central to the bitterness between downtown Jews and the ones centered on the Upper West Side, two young German-Jewish uptown women tried to bridge the gap. They were idealistic sisters named Alice and Irene Lewis, and they donated the money to build the Neighborhood Playhouse in the heart of the downtown Jewish ghetto.

The Playhouse, they promised, would present alternating Yiddish and English productions that would make for the highest-quality theater in New York. The German Jews uptown were scandalized that two of their own would even consort with the Socialists.

Their initial effort was a play staged in English (*Jephthah's Daughter*), and the Yiddish press waxed wroth at the Lewis sisters, insisting they were merely trying to appease guilt-stricken Jews from the Upper West Side. They further damned Alice and Irene Lewis for simply patronizing the kind of Yiddish theater that the downtown immigrants were so hungry for.

Not that there was much quality theater being produced on Second Avenue, the Yiddish Theater Row. The downtown crowds that packed the theaters demanded *shund* after long days in the sweatshops. Jacob Adler (who owned his own theater, and with Boris Thomashevsky, Molly Picon, and Jacob Gordin

ranked as the leading talents in Yiddish drama), correctly rea-
soned that *shund* was what the masses wanted, so *shund* was
what they would get.

Gross earnings from the trash would keep many theaters
alive, so producers could stage more serious plays. Clifford
Odets was on the scene and inhaled the style of serious Yiddish
theater, and would later turn some of that inspiration into English proletarian work, such as *Waiting for Lefty*, the prototypical
American "workers'" play that ended with the words "Strike!
Strike! Strike."

Odets's second most famous play was *Awake and Sing!*, about
a Bronx Jewish working-class family, featuring Morris Car-
novsky, John Garfield, and Stella Adler. The play featured characters such as *Zeyde* (Grandfather) and lines such as *"boychik,
wake up!"*

Yet *shund* always won the day, and Yiddish actors continued
to make fun of their working-class audiences hungering for simple melodrama by generically calling them "Moishe," the Yiddish equivalent of "John Q. Public."

Shund had a distinct recipe as easy to make as macaroni and
cheese. Combining a truly bastardized form of Yiddish that
would make even a devoted Yinglishist cringe, with crude English slang culled from the streets, *shund* relied on plots featuring impossible coincidences, and the most sitcomlike
connect-the-dots story lines that the hack writers could invent.

The most typical device used in the narrative was to have an
elderly mother cry out as the curtain came down on the second
act, *"Oy, zi shvantzgert!"* ("Oy, she's pregnant!")

Yet *shund* was probably the most powerful form of even
quasi-culture in the Yiddish community. That "trash," along
with the serious theater that *shund*'s earnings funded, drew such
large audiences that its influence dwarfed that of any Yiddish

newspaper or the serious novelists, poets, and short-story writers they published.

(Not that that stopped the soldiers of the pen from viciously battling each other for space, money, and acclaim within the pages of the same newspapers, and who smeared each other over a split hair in ideology or one tenement's worth of readership.)

The *Forward*'s Abraham Cahan, who personally didn't seem to like any actual human beings (and the feeling was returned), was certainly never considered anti-Semitic. Yet the tone he took in deriding the Jewish underclass fans of *shund* sounds almost borderline . . . downright . . . to put it nicely . . . patronizing.

The Rise of David Levinsky was Cahan's second English-language novel following *Yekl, the Imported Bridegroom*. In it, he lifts his nose in derision at the audiences who curiously were the same people who in real life wouldn't miss a day of his newspaper's Socialist screeds. (In that regard, Cahan was no hypocrite. Every year during the paper's salad days, he donated a million dollars to Socialist causes, even if they were his many enemies favorite ones.)

Notes Cahan's David Levinsky in ridiculing Cahan's own masses as they go see a typical production of *shund*:

> An intermission in a [Yiddish] theater is almost as long as an act . . . musicians . . . were playing a Jewish melody . . . in the big auditorium. The crowd was buzzing and smiling good-humoredly, with a general air of family-like sociability, some eating apples or candy. The faces of some of the men were in need of a shave. Most of the women were in shirt-waists. Altogether, the audience reminded one of a crowd at a picnic. A boy tottering under the weight of a basket laden with candy and fruit was singing his wares. A

pretty young woman stood in the center aisle near the second row of seats, her head thrown back, her eyes fixed on the first balcony, her plump body swaying and swaggering to the music. One man, seated in a box across the theater from us, was trying to speak to somebody in the box above ours. We could not hear what he said, but his mimicry was eloquent enough. Holding out a box of candy, he was facetiously offering to shoot some of its contents into the mouth of the person he was addressing. One woman, in an orchestra seat near our box, was discussing the play with a woman in front of her. She could be heard all over the theater. She was in ecstasies over the prima donna.

"I tell you you can kill a person with her singing," she said admiringly. "She tugs me by the heart and makes it melt. I never felt so heartbroken in my life. May she live long."

Still, the very audiences the *Forward* and other papers ridiculed were the same people who made up the masses they wanted to organize and send as foot soldiers in the inevitable American-Socialist revolution. With disbelief, the few Uptown Jews who somehow knew what was going on in the Yiddish press, particularly the *Forward*, were horrified that their religious brethren were trying to overturn many of the businesses *owned* by their own.

Cahan delighted in singling out these German Jews for contempt as traitors, especially at times of tragedy involving Uptown Jewish "bosses."

Few events in his fifty years of running the *Forward* would raise the decibel level of Cahan's outrage as the Triangle Shirtwaist factory of fiery infamy. In editorial after article after sermon, he emphasized continuously that all of the exits from the building were purposely blocked to keep the workers inside, making escape impossible for the 146 people, mostly Jewish or Italian women, who perished.

Their plight, as well as those of every other oppressed worker, was exposed by Yiddish muckrakers at the *Forward*, many of its Yiddish-language competitors, and by writers dubbed the "sweatshop poets." Even Shakespeare was deemed a pen pal of these writers trapped within the "sweaters."

SONNET 29, VELVELEH SHAKESPEARE
When, in disgrace with Fortune and men's eyes,
I all alone beweep my outcast state,
And trouble deaf heaven with my bootless cries,
And look upon myself and curse my Fate,
Wishing me like to one more rich in hope . . .

Ven alts geht mir kapoir und alts iz shlecht,
Zits ich und zorg, fun meineh tzsorehs kler;
Un hob ah teineh tzu dem Oibershten—
Farvos mein mazel biter iz, und shver.
Farvos bin ich nit yener vos iz reich?

The sweatshop poets, working eighteen hours a day, somehow found the time to scribble out their accounts of bleak Jewish lives lived out for cents in front of sewing machines and needles.

Sholom Aleichem wrote about a sweatshop poet in a story about the "freedom" found in America:

You want a factory/so you have a factory.
You want to/you push a pushcart.
And if you don't/you peddle or go to work in a shop—it's a free
    country!

You may starve or drop to death/of hunger right in the street,
There's nothing to prevent you/nobody will object.

Abraham Cahan loathed Yiddish. It was only the largest of the curious ironies of an imperious man with no real personal friends who spent fifty years of his life writing passionately in the *Forverts* to unite the uneducated masses, whom he in turn attacked for their uneducated love of Yiddish popular theater, all the while partaking in vitriolic feuds with the most serious talents the stage produced.

For Cahan, socialism and Jewish assimilation into America were the most important items on his agenda for the millions of Yiddish-speaking paupers who immigrated to the United States from Poland and Russia. Unlike Yiddish purists, he championed the introduction of English words into the *mamme-loshn* vocabulary of his Yiddish readers.

He agreed with intellectual Hertz Burgin, who proclaimed in 1915 that "we write for Yiddish-speaking citizens, only because we speak their language and are acquainted with their lives. The Yiddish language is our tool."

Indeed, there was much work to do before these millions of the world's truly wretched refuse could become the kind of Socialists Abe Cahan wanted. Jewish men and women, he lectured, must lead a workers' revolution through unions battling the "bosses" for a proper workday, child labor laws, and a living wage.

First, Cahan sermonized, these future revolutionaries would need to learn how to behave and think like Americans, which meant eventually leaving behind Yiddish, the only language most knew. If they needed to be hectored and lectured about high political ideals, they first had to be taught how to blow their noses into handkerchiefs and not onto their sleeves, appreciate fine literature, and address their own problems.

Cahan, though no one could stand his presence, saw himself personally leading, indoctrinating disciples, and squeezing out a revolution from his paper. Though he feuded with virtually every organization that swayed from his self-invented party line, he continued to give huge contributions to his enemies from the ten-story *Forward* headquarters.

Located at 175 East Broadway, the *Forverts* boasted a majestic building that towered over the surrounding low-level tenements. The roof supported the largest Yiddish sign in history (it read, in enormous letters, *Forverts*). A Chinese religious organization now has the building, but its facade still bears concrete likenesses of Marx and Engels put up by Cahan.

Cahan's wars and vendettas against his competitors lasted lifetimes. He'd smear other Yiddish papers with false claims that their editors weren't Jewish, or were reactionary spies, or secret tools of the "bosses" who ran the sweatshops. He railed on behalf of the workers trying to unionize, and against what he felt was the patronizing help of the likes of the legendary social worker Lillian Wald, who came downtown from the Upper West Side enclave of wealthy German Jews.

Yet Cahan didn't spend all of his time slandering Uptown German Jews or his competitors on the downtown Yiddish newspaper scene whose anarchism, or any ism, didn't jibe with his form of socialism. He also busied himself printing the first fiction west of Warsaw of Sholem Asch, Chaim Grade, and Isaac Bashevis Singer.

Singer was on the verge of suicide, he wrote in his autobiography, *Lost in America,* at the very moment Cahan began serializing the future Nobelist's fiction. Cahan further subsidized

Singer by putting him on the *Forward's* payroll, a move that saved him from actual starvation.

True, Isaac's initial good fortune in America came from Cahan as a favor to his brother, Yiddish fiction writer I. J. Singer, already one of the superstars of the *Forverts* staff. I. B. Singer, admitted in *Lost in America* that he was profoundly grateful to Cahan when he came to the United States as the anonymous younger brother of the famous I. J. Singer, who'd already authored such Yiddish classics as *The Brothers Ashkenazi* and *Yoshe Kalb.*

Yet Cahan was more than an editor who gave in to nepotism and the back-scratching New York journalism favor bank. As a cub reporter writing for the the *Arbeter Tsaytung* (*Worker's Newspaper*) he lauded, on May 9, 1890, both his own paper and the monthly *Tsukunft,* for joining with the fledgling *Yiddishe Geverkshaften* and the Socialist Labor Party for staging a well-attended May Day demonstration.

"This imposing demonstration is the beginning of the great revolution which will overthrow the capitalist system," he wrote, "and erect a new society on the foundation of genuine liberty, equality, and fraternity."

Like these proletarians, Yiddish was Cahan's only language when he arrived as a twenty-two-year-old in 1882. He started work in a tobacco factory and quickly learned English by devouring a grammar book meant for Germans new to America. Soon, he was teaching English to immigrants at *yeshivas* (religious academies) and night schools.

AT ITS PEAK during World War I, Cahan's *Forward* had an audience of almost 1.5 million readers in New York and across the country (a 1920 study of American Yiddish newspapers by a Columbia University sociologist found that as many as seven people passed around each copy sold). The demographics of those reading these Yiddish papers were an astonishing mix.

On the bottom rung, the readers ranged from the poorest, barely literate street peddlers saving up for their own pushcarts, to freelance factory workers (known as members of the *Khazer Mark* (Pig Market), whom the Uptown German Jews with their own clothing plants would hire on a day-to-day basis because they were the cheapest labor on the market.

On the other end of the *Forverts's* readers were those who read a (translated) copy delivered each day to the Oval Office and resident presidents including Woodrow Wilson, Calvin Coolidge, Herbert Hoover, and Franklin Roosevelt.

One survey taken by Mordecai Soltes of Columbia University in 1920 was titled, *The Yiddish Press: An Americanizing Agency.* Among the leading contemporary Yiddish daily papers Soltes lists are the *Yiddish Tagebalt (Jewish Daily News),* founded in 1885; the *Forward,* established in 1897; and the *Yiddisher Morgen Journal (Jewish Morning Journal),* comprising two papers established in 1905 and 1914, then merged in 1919.

Soltes had several hundred Jews fill out questionnaires concerning their Yiddish newspaper reading habits. What he found was that the median age of readers ranged between forty-six and fifty, meaning, if they had immigrated immediately after they were born, the median years of arrival in the new world would have been between 1874 and 1920. Still, Soltes found, a surprisingly larger number of readers were between the ages of sixteen and twenty-five, who if they came over as children, would have arrived in the United States between 1895 and 1904.

Generally, the largest group of readers of the Yiddish press, he found, were those who arrived in America between 1905 and 1907, the highest years of immigration, not only because of the failed Russian Revolution of 1905, but the pogroms in Bialystock and Kishinev in 1903. The fewest number of Yiddish newspaper consumers, he found in 1923, had been in the U.S. only one to six years, a time when World War I cut Jewish immigration to America to virtually nil.

Perhaps the most interesting question posed in the study was directed at people familiar with English but who chose to read the Yiddish dailies.

Twenty percent said they read these papers for sentimental reasons, such as "Yiddish is my mother tongue, it must not die" or "If our American Jews will not read it, it will die." But the main reason people bought the papers, the study revealed, was simply to keep up with Jewish current affairs.

An average daily *Forward* offered something for everyone: national, Jewish, and workers' news for those who wanted to keep up with current events and politics; "A Bintel Brief" for sob sisters of a socialist bent; serialized literature from some of the greatest writers of the first half of the twentieth century, who'd been paid by the word; sports scores; and general features. One typical issue had ads for an upcoming lecture by Emma Goldman, as well as ads for a "Yom Kippur Ball" to be held purposely on Judaism's holiest day by Socialist atheist Yiddishists eager to thumb their noses at the bourgeois Jews flocking to synagogues for absolution of their sins.

THE ARGUABLY ANTI-SEMITIC H. L. Mencken—syndicated columnist, lexicographer, and, for the first quarter of the twentieth century, the country's best-known social and literary critic—had only kind words for the editorial mix of the *Forward*, which someone apparently translated for him in his native Baltimore.

"The *Forverts* is read most assiduously not only by the proletariat," he wrote in 1927 in *The American Mercury*, Mencken's literary monthly, "but also by that part of the Yiddish intelligentsia which criticizes it most severely. None can resist the lively, human appeal of Cahan's paper, though one may criticize it ever so often as yellow."

Though the highbrow critical attention was nice, the Yiddish papers as always relied on the pennies and goodwill of immigrants from Eastern Europe. Many had been *frum* (highly religious) greenhorns long before who, as they aged, steadfastly refused to assimilate at all to America.

Sixty years after they'd sailed into New York Harbor, the men proudly kept their beards and yarmulkes on and spoke Hebrew in the synagogue and *Yiddish* at home and in the streets. Their wives kept kosher, ran the household, and often the family business, be it a candy store or newspaper stand. They refused to jettison Yiddish, ignoring English until they died in the United States.

AMONG THE MOST entertaining features of the Yiddish newspapers were the intramural attacks they launched against one another over minute political or social editorial slants; the smear campaigns constantly being conducted by one publication against all their competitors; or the hard news and feature stories whose factual basis seemed fishy, especially on slow news days.

What was one to make of those bitter fratricidal battles among Yiddish newspapers that began in the 1890s? Why were the Socialists of the Yiddish labor unions and the anarchists of the Yiddish proletariat warring harder against each other than they were against their avowed shared enemies, the capitalist robber barons and the oppressors of the bourgeoisie?

Each movement spawned peculiar coalitions. Jewish anarchists at one time worked with the conservative American Federation of Labor, while Socialists aligned themselves with the just as conservative Knights of Labor.

Tzvay yidn, drei meinungen.
"Two Jews, three opinions."

Twenty Yiddish newspapers, thirty axes to grind.
Who would want it any other way?
Because, for the *yidn*:

Di tsung iz nit in goles.
"The tongue is not in exile."

And *that's* Yiddishkeit.

CHAPTER 15

"I'm All Verklempt!":
Yiddish and Yiddishkeit Today

In the old country, as has been mentioned, a male Jew marrying a Christian woman was never spoken of. Parents declared their son dead and went into mourning. It wasn't just the shame: In the Jewish matriarchy, the offspring of a Jewish man and Gentile woman were not deemed Jewish, while the children of a Jewish woman and a non-Jewish man were considered as Jewish as Abraham or Esther.

Still, Yiddish was aware of the allure of the *shiksa* goddess:

Tsu shikses kricht a yid.
"A Jew crawls after Gentile girls."

Even with the lures of assimilation, only around 2 to 5 percent of Jews intermarried during the decades of the great Eastern European immigration to America. Even the German Jews, who in their native land were infamous for intermarrying (or converting) for reasons of social mobility among the Christian aristocracy, were shocked (and more than a little patronizing) when it was announced that Rose Harriet Pastor, a poor, Polish-born Lower East Side immigrant who'd spent twelve of her twenty-five years rolling cigars to support her family, was marrying James Graham Phelps Stokes, the High Church Episcopalian scion of a fabulous family fortune, as well as New York's most eligible bachelor, the dashing prince of a clan that had long been cemented into the city's Social Register. They'd met while working as volunteers at community houses for the Lower East Side poor.

The *New York Times*, which never announced impending marriages on the front page unless it involved international celebrities or royalty, broke its policy on April 5, 1905, when its page-one headline read:

J. G. PHELPS STOKES
TO WED *YOUNG* JEWESS
Engagement of Member of Old
New York Family Announced

The bible of Upper West Side Jewish intelligentsia, the *Times* also noted in its subhead that "BOTH WORKED ON EAST SIDE." With Rose's father dead, and her mother able to speak only Yiddish, the *Times* was stuck with interviewing only Pastor, who, they dryly noted, "as she talks on the uplifting of the poor, her face lights up."

The *Times* was also granted an interview when the Stokeses left for a grand European honeymoon cruise, and observed a mite peevishly in its headline that the couple on vacation seemed "NOT SO BENT ON UPLIFTING."

The marriage caused another war among the leading Yiddish daily newspapers. The conservative *Tageblatt*—the Socialist *Forverts*'s leading competition in circulation as well as ideological enemy—had employed Miss Pastor for $15 a week for two years before her engagement as a Miss Lonelyhearts columnist.

The *Forverts*, whose socialism the *Tageblatt* had long called "un-Godly," viciously attacked their competition for hypocrisy, citing a recent *Tageblatt* editorial written by Rose Pastor herself blasting interfaith marriage, and, as recently published, a vituperative smear of Israel Zangwill, who'd recently married a Christian woman after authoring the charming, beautiful, and hilarious *The King of the Shnorrers*, based on the iconic character who was as much a part of any *shtetl* as the village idiot.

That was over a century ago. Now, intermarriage figures hover around 50 percent, sending many Jews into paroxysms of fear that because the *yidn*, excluding the Chasidim, have an extremely low birthrate, they are killing off their own tribe. Often cited as an alarmist warning are the thoughts of the late Jewish philosopher Emil Fackenheim, who added an extra commandment to the Torah, number 614, decreeing that "the Jews are forbidden to give Hitler posthumous victories."

Yet what is it about Jewish men and their seemingly unquenchable craving for Gentile women?

In a chapter in Philip Roth's *Portnoy's Complaint* titled "Shikses and Other Goyim," Portnoy rhapsodizes:

> But the *shikses,* ah, the *shikses* . . . how do they get so gorgeous, so healthy, so *blond*? My contempt for what they believe in is more than neutralized by my adoration of the way they look, the way they move and laugh and speak—the lives they must lead behind those *goyishe* curtains! . . . For these are the girls whose older brothers are the engaging, good-natured, confident, clean, swift, and powerful halfbacks for the college football teams called *Northwestern* and *Texas Christian* and *UCLA*. Their fathers

are men who never use double negatives. . . . Jack Armstrong, the All-American *goy!*—and Jack as in John, not Jack
as in Jake, like my father. . . . O America! America! It may
have been gold in the streets to my grandparents, it may
have been a chicken in every pot to my mother and father,
but to me . . . America is a *shikse* nestling under your arm
whispering love love love love love!

TO A LESSER extent than perhaps ever before, Jews no longer
feel the need to debase themselves in front of Gentiles with
brutally self-deprecating jokes. During vaudeville's heyday in
the first quarter of the twentieth century, "Hebe acts" flour-
ished. Usually featuring Jewish comics wearing ill-fitting
clothes and hobo hats, they spoke in hideously broad Yiddish
accents (the Jewish equivalent of Butterfly McQueen's African-
American cry in *Gone With the Wind* of "I don't know *nothin'*
'bout birthin' babies!") that made fun of Jews' un-American
cheapness.

Andy Rice's "Hebe" vanderville monologue concerned one
of his children's weddings. Speaking with an insanely over-the-
top Yiddish inflection. Rice would begin:

There were two hundred in the grand march, we invited
one hundred, expected eighty, so we ordered supper for
fifty! The supper was a success, very little pushing. The hall
was decorated with shamrocks from an Irish ball the night
before. They must have had a great time, because every
chair in the place was broken! We had three detectives
watch the presents and my three brothers watched them!
We had fine presents. Rosenbloom sent his card, the tailor
his bill, Mrs. Bloom a fruit bowl, cut glass—cut from a dol-

lar to ninety-eight cents! Stein the crockery man sent six little Steins—and *could they eat!* The wedding cake was made like a ship. The little Steins were left alone with it, and *they sunk the ship!*

And then there were popular songs like "Yonkel the Cowboy Jew: The Yiddish Comic Cow-boy Novelty Song," whose sheet music features two contrasting pictures of Yonkel. In the first drawing, he is standing under a pawnbroker's three-ball sign, grinning devilishly and ghoulishly wringing his hands while dressed like "Fagin the Jew," Charles Dickens's original name for the head pickpocket in *Oliver Twist.*

In the adjacent song sheet picture of Yonkel the Cow-boy Jew, the pawnbroker looks entirely idiotic and befuddled as he holds a six-shooter, like Don Knotts in *The Shakiest Gun in the West*, while dressed like someone who's just found out he's been asked to leave a dude ranch.

And then there were the popular series of "Cohen on the Telephone" records that Columbia Records put out in the first twenty years of the twentieth century. In "Cohen Phones the Health Department," the actor rings up the agency and asks:

"Are you the Board of Health? Well, my name is Cohen of Fluckman and Cohen. I want you should send me down a doctor to my place to fix up my office boy. He just swallowed a half dollar on us. A half a dollar, cash. We want you should send a doctor down. What do you say? If the boy swallowed a half a dollar, it won't do him no harm? Well it ain't drawing any interest there, is it?"

IN THE OLD country, Jews had to have secret codes deeper than mere superficial Yiddish vocabulary to poke fun at the Christians and Jesus. The most secret phrase, again, *nisht geshtoyen, nisht gefloyen*—"It wouldn't climb and it wouldn't fly"—concerned Jesus' resurrection.

The Three Stooges snuck Yiddish phrases into their films all the time, and not just as secret and plaintive pleas for help for the Jews of Eastern Europe, as they did in the 1940 short *You Nazty Spy*.

The Stooges also made gags, such as using the popular Yiddish phrase:

Hak mir nit kain Tsheinik?

which literally means: "Don't bang on your teakettle,"—i.e., "What the hell are you talking about?" In the American vernacular, "don't *hak* me" has come to mean "quit bothering me."

In one Three Stooges film, Larry is taking a teakettle into a pawnshop.

"Hey!" yells Moe, "don't hock my *tsainek!*"

Eventually came the out-in-the-open, new-world *shpritz*, along with African-American jazz, as the only art forms indigenous to the United States. And suddenly, American, Yiddish-based comics could stop pulling their punches and start making not nice.

The antecedents of black jazz emanated from Africa's best musicians, pounding out the magical musical rhythms of their tribes who were forever—mostly impotently—fighting the threats of slavery and colonialism. Similarly, American Jewish jazz sprung from the old-world Yiddish *badchen*, the funniest wise men of the *shtetl*.

The *badchens'* jokes came not from predigested *shtick* but wisened verbal improvisations meant to temporarily relieve the pressures foisted upon the *shtetls* and ghettos by an unfriendly outer world. Hyper-spontaneous and cleverly funny, they were hired to perform at weddings, where they were allowed to make outrageous fun of the bride for her ugliness, or her father for stupidly allowing his fortune to be lost via his *shnorring luftmentsh* of a son-in-law.

The *badchen* ad-libbed doggerel on the spot, twisting Torah portions into just-thought-up poems making fun of the entire ceremony, giving the community a much-needed release from their day-to-day horrors.

In the *shtetl*, the *badchen* was allowed to be a public *apikores*, apostate, and perform his shenanigans because he was also an intellectual who knew how to make a pun out of a paragraph of *midrash* or grab a violin and play a bar of *klezmer* music that brought tears to everybody's eyes—and then come up with an outrageous riposte that the young groom before him will certainly die before his newlywed wife, now holding his hand, because eventually he'll *want* to.

Today, Richard Belzer, the actor (*Homicide* and *Law and Order*) and comedian, is America's funniest, most extreme improvising *badchen* and *shpritzer*. (At a Friars Club roast a couple of years ago, he followed a ridiculous dance performed by Sandra Bernhard by saying, "I wouldn't fuck her with Bea Arthur's dick.")

Belzer, a student of comedy history who speaks a healthy dose of Yiddish himself, deconstructed not long ago for the *Los Angeles Jewish Journal* both the old-world and American version of the *shtetl badchen*. According to Belzer, the tiny Yiddish villages of Eastern Europe "were scandalous [and] filled with gossip."

"The [*badchen's*] essence," he said, "was to expose and make fun of things in their society. The *badchen's* society was the *shtetl*. We [Jewish comics in America] expand it to include the whole society."

In Albert Goldman's biography of Lenny Bruce, he showed the keys to the *badchen's* performance, as transported from generations upon generations of old-school *shtetl shpritzers.*

"Interior monologue, free association, stream of consciousness—these are the fancy words for the *shpritz.* To see funny, think funny, talk funny. Funny guys were the guys who told the truth . . . [who] believed that being funny was the very best quality a human could have. [He was] the Jewish equivalent of a hero, funny being equivalent to vital, strong, ethnic, honest and soulful. Funny guys were the ones who told the *truth.*"

Speed and smarts were the key to the *shpritz,* whether in the *shtetl* or performing at Chuckleheads in Sheboygan. According to the late parodist and critic Max Beerbohm:

> Laughter becomes extreme only if it be consecutive. There must be no pauses for recovery. . . . The jester must be able to grapple his theme and hang on to it, twisting it this way and that, and making it yield magically all manner of strange and precious things, one after another, without pause. He must have invention keeping pace with utterance. He must be inexaustible. Only so can he exhaust us.

By the 1950s, Jewish comedians were faced with few prohibitions short of using the "obscene" dirty words that would eventually kill Lenny Bruce. They could tell their version of the truth, no matter who they were making fun of. Mel Brooks as the Yiddish two-thousand-year-old man, sold millions of records improvising answers to curveball questions from his partner Carl Reiner:

> REINER: You're a little storekeeper in Nazareth, and
> I would like to know what happened the day

when they crucified Christ on the mountain. Did you know Christ?

BROOKS: Yes; thin, thin, nervous—wore sandals. Came in the store, didn't buy much, mainly water, wanted water—so I gave him water. Look! You have a business. You can't always make a sale. So when people want water, you give them water. But one thing I have to admit. He was a bit of a troublemaker. He beat up a couple of *rovs* [rabbis] on the steps of the *shul* [synagogue or, in this case, the Temple in Jerusalem]—and *you know you can't do that!*

But they didn't have to nail him up. They could have given him a severe lecture. I didn't agree with the punishment. Oh, such a terrible day! All that yelling and screaming from up on the mountain. I tell you it was very upsetting. In fact, it got so bad, I had to close up the store.

TODAY, LENNY BRUCE wouldn't raise an eyebrow if he told his joke that the world was lucky Jesus was executed way back when and not now, because otherwise there would be millions of Catholic schoolgirls walking around with little gold electric chairs around their necks.

He could elicit rolling waves of laughter from the audience with lines like:

Now the Jews have this holiday [purposely overpronounced] Rose-o-shonah and Yom-Kypur, where they actually celebrate the killing of Christ. Underground. You know when they all get loaded, and they just yell:

"Oh ho ho! We killed him! Ho ho! More chicken soup! Oh ho ho!"

You know, kids running around with wooden sticks in the backyard: "C'mon. Come up the hill to Gethsemane!"

AND OUT OF the mouth of a modern *badchen*, like the old-world one, the truth is the truth, the exposed truth, so help me rabbi.

Bruce was offended when *Time* magazine ran "dirty pictures" after John Kennedy was shot that showed Jackie Kennedy "when she went out of the car," climbing over the back of the presidential limousine, where she was held down by Secret Service man Clint Hill, who risked his life by chasing the speeding limo, and "shielded her, protected her."

In his routine called "Hauling Ass to Save Your Ass: The Assassination of JFK," Bruce continued:

Now the conclusion that I've formed was denied by *Time* magazine, which said that she was going to get help. Now I challenge them: to which checkpoint would she go? "Oh yes, when Jack got shot I knew and I went right off the car to get help, so I could bring back the help."

No, I think that that's bullshit. Now I challenge them. The last caption [said] that he's been helped aboard [the limousine] by Jackie. That's bullshit.

Why this is a dirty picture to me, and offensive, is because it sets up a lie, that she's going to get help, and that she was helping get [Clint Hill] aboard. Because when your daughters, if their husbands get shot, and they haul ass to save their asses, they'll feel shitty and low, because they're not that good Mrs. Kennedy who stayed there.

And *fuck it*, she *didn't* stay there! That's a *lie* they keep telling people, to keep living up to bullshit that never did exist.

NOR DID HE spare the Jews in the case, especially Jack Ruby, né Jacob Rubenstein, who was chasing after both *goyishe* and *Yiddishe nachas* in November 1963, when he gut-shot and killed Lee Harvey Oswald.

After Ruby had been wrestled to the floor, the first question posed by a Dallas policeman who knew Ruby from his *shanda* strip clubs was "Jack, why'd you do it?"

"I wanted to prove," Ruby said, "that Jews have balls."

IT MAKES SENSE. According to Lenny Bruce:

You know, Ruby did it, and why he did it was because he was Jewish—and the villain was his grandmother. I want to tell Christians that.

Why Ruby did it. You see, when I was a kid I had tremendous hostility for Christians my age. The reason I had the hostility is that I had no balls for fighting and *they* could duke. So I disliked them for it, but I admired them for it—it was a tremendous ambivalence all the time, you know, and then disliking them for it. Now the neighborhood I came from there were a lot of Jews, so there was no big problem with a balls-virility complex.

But *Ruby* came from *Texas*. They're *really* concerned with "bawls"—they got ninety-year-old men biting rattlesnakes' heads off! And shooting guns! And a Jew in Texas is a tailor. So what went on in Ruby's mind is that "Well *if I* kill the guy that killed the President, the Christians'll

go: "Whew! What bawls he had, hey? We always thought
the Jews were chickenshit, but look at that! See, a Jew at the
end saved everybody!"

And the Christians'll kiss him and hug him and they'll
lift him on high. "A JEWISH BILLY THE KID RODE OUT
OF THE WEST!"

But he didn't know that was just a fantasy from his
grandmother, the villain, telling him about the Christian
who punches everybody.

Yeah. Even the shot was Jewish—the way he held the
gun. It was a dopey Jewish way. He probably went *"Nach!"*
too!—that means "There!" in Yiddish. *Nach!*

LENNY BRUCE MADE his television network debut on Steve Allen's *Tonight Show*. The networks' standards and practices department went nuts: Who knew what this foul-mouthed, "sick,"
and *meshugge* comedian would say on television? But Allen insisted they gave him a chance, and standards and practices demanded Bruce submit beforehand every word he planned to
utter on national television. He did.

Yet when Bruce was introduced on the show, he immediately began ad-libbing. The network suits in the control room
began clutching their hearts and gasping. Yet he wasn't going to
embarrass anybody for giving him a chance.

His first joke was simply, "Is Elizabeth Taylor going to have a
Ba[t] Mitzvah?"

The crowd erupted. The *über shiksa* had just married Eddie
Fisher, who'd left his wife, Debbie Reynolds, in order to marry
his friend Flicka. In return, Elizabeth Taylor had also converted
to Judaism.

Bruce went over so well with the crowd that Steve Allen invited him back on again several months later. Unfortunately, his national debut had been universally panned by the press, and he began by reading aloud from the slew of profoundly negative reviews he'd received in the national press for his previous performance.

At the end of the riff, he said that he had been cheered by the single positive notice he'd received. Without saying another word, he took out of his jacket a copy of the Yiddish *Forverts*, written in Hebrew script, and flashed the front page with its uncomprehensible lettering and began leafing through the paper seemingly backward, befuddling the audience who didn't realize Yiddish was written left to right, as backward as Moishe Kapoyr.

As the old joke goes about the *Forverts* reporter who rushed into the office and screamed at Abe Cahan: "Stop the presses! I've got the scoop of a lifetime! Hold the back page!"

The audience erupted.

For a finale, he sang a song he'd composed, with Steve Allen accompanying him on the piano. The song, which seemed to encompass the last one thousand years of Jewish existence, when the Chosen had only the *mamme-loshn* to keep them together, was the dark side of Yiddish and Yiddishkeit.

The song was sad, sung in the minor key of a mournful *klezmer* tune, and titled "All Alone." The lyrics were a bittersweet tale of taking advantage of everything rich and glitzy secular society had to offer, having only to abandon the beliefs and simple pleasures that had comforted him all his life.

"'I'll be rich'," Bruce sang softly, finishing the song, "'but oh so, all alone'."

That was his jeremiad, perfectly fitting for American Jews

eager to shed Yiddishkeit for the wedding scene in *Goodbye, Columbus*. In less than a decade, Lenny Bruce would be dead of an overdose of what his old jazz friends at Hanson's coffee shop on Broadway would have called "so much of the *richtige vare* that it had become the 'wrong stuff'."

ABOUT FIVE YEARS ago, my other rabbi in Yiddish and Yiddishkeit, the Chasidic Yiddish scholar Manis Friedman, told me that I needed to get in touch with my past, the present, and the future. For the past, I researched what had actually happened to the half of my family that had been slaughtered by the Nazis. Thanks to captured documents introduced at the Nuremberg trials, I found out. To put it mildly, an utter drag.

To plug into my Yiddishkeit present, I made the old-country wine with the secret recipe that my late grandfather had made—with my father, whom I'd recently shamed with a personal article about our family. For the future, I decided to tutor some friends' daughter, Mira Lippold-Johnson, for her Bat Mitzvah.

She had a rough weekly portion; after chanting from the Torah, she'd have to give an explanation to the crowd about what the section meant. It seemed impossible: Her week's portion seemed an utterly random delineation of unconnected laws.

The first commandment was that newlywed men didn't have to go into the army for the first year of marriage. Well, that made sense.

The next sentence read, *"Lo ya-cha-vole ray-chai-yeem va-ra-chev key-nefesh whocho-vale."*

The translation read, "A handmill shall not be taken in pawn, for that woud be taking someone's life in pawn."

"What's a handmill?" asked the thirteen-year-old who would in a few years be heading off to Harvard.

"It's what families used to use to make bread," I explained, happy that I'd looked it up half an hour before I'd come over to the Lippold-Johnsons' house for that week's tutoring session. "It means that you can't take a family's way of making food in pawn, for how else would they eat?

"There's an explanation for this in here," I said, trying to imitate Rabbi Friedman by handing over a text. I passed an old, classic book called *Blues People*, by the Jewish musician and jazz historian Mezz Mezzrow. "Look up Charlie Parker and see if you find anything relating to this. He played saxophone just like you."

"I know Charlie Parker," Mira said. "We studied him in jazz class."

I had no idea if she knew what I was getting at—there were scores of passages about the genius they called "Bird" in Mezz's book.

When it came time a few months later for Mira's Bat Mitzvah, she refused to let me read her *D'var Torah*, her personal explanation of that week's Torah portion she'd just chanted. I nervously wondered what she was going to say about this chapter of the Bible that seemed to be about nothing in particular.

"This portion," she said to the congregation on the big day, "is about shame, and the importance of not shaming other people.

"There is the part that tells us how to get a loan back from a neighbor. It says that we cannot go into our neighbor's house to take whatever we lent them. We have to wait outside on the street. I think this is because if you go into your neighbor's house, you might embarrass them in front of their family. No one should have to be humiliated like that, so God came up with a way that both the lender and the person they lent something to are happy."

Very true. To paraphrase that one-woman piece of Yiddishkeit known as Sophie Tucker, I've been proud and I've been shamed, and proud is better.

"This commandment also fits under the theme of Loans and Pawn," Mira continued. "There is a law in my Torah portion that says you cannot take a person's means of living in pawn. It gives the example of a bread maker, but it applies to everyone. Even the famous saxophone player, Charlie Parker."

She'd worked in Charlie Parker! I'd mentioned him, but I sure didn't force-feed his story to her. Though a nice Jewish girl's viola was her main instrument, Mira, after all, played saxophone, had taken a history of jazz class that year, and if she'd ever been to Manhattan's East Village would have understood the oft-scrawled graffiti on walls about Parker that used his nickname: "Bird is God."

"Charlie Parker was once so far in debt that he had to pawn his saxophone. Luckily, he had a plastic sax, so he didn't have to forfeit any concerts. He even played one of his best concerts on his plastic sax. Eventually one of his fans got the saxophone back to him, and the plastic one is now in the Jazz Hall of Fame. If this law from the Torah was one of our laws now, this would never have been a problem. No pawnbroker would have been allowed to take Charlie Parker's saxophone."

She got it.

That was Yiddishkeit, a bittersweet part, but part sweet at least. A few years later, as a senior in high school, Mira started a *klezmer* band named *Shnoz*.

One day, listening to their ensemble of brass, woodwinds, accordions, strings, and piano rehearse their joyous songs, I closed my eyes, and thought, in Yiddish:

"Sɪᴢ ɢᴜᴛ ꜰᴜʀ *dem yidn.*"
This was good for the Jews of all religions.

This was Yiddish and Yiddishkeit. And no matter what all the doubting *alter kackers* had been predicting since the *mamme-loshn* had popped out like a daisy from under the horrors of the First Crusade, it would never die.

ACKNOWLEDGMENTS

Yiddish wasn't born to kvetch; it is a language not of whining but of magic and loss. Meantime, in my book, literally, God is Henry Ferris, William Morrow Executive Editor. Henry is the personification of that wise Hollywood mogul maxim of "think Yiddish, cast British." I've known Henry a long time, and though he feigned from the beginning that he didn't know the subtle difference between a *shmuck* and a *shmeckel*, he's never had less then a *yiddishe hartz*, a warm and understanding Yiddish heart, one of the mother tongue's highest honors, and one that has nothing to do with religion. Henry pushed me when I wanted to pull, and made it seem like it was my idea; gave me the freedom to fly my kite until it got stuck in the trees and I needed someone to figure out how to get it down; and kicked my ass when I had such sparkling notions in the first draft of perhaps starting the book with a scene at a mass grave. It's not exactly breaking news that the Yiddish word *mentsch* is the highest compliment one can give another human, and must never be used freely. Henry Ferris is a *mentsch*. So give me a Yiddish hug, *bubbelah*!

I don't think you're supposed to write anything about someone for whom you're dedicating a book. But I'm not going to let Suzanne Gluck, über agent and Senior Vice President of William Morris, Inc., off that easy. To paraphrase Maria Von Trapp, I would *shlep* up any mountain for you, babe. Besides everything else she's done for me, Suzanne also said something of profound importance to me about life at lunch while I was writing *The Story of Yiddish*. Our talk that day had nothing to do with the book business—but she gave me the most crucial advice I received during these, the suckiest years of my life, their suckiness having nothing to do with this book. Suzanne, a *groiser dank*—a whopper thanks.

Peter Hubbard, Henry Ferris's assistant at William Morrow, is going to be Max Perkins when he momentarily hits the Big Show. I'm not being a grandiose jackass with such a claim, but am speaking the *emmis*—Yiddish's truest truth. That's an embarrassing thing to be called, unless it's a lock. Bet the mortgage. Respek [*sic*]. Peter hits to all fields: he can write, calm, and edit like a mofo.

Georgia Cool, Suzanne Gluck's assistant number one during the writing of *The Story of Yiddish*, went impossibly far above and beyond her job description on behalf of it. I'll never forget her, even when these pages turn yellow. Like Peter Hubbard at Morrow, bets on Georgia, now gone over to the editing side of the publishing world, should be placed at the "win" window.

Meantime, Sarah Ceglarski, Georgia's meritorious successor, was Suzanne's assistant number two. Kind, effectively pragmatic, funny, smart, and willing to laugh at my lamest Henny Youngman jokes, Sarah never once failed to stride in from the bullpen and get the last out. Respek [*sic*].

It wasn't that I didn't like at first Sarah Burningham, Morrow's associate director of publicly; rather, it was embarrassing when, from her first press release, it was obvious she could write better than me. Thank God I got over my jealousy, Sarah. For beyond your kindness and professionalism, you got the word out to Yechupitzville and beyond, instead of from Minsk to Pinsk.

My father, Markle Karlen, served as my official translator of Yiddish and Yiddishkeit. All mistakes are his own. He is a native speaker and spells Yiddish any damn way he pleases. In a move certain to be dismissed by all how-to-spell-Yiddish mavens, I have tried to combine all available sources for official spellings: YIVO; Philip Roth, Sholom Aleichem, Lenny Bruce; and most important, the Minneapolis Jewish Community Center of Minneapolis' *Yiddish Vinkl*.

Elianna Lippold-Johnson was the best researcher I've ever had.

Heather Farnharm was a swell proofreader blessed with an amazing ear.

Amanda Seigel of the New York Public Library's D'Orot division is the symbol of the future of Yiddish and klezmer.

My rabbi at the University of Minnesota's Graduate School of Journalism and Mass Communication was Chairman Al Tims; my thesis committee of professors Kathy Forde-Roberts, Stephen Feinstein, and Michael Stamm got me to think linearly, while Nancy Roberts, now chair of the State University of New York at Albany's journalism school, got me into college teaching in the first place.

In Yiddish-land, each generation of authors stands not on mere shoulders, but the equivalent top head of the Flying Wallendas nine-head high-wire balancing act. (Block that metaphor! Except when it's the absolute *emmis*. Many of the following authors, many who's life work included Yiddish or Yiddishkeit, hate, or hated, each other. Some grudges have lasted so long more would want to be taken off any list where an enemy was mentioned.) Once again, read Cynthia Ozick's *Envy: Or Yiddish in America*.

Then again, what would Max Weinreich, author of the majestic four-volume *Geshikhte fun der Yidisher Sprak* (History of the Yiddish Language), say to Ellis Weiner and Barbara Davidman, authors of the equally brilliant *Yiddish With Dick and Jane?*

I know I am missing many names, and I apologize. I have left off the usual suspects—Kazin, Rosten, and the brilliant hatah' and lover of ideas, Irving Howe—because they are the usual suspects. I've never met any of you, but I loved what you were or had been up to in Yiddish. Check 'em out.

The late Dina Abramowitz, Yosl Alpert, Zachary M. Bakker, Sandra Bark, Ira Berkow, Stephen Birmingham, Ken Blady, Rabbi Benjamin Blech, Douglas Century, Melvin Connor, Michael Chabon, Rich Cohen, S. M. Dubnow; Eli Evans, Neal Gabler, Rabbi Manis Friedman, Steven Gaines, Sol Gittleman; Emanuel Goldsmith, Bill Graham, Alexander Harkavy, Benjamin Harshav, Ben Hecht, J. Hoberman, Dovid Katz, Menke Katz, Dov-Ber Kerler, Fred Kogos, Stefan Kanfer, Shirley Kumove, Paul Kriwaczek, David Margolick, Mezz Mezzrow, Francine Prose, Ann Roiphe Robert Rockaway, Maurice Samuel,

Ronald Sanders, Nahma Sandrow, Jeffrey Shandler, Richard F. Shepard and Vicki Gold Levi, Mordecai Spector, Sol Steinmetz, Ilan Stevens, Rabbi Joseph Telushkin, Ellis Weiner and Barbara Davidman, Beatrice, Gabriel, Max, and Uriel Weinreich, Miriam Weinstein, and Ruth R. Wisse.

Aaron Lansky, founder of the Yiddish Book Center in Amherst, Massachusetts, deserves his own paragraph. Actually, young Lansky, a MacArthur Genius winner and the savior of Yiddish libraries via Dumpsters and bequests, deserves his own book, which thankfully already exists: *Outwitting History.*

Among other online sources do not miss:

Der Bay: Philip "Fishl" Kutner, 1128 Tangelwood Way, San Mateo, California 94403, FISHL@derbay.org

Mendele: Forum for Yiddish Literature and Yiddish Language at http://www2.trincoll.edu/~mendele/index.htm.

Yosl Alpert: mysite.verizon.net/jialpert/index.html

Peggy Orenstein, Art Simon, Barb Berger. Emily Goldberg, Monica Schmidt, Bill Bates. Mark Ehling. The Lippold-Johnsons. Karen Cleveland, Andrea Leap, Rabbi Manis Friedman, Southern Baptist Minister Jim Nelson; Street Preacher Richard Mammen.

The rest know who you are and I'll thank you . . . in better than a phone-book list.

NOTES

Epigraph

vii McQueen's first role was in Yiddish: Amanda (Miryem-Khaye) Seigel, Dorot Jewish Division, New York Public Library.

vii Jenny McCarthy speaks Yiddish: *Stacked,* Fox Television sitcom, November 16, 2005.

Chapter 1

1 Steve McQueen: op. cit.

1 Jimmy Cagney fluent in Yiddish: Catherine Seipp, "Reds a Star," *National Review,* 1 April 2000, and Cagney's autobiography, spoke Yiddish in several movies, including *Taxi* (1932).

1 General Colin Powell: government report, "Visit of the Secretary of State Colin Powell to the Middle East," U.S. Dept. of State. On that May 2003 trip, Powell told a news conference attended by international reporters that he remembers "a *bisseleh*" (a little) of the Yiddish he learned as a child while working at a New York toy store owned by his second family, an old Yiddish-speaking-only family. A backlash at Powell and his supposed knowledge of Yiddish backfired—he stopped publicly talking in Yiddish.

1 Adolf Eichmann tried to learn Yiddish: Hannah Arendt, *Eichmann in Jerusalem: A Report on the Banality of Evil* (New York: Penguin Classics, 1994).

3 "Just take what you need and leave the rest": Robbie Robertson, "The Night They Drove Old Dixie Down," 1969, performed with the Band.

4 Yiddish as a "nation of words": Miriam Weinstein, *Yiddish: A Nation of Words.*

4 "a fraternity of survivors": Irving Howe, quoted in Rabbi Benjamin Blech, *The Complete Idiot's Guide to Learning Yiddish.*

4 "Eleven million *lantzmen*": National Yiddish Book Center.

6 "Yiddish is the Robin Hood of languages": Leo Rosten, *The Joys of Yiddish*, 1968 printing, xviii.

6 "One Piece at a Time": Johnny Cash, on album "One Piece at a Time," 1976.

6 Nobel speech by Singer: *New York Times*, 8 December 1978.

9 "Couldn't you choose someone else for a while?": Zero Mostel, the original and best Tevye ever in *Fiddler on the Roof,* with the play's book by Joseph Stein, music by Jerry Bock, and lyrics by Sheldon Harnick; original cast soundtrack album, 1964, RCA Records, 1963.

10 Jews expelled from England for allegedly practicing voodoo: Jonathan Haeber, "The Primary Force in Medieval Anti-Jewish Violence: Using Haitian Voodoo as a Case Study" (Jerusalem: The Jewish History Resource Center at Hebrew University 20 April 2004).

11 "hold up de *hends*—please!": Rabbi Benjamin Blech, *The Complete Idiot's Guide to Learning Yiddish*, 21.

11 "*Guten erev Shabbos,* Madame Chairman": Rosten, *Joys of Yiddish*, 20.

Chapter 2

16 "Stop or we'll shoot!": William Novak and Moshe Waldocks, editors and annotators, *The Big Book of Jewish Humor*, 116.

17 Rabbi Hillel's Golden Rule, "hateful to you": Babylonian Talmud, tractate Shabbat 31a.

17 "biblical precept": Leviticus 19:18.

18 Lenny Bruce's death: Ronald K. L. Collins and David M. Skover, *The Trials of Lenny Bruce: The Rise and Fall of an American Icon* (Naperville, Ill.: Sourcebooks, Inc., 2002), 339.

18 Leo Frank gets lynched: Steve Oney, *And the Dead Shall Rise: The Murder of Mary Phagan and the Lynching of Leo Frank* (New York: Pantheon, 2003).

19 "A *mezuzah* is Jewish chap stick": Lenny Bruce, compiled and edited by John Cohen, *The Essential Lenny Bruce*, 34.

20 Kabbalah Center scam: author attendance at meeting in Minneapolis, 2003.

22 Young, unknown, Yiddish-spouting comedians at Hanson's drugstore: Albert Goldman, *Ladies and Gentlemen, Lenny Bruce!*, 105.

23 drove you to work—with a whip!: Henny Youngman, author interview, 1990.

24 "Potent marijuana" in Yiddish: Goldman, 119.

26 Jimmy Cagney speaking potent Yiddish as a cabdriver in the film *Taxi!* (1932): Al Grand, *Mendele: Yiddish Literature and Language*, 10 October 2004.

27 *Ladino* as "kitchen language" to Mom who speaks it: Gabriel Sanders, *Forward*, 19 January 2007, forward.com.

29 "Get lost," etc.: Rosten and Bush, *The New Joys of Yiddish*, xiv.

29 Art Spiegelman's father speaking Yiddish as English: Art Spiegelman, *Maus: A Survivor's Tale* (New York: Pantheon Books, 1986), quoted by Pekka Pietkainen, "Yiddish Influence on American English," Department of Translation Studies, University of Tampere, Finland (2004).

30 Singer and how "ghosts love Yiddish": Isaac Singer, in his Nobel banquet talk, *New York Times*, 12 August 1978.

31 "Yiddish language is dying": Gary Rosenblatt, "Yiddish Still Dying," *Moment* magazine, 1978.

34 Segal's Café on "Knish Alley" as gangster hangout: Richard F. Shepard and Vicki Gold Levi, *Live and Be Well: A Celebration of Yiddish Culture in America*, 148.

35 "Dopey Benny": ibid., 148, quoting Shoenfeld from Albert Fried's *The Rise and Fall of the Jewish Gangster in America*.

36 "Battling Levinsky": Ken Blady, *The Jewish Boxers Hall of Fame: A Who's Who of Jewish Boxers*.

36 Battling Levinsky, Benny Leonard, et al: Allen Bodner, *When Boxing Was a Jewish Sport*.

39 Yiddish has only "two names for flowers (rose, violet) and none for wild birds": Lionel Trilling, introduction to *Isaac Babel: The Collected Stories* (New York: Plume Publishers, 1955), 24. Trilling attributed the findings to

late Yiddish *maven* Maurice Samuel and his classic *The World of Sholom Aleichem* (New York: Vintage Books, 1973).

Chapter 3

43 *"feh!,"* as "Jewish seagull": *Lenny*, directed by Bob Fosse, 1974.

43 *"Feh! I* salute you!*"*: Rosten and Bush, 104.

44 "Hebe" acts: Joe Laurie, Jr., *Vaudeville: From the Honky Tonks to the Palace*, 200.

45 The Three Stooges talking Yiddish in *You Nazty Spy!* (1940): Joyce Millman, "Nyuk, Nyuk, Nyuk, Wanna Talk About the Three Stooges? Soitenly!," *Salon*, 4 April 2000, International Movie Data Base, IMDB. com.

45 Sidney Lumet's worst film: Melanie Griffith as a Chasid in Lumet's 1992 *A Stranger Among Us*, IMDB.com.

46 Artie Heyman and Moses "The Rabbi of Swat" Solomon: Jesse Silver, Roy Silver, Bernard Postal, *Encyclopedia of Jews in Sport* (New York: Bloch Publishing, 1965).

50 Meyer Lansky's encyclopedias: Robert Lacey, *Little Man: Meyer Lansky and the Gangster Life* (Little, Brown and Company, 1991).

51 Henry Kissinger to Richard Nixon, who calls him "Jewboy" to his face: Evan Thomas, "The Oddest Couple," *Newsweek*, 5 May 2007.

52 Heinrich Heine's poem about being such a rotten Jewish son: Marie B. Jaffe, *Gut Yuntif, Gut Yohr: A Collection in Yiddish of Original Holiday Verses and Popular English Classics in Translation*, 96–97.

53 Mel Brooks: Kenneth Tynan, *Show People: Profiles in Entertainment*, 213.

53 Sigmund Freud says "I do not know": quoted in Novak and Waldoks, 11.

54 Cynthia Ozick kicks the ass of old Yiddishist smarties: Cynthia Ozick, "Yiddish: Or Envy in America," from *The Pagan Rabbi and Other Stories*, 43.

55 *The King of the Shnorrers*: Israel Zangwill, quoted by *Chicago Jewish News*, 3 March 2006.

55 Bad news for Yiddish: "Enlightenment as assimilation": Howe and Greenberg, 18.

56 "[Yiddish] is vulgar," wrote David Friedlander, following his leader Moses Mendelssohn as a German self-loathing Jew: David Friedlander, *Epistle to the German Jews* (Berlin: 1788), quoted in Dovid Katz, *Words on Fire: The Unfinished Story of Yiddish*, 180–181.

57 "The past isn't dead. It isn't even past": William Faulkner, *Requiem for a Nun* (Cambridge, Mass.: Vintage, 1975).

Chapter 4

58 "Let's flee through the valley of the Shadow of Death": Woody Allen, *Love and Death*.

59 "By thy sword": Genesis 27:40.

59 God approached other tribes with the Torah with no success until "He came to the Jews": Dr. Melvin Konner, *Unsettled: An Anthropology of the Jews*, 114.

59 Literally hell to pay for the Jews: Rabbi Benjamin Blech, *Eyewitness to Jewish History*, 59–60.

62 Jewish "anxiety and skepticism": Novak and Waldoks, 17.

63 "Two tickets": Rosten, 1968 edition, 22.

64 expulsions of Jews: Blech, *Eyewitness* 15; quoting Don Isaac Abravanel, *Commentary to the Prophets*, translated from the Hebrew by Blech.

68 "a wholesale massacre": ibid., quoting from the *Jewish Chronicle*, London, 5 June 1888, 208–209.

69 The glorious *shnorrer* and the Marx Brothers: *Shnorrer* jokes, author interviews with Henny Youngman, 1990–1991, reproduced here from Novak and Waldoks, 178.

72 The stoned and solitary writer on *Pesach* (Passover): Jeff Goldblum "looking for the *afikomen* all by myself," from the film *Between the Lines*, directed by Joan Micklin Silver, 1977.

Chapter 5

75 "Do you understand Yiddish?": Novak and Waldoks, 25–26.

77 Cannery Row . . . "a poem, a stink, a grating noise": John Steinbeck, *Cannery Row* (New York: Bantam Books, 1982), quoted in Neal Karlen, *The Complete Armchair Book of Baseball* (New York: Scribners, 1997), 623.

77 Shylock in Yiddish: *"Ich bin ein Yid. Hot a Yid nisht kine oigen?"* (I am a Jew. Hath not a Jew eyes?): William Shakespeare, *The Merchant of Venice*, Act III, pp. 60–63, 1989 edition, translated into the Yiddish by Dr. Markle Karlen.

78 Maurice Schwartz makes a ruckus: "When you went to see [Maurice] Schwartz in Yiddish, "you always know that you are not in a library.": Shepard and Gold Levi.

79 "And the audience, which is composed of Jewish people who have troubles of their own": Novak and Waldoks, quoting Allan Sherman, 302.

80 "A language is a dialect with an army and a navy": attributed to Max Weinreich, "YIVO and the problems of our time," *Yivo-bleter* 25, no. 1 (1945): 13.

81 "Yiddish is a hard language, Miss Rose": Saul Bellow, *Him with His Foot in His Mouth and Other Stories*.

82 "My mother tongue is unpolished as a wound . . . a love-starved kiss": Menke Katz, from *Land of Manna* (Athens, Greece: Alvin Redman Hellas publishers, 1968), Dovid Katz's father's poem reprinted in Katz, epigraph.

82 S. H. Chang, Chinese Yiddishist: "Points East: Language News and Notes from Taiwan," Sino-Judaic Institute, 3 June 2006; also, Mendele, Hersh Hartman, "Yiddish in China," *Mendele*, 22 May 2005, www2.trincoll.edu.

83 Actors, trained to sound like the yidn "even by my worst enemy it shouldn't happen.": Lewis Herman and Marguerite Herman, *Foreign Dialects; a Manual for Actors, Directors, and Writers* (New York: Theatre Arts Books, 1943), 392–415; and Ari Y. Kelman, in *Shofar: An Interdisciplinary Journal of Jewish Studies*, 2006, 132.

84 "When we see men grow old and die": Robert McCrum, et al., quoting Samuel Johnson in *The Story of English* (New York: Penguin, 1986), epigraph.

Chapter 6

88 "Queer Yiddishkeit gives permission": Kathleen Peratis, quoting Sara Felder, "And the Award Goes to: Queer Yiddishkeit: Only Human," *Forward*, 23 February 2007, forward.com.

89 "the marginalized status of Yiddish": ibid., Alisa Solomon quoted.

89 "double fault": Ruth Wisse, *Commentary* article, quoted by Gabriel Sanders in "Mamaloshn: Why the Gay Connection?" *Forward*, 2 March 2007, forward.com.

89 Faith Jones on Professor Wisse: "they [gay Yiddishists] are [Professor Wisse's] her own students," ibid.

95 "[Yiddish] was spoken [growing up] . . . as the language of secrecy, the language of surprise and chagrin": Philip Roth, edited by George J. Searles, *Conversations with Philip Roth*, 3.

95 Onan's crime into a large lump of liver: Philip Roth, *Portnoy's Complaint*.

100 "The Provincetown Players have come to life again. In their reincarnation they speak Yiddish": *New York Times*, 1934.

101 "[I am a] native listener of Yiddish": Jeffrey Shandler, *Adventures in Yiddishland: Postvernacular Language and Culture*.

101 "A living language is like a man suffering": Robert McCrum and others, quoting H. L. Mencken, epigraph.

102 "Who do you have to fuck to get a break in this town?": The Three Stooges, *You Nazty Spy!*, 1940.

103 Homage to the Stooges' secret effrontery: Mel Brooks, *The Producers*, "The King of Broadway," original cast soundtrack, Nathan Lane, Matthew Broderick, et al., 2001.

104 "The Yiddish mentality is not haughty": Isaac Singer, text of Nobel speech, *New York Times*, op. cit.

105 "If Yiddish has a future on college campuses": Anthony Weiss, *Forward*, 24 March 200.

105 "many [academics] never master Yiddish as a language of conversation.": ibid. Schiffman quoted.

106 "Yiddish was primarily a language of conversation": Harshav, Chapter 8, "Semiotics of Yiddish Communication." op. cit.

107 "Keeping alive a dead language has become an academic field": Anthony Weiss, quoting Lawrence H. Schiffman, *Forward*, 24 March 2006, forward.com.

Chapter 7

110 The first written Yiddish accompanied by a date: Katz, 48.

110 Jews' synagogues and schools should be put to the torch: Martin Luther, *On the Jews and their Lies*, 1543; now in print as Martin Luther, *The Jews and their Lies* (Reedy, W.Va.: Liberty Bell Publications, 2004).

110 "Yiddish wasn't just words": Erica Jong, quoted in Blech, *Guide to Learning Yiddish*, 12.

111 *Zi veys take vi tsu tantsn matratsn-polke*; Jason Yusl Alpert, mysite. verizon.net/Jialpert/Yiddish glossary.

112 *"Koosh mir in tuchus!"* ("Kiss my ass!"): Romain Gary, *The Dance of Genghis Cohn* (New York: World Publishing Company, 1968).

112 Barbra Streisand's already built mausoleum: Committee on Jewish Law and Standards, "May a Mausoleum Be Used for Jewish Burials?" (New York: Rabbinical Assembly, 1988).

119 Stalin-Trotsky joke: Novak and Waldoks, 97.

120 Yiddish-style questions in doctor's office: ibid., 121.

122 Yeshiva-students with "spectacles on their nose and autumn in their hearts": Isaac Babel, 31.

123 "Now, honestly—how can you have a Yiddish dictionary without the word *tuchus*?": Alpert, op. cit.

123 Number of Yiddish speakers in 1939: Fact sheet, National Yiddish Book Center, 2007.

123. Yiddish among Jews is "running dry.": Rosten, 1968 edition, xii.

124 "To all the *shlemiels*": attributed on the Internet to Jackie Mason, 2007.

125 "Excuse me, Miss Blondie, do you speak Yiddish?": Author interviews with Henny Youngman, 1990–1991; joke also recounted in Novak and Waldoks.

126 Lenny Bruce, *"fressing"*: *The Essential Lenny Bruce*, editor Cohen, "There's Nothing Dirty About Yiddish" routine, 33.

Chapter 8

142 Sandy Koufax not pitching on Yom Kippur: Sandy Koufax with Ed Linn, *Koufax* (New York: Viking, 1966).

144 Abbie Hoffman decrying that "nostalgia is just another form of depression.": Neal Karlen, "Abbie Hoffman's Second Stage," *Newsweek*, 20 August 1984, 11.

144 Yippie co-founder Abbie Hoffman yelling at Judge Julius Hoffman (no relation) that the Jewish judge was *"a shanda fur di goyim"* in the middle of his Chicago Seven conspiracy trial: J. Anthony Lukas, *The Barnyard Epithet and Other Obscenities: Notes on the Chicago Conspiracy Trial* (New York: Harper and Row, 1970).

Chapter 9

146 Chasidic history and biographies: Manis Friedman, *Doesn't Anyone Blush Anymore?*

———Yale Strom, *The Hasidim of Brooklyn* (Northvale, N.J. Jason Aronson Inc., 1993).

———R.J. Zwi Werblowsky and Geoffrey Wigoder, eds., *The Encyclopedia of the Jewish Religion.*

———David Gonzales. "'A Family in Stress' Over Its Stricken Rebbe; The Unspoken Question Among Lubavitchers: Who Is Going to Succeed Their Leader?" *New York Times*, 12 March 1994, sec. 1, p. 23.

———David Gonzales. "Lubavitchers Learn to Sustain Themselves Without the Rebbe," *New York Times*, 8 November 1994, sec. B, p. 3.

161 Duchess Fergie visits Rabbi Manis: Nadine Brozan. "Chronicle," *New York Times*, 28 May 1997, sec. A, p. 22.

Chapter 10

169 Professor Ilan Stavans sticks up for the dead Leo Rosten: Ilan Stavans. "O Rosten! My Rosten!" *Pakn Treger* 52 (fall 2006).

170 *Greener* with jealousy: Cynthia Ozick, *The Pagan Rabbi and Other Stories*.

173 Chaim Grade's almost Pulitzer: Chaim Grade, *Rabbis and Wives* (New York: Alfred A. Knopf, 1982).

175 [Isaac] Singer said, "eight people and nine spits!": *Partisan Review*, February 2002.

Chapter 11

186 Russian army "recruitment": Rabbi Benjamin Blech, *Eyewitness to Jewish History*, taken from S. M. Dubnow, *History of the Jews in Russia and Poland*, 210–211.

189 Author interview: with Markle Karlen, 20 June 2001.

191 Yiddish "optimistic in the long run, but pessimistic about the present and the immediate future": William Novak and Moshe Waldoks, eds., *The Big Book of Jewish Humor*.

196 Ben Hecht's story: Ben Hecht, *A Child of the Century*.

203 "The Golem": I. L. Peretz, as reprinted in Irving Howe and Eliezer Greenberg, eds., *A Treasury of Yiddish Stories*, 245–246.

Chapter 12

211 Come back, Tom Lehrer: Tom Lehrer. "National Brotherhood Week Lyrics," www.sing365.com/music/lyric.nsf/National-Brotherhood-Week-lyrics-Tom-Lehrer/625DBDA1F04F231148256A7D0025A2FC.

215 Said's notion of Orientalism: Edward Said, *Orientalism*.

216 The Upper West Side was "inhabited chiefly . . . by New York–born Jews": Steven Gaines, *The Sky's The Limit: Passion and Property in Manhattan*.

216 Times Square language as Yiddish showbiz and the midway: James Traub, *The Devil's Playground*, 98.

218 Take Mrs. Phillip J. Goodhart, née Lehman: Steven Birmingham, *Our Crowd: The Great Jewish Families of New York.*

219 Jewish four hundred: Gaines, *The Sky's The Limit: Passion and Property in Manhattan.*

220 Moses Mendelssohn says, "Yiddish was an archenemy of the people.": Dovid Katz, *Words on Fire.*

221 German-Jewish assimilation: Birmingham, *Our Crowd.*

Chapter 13

231 Kenneth Tynan and Mel Brooks: Kenneth Tynan, *Show People: Profiles in Entertainment.*

236. *The Other Half:* Jacob Riis and Luc Sante, eds., *How the Other Half Lives.*

239 *Laugh, Jew, Laugh:* B. Kovner, *Laugh, Jew, Laugh.*

242 Once upon a time, a Talmud teacher: Menachem Dolitsky quoted by Irving Howe, *World of Our Fathers.*

243 Kovner interview with Maxie Shapiro: Allen Bodner, *When Boxing Was a Jewish Sport.*

Chapter 14

258 Now everyone had a newspaper: Ronald Sanders, *The Downtown Jews: Portraits of an American Generation.*

259 Irving Howe's "step toward modern consciousness": Howe, *World of Our Fathers.*

261 The first Ann Landers: Isaac Metzger, ed., *A Blintel Brief: Sixty Years of Letters from the Lower East Side to the Jewish Daily Forward.*

264 Cahan's New Journalism: Abraham Cahan and Moses Rischin, eds., *Grandma Never Lived in America: The New Journalism of Abraham Cahan.*

267 *shund:* Abraham Cahan, *The Rise of David Levinsky.*

Chapter 15

282 Rose Pastor marries an aristocrat: Stephen Birmingham, *The Rest of Us: The Rise of America's Eastern European Jews.*

283 The biggest *schnorrer* ever: Israel Zangwill, *The King of Schnorrers.*

284 "Hebe" vaudeville monologues: Joe Laurie, Jr., *Vaudeville: From the Honky Tonks to the Palace,* 178.

287 Shtetl *badchens* versus American comedians: Rob Eshman. "My Culture War," *Los Angeles Jewish Journal,* 3 March 2004, <http://www.jewishjournal.com/home/preview.php?id=11952>.

288 Goldman, p. 109.

288 Max Beerbohm: quoted in Tynan, p. 216.

290 Jackie Kennedy and Lenny Bruce: John Cohen, ed., *The Essential Lenny Bruce.*

BIBLIOGRAPHY

Aleichem, Sholom. *Collected Stories of Sholom Aleichem: The Old Country* (New York: Crown Publishers, 1946).

———. *Collected Stories of Sholom Aleichem: Tevye's Daughters* (New York: Crown Publishers, 1946).

———. *Tevye the Dairyman and the Railroad Stories* (New York: Schocken Books, 1996).

Alpert, Yosl. *Kosher Yiddish Website* <http://mysite.verizon.net/jialpert/index.html>.

Babel, Isaac. *Benya Krik, the Gangster, and Other Stories* (New York: Schocken Books, 1987).

Babel, Isaac, with an introduction by Lionel Trilling. *Isaac Babel: The Collected Stories* (New York: Simon and Schuster, World Publishing, 1972).

Bader, David. *Haikus for Jews: For You a Little Wisdom* (New York: Harmony Books, 1999).

Baker, Zachary M., "An Embarrassment of Riches: A Distinguished Bibliographer Chooses 1,000 Definitive Yiddish Titles," in *Pakn Treger*, Nancy Sheman, editor, Aaron Lansky, publisher (Amherst, Mass.: The National Yiddish Book Center, spring 2006).

Bark, Sandra, ed., with an introduction by Francine Prose. *Beautiful as the Moon, Radiant as the Stars: Jewish Women in Yiddish Stories: An Anthology* (New York: Warner Books, 2003).

Bellow, Saul. *Him with His Foot in His Mouth* (New York: Penguin Classics, 1998).

———. *Humboldt's Gift* (New York: Penguin Classics, 1996).

Berg, A. Scott. *Goldwyn: A Biography* (New York: Riverhead Trade, 1998).

———. *Lindbergh* (New York: Putnam, 1998).

Berkow, Ira, *Maxwell Street, Survival in a Bazaar* (New York: Doubleday & Co., 1977).

Birmingham, Stephen. *The Grandees: America's Sephardic Elite* (New York: Harper & Row, 1971).

———. *Our Crowd: The Great Jewish Families of New York* (New York: Dell Publishing Company, 1967).

———. *The Rest of Us: The Rise of America's Eastern European Jews* (Boston: Little, Brown and Company, 1984).

Blady, Ken, with a foreword by Ray Arcel and introduction by Hank Kaplan. *The Jewish Boxers Hall of Fame: A Who's Who of Jewish Boxers* (New York: Shapolsky Publishers, Inc., 1988).

Blech, Rabbi Benjamin. *The Complete Idiot's Guide to Learning Yiddish* (Indianapolis: Alpha Books, 2000).

———. *Eyewitness to Jewish History* (Hoboken, N.J.: John Wiley and Sons, Inc., 2004).

Bluestein, Gene. *Anglish/Yinglish: Yiddish in American Life and Literature* (Lincoln, Neb., and London, England: University of Nebraska Press, 1998).

Bodner, Allen, with a foreword by Budd Schulberg. *When Boxing Was a Jewish Sport* (Westport, Conn.: Praeger Publishers, 1997).

Bryson, Bill. *The Mother Tongue* (New York: William Morrow and Company, Inc., 1990).

Cahan, Abraham. *The Education of Abraham Cahan [Bleter Fun Mein Leben]*, vols. 1 and 2 (Philadelphia: Jewish Publication Society of America, 1969).

———. *The Rise of David Levinsky* (New York: Penguin Publishers, 1993).

———. *Yekl the Imported Bridegroom and Other Stories of Yiddish New York* (New York: Dover Publications, 1990).

Cahan, Abraham, and Moses Rischin, eds. *Grandma Never Lived in America: The New Journalism of Abraham Cahan* (Bloomington: Indiana University Press, 1985).

Century, Douglas. *Barney Ross* (New York: Shocken Books, 2006).

Chabon, Michael. *The Yiddish Policemen's Union: A Novel* (New York: HarperCollins, 2007).

Cohen, John, ed. *The Essential Lenny Bruce* (New York: Douglas Books, 1970 edition).

Cohen, Rich. *Tough Jews: Fathers, Sons, and Gangster Dreams* (New York: Simon and Schuster, 1998).

Corenthal, Michael G. *Cohen on the Telephone: A History of Jewish Recorded Humor and Popular Music, 1892–1942* (Milwaukee: Yesterday's Memories Publishers, 1984).

Dershowitz, Alan M. *The Vanishing American Jew: In Search of Jewish Identity for the Next Century* (New York: Touchstone, 1998).

Dimont, Max I. *The Indestructible Jews: Is There a Manifest Destiny in Jewish History?* (New York: New American Library, 1971).

Dubnow, S. M. *History of the Jews in Russia and Poland: From the Earliest Times Until the Present (1915)* (Jerusalem: Avotaynu Inc., Hebrew University of Jerusalem, 2000).

Evans, Eli. *Judah P. Benjamin: The Jewish Confederate* (New York: Free Press, 1989).

Flexner, Stuart Berg. *I Hear America Talking: An Illustrated History of American Words and Phrases* (New York: Van Nostrand Reinhold, 1976).

Freud, Sigmund, James Strachey, and Angela Richards, eds. *Jokes and Their Relation to the Unconscious* (New York: The Pelican Freud Library, 1976).

Fried, Albert, *The Rise and Fall of the Jewish Gangster in America* (New York: Columbia University Press, 1994).

Friedman, Manis. *Doesn't Anyone Blush Anymore? Reclaiming Intimacy, Modesty and Sexuality* (San Francisco: HarperSanFrancisco, 1990).

Gabler, Neal. *An Empire of Their Own: How the Jews Invented Hollywood* (New York: Anchor Books, 1989).

Gaines, Steven. *The Sky's the Limit: Passion and Property in Manhattan* (New York: Little, Brown and Company, 2005).

Gittleman, Sol. *From Shtetl to Suburbia: The Family in Jewish Literary Imagination* (Boston: Beacon Press, 1978).

Gold, Michael. *Jews Without Money: A Novel* (New York: Carroll and Graf, 2004).

Golden, Harry, with a foreword by Carl Sandburg, *Only in America* (New York: World Publishing, 1958).

Goldman, Albert, *Ladies and Gentlemen, Lenny Bruce!* (New York: Ballantine Books, 1974).

Goldsmith, Emanuel. *Modern Yiddish Culture: The Story of the Yiddish Language Movement* (New York: Fordham University Press, 1997).

Goren, Arthur A. *New York Jews and the Quest for Community: The Kehillah Experiment, 1908–1922* (New York: Columbia University Press, 1970).

Gottlieb, Jack. *Funny, It Doesn't Sound Jewish: How Yiddish Songs and Synagogue Melodies Influenced Tin Pan Alley, Broadway, and Hollywood* (Washington, D.C.: State University of New York Press and the Library of Congress, 2004).

Graham, Bill, and Robert Greeenfield, with a preface by Pete Townshend. *Bill Graham Presents: My Life Inside Rock and Out* (Cambridge, Mass.: Di Capo Press, 2004).

Harshav, Benjamin. *The Meaning of Yiddish* (Stanford, Calif.: Stanford University Press, 1999).

Hecht, Ben. *A Child of the Century* (New York: Simon and Schuster, 1954).

Hertzberg, Arthur. *The Jews in America* (New York: Columbia University Press, 1998).

Howe, Irving. *World of Our Fathers: The Journey of the East European Jews to America and the Life They Found and Made* (New York: Harcourt Brace Jovanovich, 1976).

Howe, Irving, and Eliezer Greenberg, eds. *A Treasury of Yiddish Stories* (New York: Schocken Books, 1973).

Howe, Irving, and Kenneth Libo. *How We Lived* (New York: Richard Marek Publishers, 1979).

Jaffe, Marie B. *Gut Yuntif, Gut Yohr: A Collection in Yiddish of Original Holiday Verses and Popular English Classics in Translation* (New York: Citadel Press, 1991).

Katz, Dovid. *Words on Fire: The Unfinished Story of Yiddish* (Cambridge, Mass.: Basic Books, 2004).

Kavieff, Paul R. *The Life and Times of Lepke Buchalter* (New Jersey: Barricade Books, 2006).

Kerler, Dov-Ber, ed. *The Politics of Yiddish* (Walnut Creek, Calif.: Altamira Press, 1988).

Kogos, Fred. *A Dictionary of Yiddish Slang and Idioms* (Secaucus, N.J.: Citadel Press, 1999).

Konner, Melvin. *Unsettled: An Anthropology of the Jews* (New York: Viking Penguin, 2003).

Kovner, B. (pseudonym for Jacob Adler). *Laugh, Jew, Laugh* (New York: Bloch Publishing Company, 1936).

Kraut, Alan M. *The Huddled Masses: The Immigrant in American Society, 1880–1921* (Arlington Heights, Ill.: Harlan Davidson Publishers, 1982).

Kriwaczek, Paul, *Yiddish Civilisation, the Rise and Fall of a Forgotten Nation* (New York: Alfred A. Knopf, 2005).

Kumove, Shirley, compiler. *Words Like Arrows: A Collection of Yiddish Folk Sayings* (New York: Schocken Books, 1985).

———. *More Words Like Arrows: A Further Collection of Yiddish Folk Sayings* (Detroit: Wayne State University Press, 1999).

Lacey, Robert. *Little Man: Meyer Lansky and the Gangster Life* (Boston: Little, Brown and Company, 1991).

Lansky, Aaron. *Outwitting History* (Chapel Hill, N.C.: Algonquin Books, 2004).

Laurie, Joe, Jr., with a foreword by Gene Fowler. *Vaudeville: From the Honky Tonks to the Palace* (New York: Henry Holt and Company, 1953).

Leftwich, Joseph, ed. *The Way We Think: A Collection of Essays from the Yiddish*, vols. 1 and 2 (Cranbury, N.J.: A. S. Barnes and Company, Inc., 1969).

Levine, Dr. Peter. *Ellis Island to Ebbets Field: Sport and the American Jewish Experience* (New York: Oxford University Press, 1988).

Lewin, Rhoda. *Jewish Community of North Minneapolis* (Chicago: Arcadia Publishing, 2001).

Liebling, A. J., selected by William Cole. *The Most of A. J. Liebling* (New York: Simon and Schuster, 1963).

Liebling, A. J., with an introduction by David Remnick. *Just Enough Liebling* (New York: North Point Press, 2004).

Lisitzky, Ephraim E. *In the Grip of Cross Currents* (Jacksonville, Fla.: Bloch Publishing, 2001).

Margolick, David. *Beyond Glory: Joe Louis vs. Max Schmeling, and a World on the Brink* (New York: Alfred A. Knopf, 2005).

Mason, Jackie, with Ira Berkow. *How to Talk Jewish* (New York: St. Martin's Press, 1990).

Matisoff, James A. *Blessings, Curses, Hopes, and Fears: Psycho-Ostensive Expressions in Yiddish* (Stanford, Calif.: Stanford University Press, 2000).

McCrum, Robert, William Cran, and Robert McNeil. *The Story of English* (New York: Penguin Publishers, 1986).

Mencken, H. L. *The American Language: An Inquiry into the Development of English in the United States* (New York: Alfred A. Knopf, 1980).

————. *Treatise on the Gods* (New York: Blue Ribbon Publishers, 1932).

Mendele:Forum for Yiddish Literature and Yiddish Language, http://www2.trincoll.edu/~mendele/index.htm.

Metzger, Isaac ed. with foreword and notes by Harry Golden. *A Bintel Brief: Sixty Years of Letters from the Lower East Side to the Jewish Daily Forward* (New York: Doubleday and Sons Publishers, 1971).

Mezzrow, Mezz, and Bernard Wolfe. *Really the Blues* (New York: Random House, 1946).

Michels, Tony, *A Fire in Their Hearts: Yiddish Socialists in America* (Cambridge: Harvard University Press, 2005).

Montague, Art. *Meyer Lansky: The Shadowy Exploits of New York's Master Manipulator* (Alberta: Altitude Publishing Ltd., 2005).

Moore, Deborah Dash. *GI Jews: How World War II Changed a Generation* (Cambridge: Harvard University Press, 2004).

Mr. "P." *The World's Best Yiddish Dirty Jokes* (Secaucus, N.J.: Citadel Press, 1984).

Neugroschel, Joachim, ed. and trans. *Great Tales of Jewish Fantasy and the Occult: The Dybbuk and Thirty Other Classic Stories* (Woodstock, N.Y.: The Overlook Press, 1987).

————. *Shtetl: A Creative Anthology of Jewish Life in Eastern Europe* (Woodstock, N.Y.: The Overlook Press, 1979).

Noiville, Florence, and Catherine Temerson, trans. *Isaac B. Singer: A Life* (New York: Farrar, Straus and Giroux, 2006).

Novak, William, and Moshe Waldoks, eds. *The Big Book of Jewish Humor* (New York: Harper and Row, 1981).

Ozick, Cynthia, *The Pagan Rabbi and Other Stories* [The Library of Modern Jewish Literature] (Syracuse, N.Y.: Syracuse University Press, 1995).

Passow, David. *The Prime of Yiddish* (Jerusalem: Gefen Publishing House, Ltd., 1996).

Richler, Mordecai. *The Apprenticeship of Duddy Kravitz* (Toronto: McClelland & Stewart, 1969).

———. *Solomon Gursky Was Here* (Rutherford, N.J.: Penguin USA, 1991).

———. *St. Urbain's Horseman* (New York: Bantam Books, 1972).

Riis, Jacob A., and Luc Sante, eds. *How the Other Half Lives* [original subtitle: *Studies Among the Tenements of New York*] (New York: Penguin Classics, 1997).

Rockaway, Dr. Robert. *But He Was Good to His Mother: The Lives and Crimes of Jewish Gangsters* (Jerusalem: Gefen Publishing House, Ltd., 2000).

Rome, David, trans. *Through the Eyes of the Eagle: The Early Montreal Yiddish Press 1907–1916* (Montreal: Vehicule Press, 2001).

Rosenfield, Max, ed. and trans. *Pushcarts and Dreamers: Stories of Jewish Life in America* (Philadelphia: Sholom Aleichem Press, 1993).

Roskies, David G. *Against the Apocalypse: Responses to Catastrophe in Modern Jewish Culture* (Cambridge: Harvard University Press, 1984).

Roskolenko, Harry. *The Time That Was Then* (New York: Dial Press, 1971).

Rosten, Leo. *The Education of H★Y★M★A★N K★A★P★L★A★N* (New York: Harcourt Brace and Company, 1937).

———. *The Joys of Yiddish* (New York: McGraw-Hill, 1968).

Rosten, Leo, revisions and commentary by Lawrence Bush, illustrations by R. O. Blechman. *The New Joys of Yiddish: Completely Updated* (New York: Three Rivers Press, 2001).

Roth, Henry. *Call It Sleep: A Novel* (London: Picador, 2005).

Roth, Philip, *Goodbye, Columbus: And Five Short Stories* (New York: Vintage, 1994).

———. *Portnoy's Complaint* (New York: Vintage, 2005).

Roth, Philip, and George J. Searles. *Conversations with Philip Roth* (Jackson: University Press of Mississippi, 1992).

Said, Edward. *Orientalism* (New York: Pantheon Books, 1978).

Samuel, Maurice. *In Praise of Yiddish* (Chicago: Cowles Book Company, 1971).

Sanders, Ronald. *The Downtown Jews: Portraits of an American Generation* (New York: Signet Publications, 1969).

Sandrow, Nahma. *Vagabond Stars: A World History of Yiddish Theater* (New York: Harper and Row, 1997).

Schloff, Linda Mack. *"And Prairie Dogs Weren't Kosher"* (St. Paul: Minnesota Historical Society Press, 1996).

Shandler, Jeffrey. *Adventures in Yiddishland: Postvernacular Language and Culture* (Berkeley: University of California Press, 2005).

Shakepeare, William "Velvele." *The Merchant of Venice* (New York: Signet Classics, 2004).

Shepard, Richard F., and Vicki Gold Levi. *Live and Be Well: A Celebration of Yiddish Culture in America* (New York: Ballantine Books, 1982).

Singer, Isaac Bashevis. *Enemies: A Love Story* (New York: Signet Movie Tie-In, 1989).

———. *Lost in America* (New York: Doubleday and Sons Publishers, 1981).

Singer, Isaac Bashevis, and Saul Bellow, trans. *Gimpel the Fool and Other Stories* (New York: Farrar, Straus and Giroux, 1988).

Singer, Isaac Bashevis, and Richard Burgin. *Conversations with Isaac Bashevis Singer* (New York: Doubleday and Sons Publishers, 1985).

Singer, I. J., Maurice Samuel trans. *Yoshe Kalb* (New York: Liveright, Inc., 1933). With an introduction by I.B. Singer, 1965.

Soltes, Mordecai. *The Yiddish Press: An Americanizing Agency* (New York: Arno Press and the *New York Times*, 1969).

Spears, Richard A. *Hip Hot! A Dictionary of 10,000 American Slang Expressions* (New York: Gramercy Books, 1997).

Steinmetz, Sol. *Yiddish and English: The Story of Yiddish in America* (Tuscaloosa: University of Alabama Press, 2001).

Stevens, Payson R., Charles M. Levine, and Sol Steinmetz. *Meshuggenary: Celebrating the World of Yiddish* (New York: Simon and Schuster, 2002).

Strom, Yale. *The Hasidim of Brooklyn* (Northvale, N.J.: Jason Aronson Inc., 1993).

Telushkin, Rabbi Joseph. *Jewish Humor* (New York: William Morrow and Company, Inc., 1992).

Tidyman, Ernest. *Shaft Among the Jews* (New York: The Dial Press, 1972).

Traub, James. *The Devil's Playground* (New York: Random House, 2004).

Turan, Kenneth. "Singer Redux," *Pakn Treger* 25, no. 48" (Amherst, Mass.: The National Yiddish Book Center, summer 2005).

Tynan, Kenneth. *Show People: Profiles in Entertainment* (New York: Simon and Schuster, 1979).

Weeks, Dr. David, and Jamie James. *Eccentrics: A Study of Sanity and Strangeness* (New York: Kodansha American, 1995).

Weiner, Ellis, and Barbara Davidman. *Yiddish with Dick and Jane* (New York: Little, Brown and Company, 2004).

Weinreich, Beatrice Silverman, ed. *Yiddish Folktales* [Library of Yiddish Classics] (New York: Pantheon Books and YIVO Institute for Jewish Research, 1988).

Weinreich, Gabriel. *Confessions of a Jewish Priest: From Secular Jewish War Refugee to Physicist and Episcopal Clergyman* (Cleveland: Pilgrim Press, 2005).

Weinreich, Max. *Geshikhte fun der Yidisher sprakh* [*History of the Yiddish Language*], vols. 1 and 2 (Chicago: University of Chicago Press, 1980).

Weinreich, Uriel. *College Yiddish: An Introduction to the Yiddish Language and to Jewish Life and Culture* (New York: YIVO Institute for Jewish Research, 1949).

———. *Modern English-Yiddish Dictionary* (New York: Schocken Books, 1987).

Weinreich, Uriel, and Beatrice Weinreick. *Say It in Yiddish* (New York: Dover Publishers, 1958).

Weinstein, Miriam. *Yiddish: A Nation of Words* (New York: The Ballantine Publishing Group, 2001).

Weiser, Chaim. *Frumspeak: The First Dictionary of Yeshivish* (Lanham, Md.: Jason Aronson Books, 1995).

Werblowsky, R.J. Zwi, and Geoffrey Wigoder, eds. *The Encyclopedia of the Jewish Religion* (New York: Holt, Rinehart, and Winston, Inc., 1965).

Wieseltier, Leon. *Kaddish* (New York: Vintage, 2000).

Winchester, Simon. *The Meaning of Everything: The Story of the Oxford English Dictionary* (Oxford: Oxford University Press, 2003).

Wisse, Ruth R. *The Schlemiel as Modern Hero* (Chicago: University of Chicago Press, 1971).

Yiddish B'Israel Mad-reech Informater, Chasidic Yiddish phone book (Brooklyn, 1992).

Youngman, Henny, with Neal Karlen. *Take My Life, Please!* (New York: William Morrow and Company, Inc., 1991).

Zamir, Israel. *Journey to My Father, Isaac Bashevis Singer* (New York: Arcade Publishing, 1996).

Zangwill, Israel. *The King of Schnorrers* (New York: Macmillan and Company, 1909 ed.).

Zion, Sidney. *Read All About It: The Collected Adventures of a Maverick Reporter* (New York: Summit Books, 1982).

———. *Trust Your Mother but Cut the Cards* (Fort Lee, N.J.: Barricade Books, 1993).

Zurawik, David. *The Jews of Prime Time* (Lebanon, N.H.: Brandeis University Press, 2003).